A CHASTENED COMMUNION

Irish Studies
James MacKillop, *Series Editor*

Other titles from Irish Studies

Collaborative Dubliners: Joyce in Dialogue
Vicki Mahaffey, ed.

Ireland in Focus: Film, Photography, and Popular Culture
Eóin Flannery and Michael Griffin, eds.

The Irish Bridget: Irish Immigrant Women in Domestic Service in America, 1840–1930
Margaret Lynch-Brennan

Irish Theater in America: Essays on Irish Theatrical Diaspora
John P. Harrington, ed.

Joyce, Imperialism, and Postcolonialism
Leonard Orr, ed.

Making Ireland Irish: Tourism and National Identity since the Irish Civil War
Eric G. E. Zuelow

Memory Ireland. Volume 1: History and Modernity; Volume 2: Diaspora and Memory Practices
Oona Frawley, ed.

The Midnight Court/Cúirt an Mheán Oíche
Brian Merriman; David Marcus, trans.; Brian Ó Conchubhair, ed.

Modern Irish Drama: W. B. Yeats to Marina Carr, Second Edition
Sanford Sternlicht

A CHASTENED COMMUNION

Modern Irish Poetry and Catholicism

ANDREW J. AUGE

SYRACUSE UNIVERSITY PRESS

Syracuse, New York 13244-5290

First Edition 2013
13 14 15 16 17 18 6 5 4 3 2 1

∞ The paper used in this publication meets the minimum requirements of the American National Standard for Information Sciences—Permanence of Paper for Printed Library Materials, ANSI Z39.48-1992.

For a listing of books published and distributed by Syracuse University Press, visit our website at SyracuseUniversityPress.syr.edu.

ISBN: 978-0-8156-3329-7 (cloth) 978-0-8156-5239-7 (e-book)

Library of Congress Cataloging-in-Publication Data

Auge, Andrew J.

A chastened communion : modern Irish poetry and Catholicism / Andrew J. Auge. — First Edition.

pages cm. — (Irish studies)

Includes bibliographical references and index.

ISBN 978-0-8156-3329-7 (cloth : alk. paper) 1. Irish poetry—History and criticism. 2. Catholic Church—In literature. 3. Religion in literature. I. Title.

PB1331.A97 2013

821'.900938282—dc23 2013031278

Manufactured in the United States of America

In memory of my parents

Thomas E. Auge (1923–2002)

M. Theresa (Moffitt) Auge (1922–2009)

Andrew J. Auge is professor of English at Loras College in Dubuque, Iowa. He has published articles on Irish poetry in *LIT: Literature Interpretation Theory*, *New Hibernia Review*, *Contemporary Literature*, and *An Soinnach*.

Contents

Acknowledgments

That no one writes a book single-handedly may be a cliché, but in this case, it happens to be particularly true. Had Loras College not granted me the O'Connor Chair for Catholic Thought in 2007–2008 and a semester sabbatical in 2009, this book would not have been written. Nor would it have come to fruition without the encouragement and assistance of my colleagues at Loras and elsewhere. The sadly defunct Redactor's Group, under the leadership of the inestimable Fred Morton, provided a forum for the critique of my early work on contemporary Irish poetry. Kevin Koch, David Cochran, and John Waldmeir offered helpful feedback on various sections of this book. Bob Beck, who has read everything that I have written over the last twenty-five years, provided unstinting support and illuminating advice, including most notably his suggestion that I regard this project as an autobiographical inventory of my own deep immersion in Catholicism. Jim Rogers of the University of St. Thomas welcomed a mid-career interloper into the field of Irish studies. Stephanie Rains and Nick Daly exceeded even the traditional standards of Irish hospitality by graciously hosting me throughout the six weeks when I was in Dublin conducting research for the book. The anonymous readers of the manuscript suggested several important revisions that improved the clarity and coherence of the book's overarching argument. I have been especially fortunate to work with Jennika Baines, acquisitions editor at Syracuse University Press; no author could wish for a better advocate for their book. The Kucera Center at Loras College, under the directorship of David Cochran, generously provided funds to help offset the cost of permissions.

Above all, I am grateful to my family. Finnegan, our Irish wheaten terrier, was a constant companion throughout the lonely process of writing.

My children, Jane and Thomas, provided welcome distraction from what they came to call "Dad's so-called book." They also generously accommodated my absences during research forays to Ireland and the many hours in which I was sequestered in my study. I owe my deepest debt of gratitude to my wife, Mary Ellen McKinstra-Auge. She offered encouragement during those times when my belief in the project flagged, and she made innumerable sacrifices to allow me the time and space in which to complete this endeavor.

An earlier version of chapter 5, "Sifting the Remains of Irish Catholicism: Relics and Nuns in Eiléan Ní Chuilleanáin's Poetry," appeared in *Contemporary Catholicism in Ireland: A Critical Appraisal*, ed. John Littleton and Eamon Maher (Dublin: Columba, 2008), 220–41. Similarly, chapter 7 appeared in an altered form as "The Apparitions of 'Our Lady of the Facts of Life': Paula Meehan and the Visionary Quotidian," *An Sionnach* 5, no. 1 and 2 (Spring and Fall 2009): 50–64.

Excerpts from Denis Devlin's "Est Prodest" are reprinted by permission of Dedalus Press (http://www.dedaluspress.com) and Wake Forest University Press. Material from Austin Clarke's *Collected Poems* has been reproduced by the gracious permission of R. Dardis Clarke, 17 Oscar Square, Dublin 8, Ireland. Lines from the poetry of Patrick Kavanagh are reprinted from *Collected Poems*, edited by Antoinette Quinn (Allen Lane, 2004), by kind permission of the trustees of the estate of the late Katherine B. Kavanagh, through the Jonathan Williams Literary Agency. Excerpts from the poetry of John Montague are reprinted from *New Collected Poems* (2012) by kind permission of the author and the Gallery Press, Loughcrew, Oldcastle, County Meath, Ireland and Wake Forest University Press. Excerpts from *Opened Ground: Selected Poems 1966–1996* by Seamus Heaney (@ 1998 by Seamus Heaney; reprinted by permission of Farrar, Straus and Giroux). Excerpts from "The Milk Factory," "Squarings X," and "Squarings XLVII" by Seamus Heaney, reprinted by permission of Faber and Faber. Excerpts from the poetry of Eiléan Ní Chuilleanáin are reprinted from *The Magdalene Sermon* (1989), *The Brazen Serpent* (1994), and *The Girl Who Married the Reindeer* (2001) by kind permission of the author and the Gallery Press, Loughcrew, Oldcastle, County Meath, Ireland (http://www.gallerypress.com) and Wake Forest University Press. Excerpts from *Life Is a Dream: Forty Years Reading Poems 1967–2007* (copyright @ 2009 Paul Durcan) reproduced by permission of the author c/o Rogers, Coleridge and White Ltd., 20 Powis Mews, London W11 1JN. Excerpts from "Letter to the Archbishop of Cashel and Emly" and "First and Last Commandments of the Commander-in-Chief" from *Greetings to Our Friends in Brazil* by Paul Durcan, published by Harvill Press, are reprinted by permission of Random House Group. Lines from the poetry of Paula Meehan are reprinted from *Return and No Blame* (1984), *Reading the Sky* (1985), *The Man Who Was Marked by Winter* (1991), *Pillow Talk* (1994) by the gracious permission of the author. Excerpts from Paula Meehan's *Dharmakaya* (2002) and *Painting Rain* (2009) are reprinted by permission of the author and Carcanet Press and Wake Forest University Press. Excerpts from Seán Dunne's *Collected* (2005) are reprinted by permission of the estate of Seán Dunne and the Gallery Press. Extracts from Dennis O'Driscoll's "Missing God" are reprinted from *New and Selected Poems* (2004) by kind permission of the author and Anvil Press.

Abbreviations

BS	Eiléan Ní Chuilleanáin, *The Brazen Serpent*
BWC	Paul Durcan, *The Berlin Wall Café*
CPC	Austin Clarke, *Collected Poems*
CPK	Patrick Kavanagh, *Collected Poems*
CPM	John Montague, *Collected Poems*
D	Paula Meehan, *Dharmakaya*
FW	Seamus Heaney, *Field Work*
GB	Paul Durcan, *Greetings to Our Friends in Brazil*
GWMR	Eiléan Ní Chuilleanáin, *The Girl Who Married the Reindeer*
GT	Seamus Heaney, *The Government of the Tongue*
LD	Paul Durcan, *Life Is a Dream: Forty Years Reading Poems, 1967–2007*
MS	Eiléan Ní Chuilleanáin, *The Magdalene Sermon*
MW	Paula Meehan, *The Man Who Was Marked by Winter*
OG	Seamus Heaney, *Opened Ground: Selected Poems, 1966–1996*
P	Seamus Heaney, *Poems, 1965–1975*
PR	Paula Meehan, *Painting Rain*
PT	Paula Meehan, *Pillow Talk*
RNB	Paula Meehan, *Return and No Blame*
RP	Seamus Heaney, *The Redress of Poetry*
RS	Paula Meehan, *Reading the Sky*
SI	Seamus Heaney, *Station Island*
ST	Seamus Heaney, *Seeing Things*

A CHASTENED COMMUNION

Introduction

At the close of the first decade of the twenty-first century, Irish Catholicism bears little trace of its once preeminent status among the branches of the Roman Catholic Church. It appears instead to be an increasingly endangered religious species. With the release in 2009 of two governmental inquires, commonly referred to as the Ryan and Murphy reports after the justices who presided over them, two decades of shameful revelations about sexual and physical abuse perpetrated by Catholic priests, brothers, and nuns have reached a horrifying culmination. The Ryan Report detailed a pervasive culture of abuse that had been fostered in Church-run reformatories and industrial schools since the 1930s and purposively concealed by both the Catholic hierarchy and the state government. The Murphy Report needed over two thousand pages to catalogue the incidents of abuse that had occurred within and been covered up by the Archdiocese of Dublin. Reading these reports is a harrowing experience. Confronted with the terrible suffering of the innocent victims of this abuse and the Church's decades-long sanctioning of it, even the most devout Irish Catholics have been forced to acknowledge the stigma now attached to their faith.

For some it is more than they are willing to bear. A website, Count MeOut.ie, established in the aftermath of the Ryan and Murphy reports provided Irish Catholics with a protocol and form for terminating their membership in the Church. In the succeeding months, twelve thousand Irish men and women availed themselves of this means to put a formal end to their relationship with the Catholic Church.[1] In the case of modern Irish literature, critics and scholars often seem eager to effect a similar severance. To preserve the literary work from the taint surrounding a corrupt and regressive institution, any connections to it are either downplayed or cast as purely oppositional. Such tactics obscure the potency of Catholicism as a "cultural system" in twentieth-century Ireland, its formative influence upon social practices and individual psyches, including even those who actively resisted it.[2] But more significantly, this annulling of the shaping power of Irish Catholicism diminishes the creative efficacy of those artists who actively reshaped what had been imposed upon them, rendering obdurate doctrines and rituals into something more spiritually enlivening. This process of transformation reached its apogee, as I explain below, in the poetry written by Irish Catholics in the aftermath of Yeats.

Early immersion in a world saturated with Catholicism is, according to Seamus Heaney, the best-known Irish poet of the post-Yeats era, what differentiates his poetic career from that of his Anglo-Irish predecessor. In interviews with Dennis O'Driscoll, Heaney attributes to his Catholic upbringing the ready-to-hand presence of a sustaining mythos that Yeats lacked. Having been raised in a quintessential Victorian atmosphere of disbelief, Yeats was forced to buttress his imagination with, as Heaney paraphrases Yeats, "a do-it-yourself religion [constructed] out of 'a fardel of old stories.'"[3] In contrast, Heaney describes himself as the legatee of an intricate system of beliefs:

> Far from being deprived of religion in my youth, I was oversupplied. I lived with, and to some extent lived by, divine mysteries: the sacrifice of the Mass, the transubstantiation of bread and wine into the body and blood of Christ, the forgiveness of sin, the resurrection of the body and the life of the world to come, the whole disposition of the cosmos from celestial to infernal, the whole supernatural population, the taxonomy of virtues and vices and so on.[4]

This is not a declaration of faith. It is instead an acknowledgment of the perdurability of childhood imprinting, an admission that the "whole underlife or otherlife of religious devotion, known from childhood," as O'Driscoll refers to it, remains indelibly stamped upon the poet's consciousness.[5] The other poets surveyed in this book each bear the watermark of this Catholic matrix. All of them came of age during the period when Catholicism penetrated most deeply and pervasively into Irish life.

In the latter half of the nineteenth century, the Irish Catholic Church under the guidance of Paul Cardinal Cullen, Archbishop of Armagh and then of Dublin, consolidated its authority and formalized its practices. This so-called Devotional Revolution, which continued unabated until Vatican II, not only increased participation in the central sacraments of confession and communion but established an intricate apparatus of subsidiary rituals—novenas, retreats, missions, recitation of the rosary, devotion to the Sacred Heart, eucharistic adoration—which greatly intensified the Church's presence in the everyday lives of individuals.[6]

Few of the poets analyzed here are as overt as Heaney in pointing to the influence of Catholicism upon their work. But their poetry often belies their reticence as it draws both ballast and fodder from their inherited faith. Whether acknowledged or not, the relationship remains deeply vexed. Whatever imaginative sustenance these poets may have derived from this Catholic atmosphere was offset by the miasma of clerical authoritarianism, narrow moralizing, and sexual repression polluting it. The anatomizing of this profoundly mixed cultural inheritance eventuates for each of them in a process of sublation that nullifies some aspects of the original construct while transmuting others. However divergent their poetic styles may be, a common pattern persists: a demythologizing critique of some elemental feature of Irish Catholicism—the sacraments of confession and the Eucharist, the pilgrimages to holy wells and Lough Derg, the worshipping of relics and veneration of the Blessed Virgin, the imperative to self-sacrifice, the narrowly patriarchal nature of the institution—elicits, in turn, a radical reshaping of these traditional religious phenomena. Through this dialectical engagement with Irish Catholicism, these poets engender new forms of spiritual vision and praxis that blur the sharp lines of demarcation interposed by institutionalized religion between belief and unbelief, secular and sacred. But a full understanding of the significance as well as the precise nature of these poetic transfigurations requires a deeper awareness of their cultural provenance.

In Heaney's evocation of his Catholic background as the feature that distinguishes his work from that of Yeats, there is a distant echo, albeit shorn of the nativist overtones, of the early twentieth-century Irish Ireland movement, which insisted that Catholicism, even more than the Irish language, was the cornerstone of genuine Irish culture. The most significant assertion of this viewpoint in a literary context was Daniel Corkery's influential *Synge and Anglo-Irish Literature* (1931). Fashioning himself as a cultural arbiter for the nascent Irish Free State, Corkery issued a clarion call in this most significant of his critical works for an Anglo-Irish literature, that is, an Irish literature written in English that would be authentically rather than just nominally Irish. From Corkery's nativist perspective, this new Anglo-Irish literature would be purged of the colonial influences that rendered its pre-Independence precursor a counterfeit. The cultural essentialism that undergirds Corkery's argument obscures the legitimacy of his appeal for an Irish literary movement that would bridge the gap between the cultural elite and the masses. That such a gap existed was starkly evident to him when he found himself in a crowd of thirty thousand of his countryman at the championship hurling match in Thurles:

> It was while I looked around on that great crowd I first became acutely conscious that as a nation we were without self-expression in literary form. The life of this people I looked upon—there were all sorts of individuals present, from bishops to tramps off the road—was not being explored in a natural way by any except one or two writers of any standing.[7]

For Corkery, the characteristics that distinguished the collective consciousness of this crowd had not yet been adequately articulated in the nation's literature. Among these, religion was foremost. While he asserted that the attachment of the Irish to nation and land had also not been sufficiently represented, it was the absence of any significant literary trace of the crowd's deeply entrenched Catholicism that rankled him most. He deplored the fact that a young Irish boy (Corkery's chauvinism, like so many of his fellow cultural nationalists, extended to gender as well as ethnicity) would find in the literature presented to him at school no acknowledgment of such a pervasive and central aspect of his experience as Mass.[8] Corkery was particularly scornful of the Celtic Revivalists for having "cut out the heart of the mystery" of the religious consciousness of the Irish people by substituting for the lived practice of their Catholic faith "wraith-like wisps of vanished beliefs."[9] If Irish poets wanted genuinely to learn their trade, Corkery argued, they must turn not to "the all too sophisticated alien-minded poetry of the 'Celtic Revival' school" but rather to base-born popular poetry of the sort collected in Stopford Brooke and T. W. Rolleston's *A Treasury of Irish Poetry in the English Tongue* (1900). However aesthetically deficient, only "this simple poetry" arising from the heart of the folk could provide a suitable foundation for a more authentic Anglo-Irish poetic tradition. There the defining characteristics of the newly constituted Irish people—Religion, Nationalism, and the Land—would "find intense yet chastened expression."[10]

Ironically, Brooke and Rolleston's anthology provides many more examples of the ersatz Celtic Revival spirituality that Corkery denounced than of the religious consciousness of the Irish Catholic masses that he claimed to be manifested there. So what was the indigenous religious verse whose themes he believed should be refined and developed by present and future generations of Irish poets? One gets some sense of this from a few of the poets whose work is sampled in *A Treasury of Irish Poetry in the English Tongue*: most notably, Ellen Mary Downing (1828–1869) and Katharine Tynan-Hinkson (1861–1931). Known as "Mary of *The Nation*," Downing was one of the few poets associated with that mid-nineteenth-century coterie of nationalist poets to write on explicitly religious themes. "The Old Church at Lismore," one of the two Downing poems collected in this anthology, laments the desecration of the Catholic Church in the village of Lismore—the removal of altar, cross, and statuary that accompanied its transformation into a Protestant chapel. The poem ends with a rousing plea for the Irish people to preserve their dedication to the Catholic Church despite the loss of its physical habitation:

> Oh, let us lose no single link that our dear Church has bound,
> To keep our hearts more close to Heaven, on earth's ungenial ground;
> But trust in saint and martyr yet, and o'er their hallowed clay,
> Long after we have ceased to weep, kneel faithful down to pray.[11]

Such heartfelt piety received a thin veneer of formal polish in the poetry of Katharine Tynan.

Of these two poets, Tynan alone carved a niche for herself, however small, in Irish literary history. She came to prominence through her involvement in the production and publication of *Poems and Ballads of*

Young Ireland (1888), an enterprise spearheaded by such preeminent figures in the Irish Literary Revival as Douglas Hyde and W. B. Yeats and intended to revitalize an indigenous poetic tradition that had fallen dormant in the forty years since the heyday of *The Nation*. Remembered now mostly for the close relationship that she established with the young Yeats, Tynan's reputation in her own lifetime centered upon her poetry's affiliation with Catholicism. Indeed, in *Ireland's Literary Renaissance* (1916), the first full literary history of the Celtic Revival, the Irish writer and critic Ernest Boyd identified Tynan as "the only important Catholic poet in Ireland," "the only [Irish] writer of any importance whose Catholicism has found literary expression."[12] Like most commentators on her poetry, Boyd notes the simple charm and thoroughgoing conventionality of her religious verse, qualities readily evident in the two religious poems of hers included in *A Treasury of Irish Poetry*, "Lux in Tenebris" and "St. Francis and the Wolf." The second poem, one of series inspired by the legends associated with St. Francis, elicits a modicum of aesthetic interest through its deftly managed allegorical narrative of St. Francis's conversion of Brother Wolf from malicious beast to docile penitent.[13] But the religious attitudes expressed there are cloyingly familiar and never move beyond a sincere yet bland devotion. The fact that "one does not find her expressing the profounder aspects of Catholicism, the exaltation and rapture of belief" is, according to Boyd, due not just to her limitations as a poet but to the deep-seated deficiencies of Irish Catholicism.[14] For Boyd, Irish Catholicism never overcame the pinched nature into which it was coerced during the period of the Penal Laws. It retained the "narrowness and hardness" of a persecuted sect, assimilating from the dominant Protestant church only its puritanical ethos without any trace of its more liberating elements.[15] The poetic vitality of Irish Catholicism evinced in Douglas Hyde's *Religious Songs of Connacht*, his collection of Irish-language religious poetry from previous centuries, had been lost. In its modern formation, Irish Catholicism was seemingly doomed to aesthetic sterility. While its European counterparts generated an artistic efflorescence even into the late nineteenth century, "the artistic influence of Catholicism in Ireland" was and would remain, Boyd implied, "slight."[16] Corkery and Boyd each traced the absence of literary expressions of Irish Catholicism to the deleterious effects of colonialism, the former seeing it as a consequence of Irish writers' failure to free themselves from the lingering influence of the imperial metropolis, the latter as the result of the Irish Catholic Church's enervation in the aftermath of centuries of Protestant domination. Yet even as these critics were in the process of lamenting this lacuna in the national literature, it was being filled to repletion, albeit in a manner that neither Boyd nor Corkery would approve.[17]

It is not altogether surprising then that it was John Eglinton, an Anglo-Irish Protestant, who, writing in *The Dial* in 1929, identified James Joyce as having inaugurated an Anglo-Irish literature that at last gave voice to the distinctive experience of Irish Catholics:

> In him, for the first time, the mind of Catholic Ireland triumphs over the Anglicism of the English language, and expatiates freely in the element of a universal language: an important achievement, for what has driven Catholic Ireland back upon the Irish language is the ascendancy in the English language of English literature, which, as a Catholic clergyman once truly asserted, is "saturated with Protestantism." In Joyce, perhaps for the first time in an Irish writer, there is no faintest trace of Protestantism: that is, of the English spirit . . . we are obliged to admit that in Joyce literature has reached for the first time in Ireland complete emancipation from Anglo-Saxon ideals.[18]

Fellow Irish Catholics as divergent as the "peasant" poet Padric Collum and the cosmopolitan Thomas MacGreevy followed Eglinton in asserting that Joyce's work spoke from the heart of their inherited faith. Collum's review of *A Portrait of the Artist as a Young Man* described it as "profoundly Catholic." MacGreevy went even further, claiming that *Ulysses* manifested a "deep-rooted Catholicism," which was unrecognizable to the British literary establishment because it emerged not from their own more urbane variants of Catholicism but from the "more profound 'regular' Catholicism of Ireland."[19] A more typical Irish Catholic response was that of the convert Shane Leslie, who characterized *Ulysses* as "devilish drench" and called for it to be placed on the *Index Expurgatorius*, the Vatican's list of forbidden books. But even those Irish Catholics who, like Leslie, deplored Joyce's representation of their faith acknowledged that the novelist's work was thoroughly steeped in "Catholic lore and citation."[20] Generations of subsequent scholars have precisely catalogued Joyce's many debts to Catholic ritual and theology: ranging from evocations, both realistic and parodic, of Catholic sacraments and liturgical devotions; to extensive borrowings from Church fathers and doctors, most notably St. Thomas Aquinas; to the appropriation of such distinctively Catholic forms of discourse as the catechism and the litany. However, the issue of the governing attitude towards Catholicism that undergirds Joyce's works remains as contested now as it was in the immediate aftermath of their publication. Thus, two recent book-length studies of Joyce's relationship to Catholicism arrive at starkly antithetical assessments. In *Ulysses and the Irish God*, Frederick Lang casts Joyce as a "hostile unbeliever" who wages war on the Church by constructing his masterwork around "sacrilegious" acts of "desecration," perhaps the most notorious being the precise paralleling in the "Nausicaa" episode of Bloom's masturbation with the Benediction of the Blessed Sacrament taking place during a temperance retreat at a nearby church.[21] Focusing on some of the same fictional episodes, Mary Lowe-Evans in *Catholic Nostalgia in Joyce and Company* argues contrarily that Joyce's fiction is driven by a nostalgic desire to recuperate the Catholic beliefs with which he was indoctrinated as a young man, specifically that of the immortality of the soul. Regardless of Joyce's heretical tendencies, Lowe-Evans ultimately concludes that his artistic "forays into his Catholic past, as often as not, enable rather than dismantle the institutional Church."[22]

This tendency toward extreme bifurcation in the categorizing of Joyce's relationship to Catholicism arises to some extent from the prevailing conception of modern secularity. In the standard version of the rise of secularism, the steady advance of scientific discovery, instrumental rationality, and economic and political specialization leads to an inexorable waning of religious belief. Within such a framework, one is either aligned with the progressive forces of unbelief or cast as anachronistically holding onto an outworn creed, or, perhaps worst of all, seen as blindly veering back and forth between these opposing poles. Charles Taylor's recent revisionary account of the development of the secular West enables a more nuanced perspective on the nature of religious experience available in the modern age. According to Taylor, secularity does not so much involve the eclipse of religious faith by a burgeoning rationality as it does the gradual detachment of faith from its secure moorings in collective political and social identities. This decoupling of religious belief from any authorizing civic framework, together with an abiding sense of lack that can only be redressed through "solicitations of the spiritual," has opened up an intermediate zone between the poles of dogmatic faith and thoroughgoing atheism.[23] The creation of "this free and neutral space" gives rise to what Taylor refers to as the "nova effect," the proliferation in modernity of diverse and hybrid variants of belief and unbelief—all of which remain conditional, cut loose from any overarching societal legitimation.[24] This effect did not occur synchronically throughout the Western world. It was especially delayed, Taylor notes, in countries such as Ireland and Poland where nationalist aspirations had long been thwarted and where Catholicism remained linked to national identity throughout much of the twentieth century.[25] This absence in Ireland of any cultural zone for free thinking about religion is, more than anything else, what drove Joyce into exile from his homeland.

In his recent work, the contemporary Irish philosopher Richard Kearney provides a more detailed mapping of the hermeneutical activities associated with this liminal territory, where "the free decision to believe or not believe is not just tolerated, but cherished."[26] Located outside the citadel of faith but not within the comfortable precincts of a secure atheism, the domain of "anatheism" is distinguished by plurality, ontological uncertainty, and transitivity. It elicits from those who venture there a willingness not only to critique the tenets and rituals of inherited creeds, but also to refashion them. These salvaging operations approach but do not necessarily cross over the border of religious belief. Indeed, for Kearney, it is the incessant "wagering between belief and nonbelief" that demarcates this discursive space.[27] Kearney draws his understanding of the anatheist habit of mind from the hermeneutic philosophy of his mentor, the French philosopher Paul Ricoeur. The imperative that lies at the heart of Ricoeur's religious thinking requires a passage from the naïve "immediacy of belief" to the "second naivete" of a critically chastened, demythologized rendition of the original belief. Through such a movement, Ricoeur suggests, "'modernity' transcends itself," overcoming the annulling of the sacred that for many constitutes its essence.[28] Kearney invests anatheism with a similar promise and, tellingly, identifies Joyce's fiction as a site where that promise has been realized. In Kearney's reading, Stephen Dedalus's aesthetic redaction of the Eucharist near the end of *A Portrait of the Artist as a Young Man*—his intention to become "a priest of the eternal imagination, transmuting the daily bread of experience into the radiant body of everliving life"—is embraced by Joyce himself and brought to fruition in *Ulysses*.[29] But this only happens after Joyce subjects the "official" Catholic version of the Eucharist to a variety of parodic iterations and, thereby, demystifies it. That frees the novel to pursue, as it does so brilliantly, the incarnational possibilities of the quotidian, a process that culminates in Molly's final unconditional affirmation of existence. Her full-throated embrace of life constitutes, to adapt a term from Ricoeur, a postcritical hierophany.[30] For Kearney, it "epitomizes" the "anatheist move."[31]

In his re-tailoring of the remnants of a deconstructed Catholicism to fashion ad hoc forms of sacrality, Joyce establishes a paradigm for subsequent Irish Catholic writers. But the pattern is not realized in the expected literary locations. As many scholars have noted, the fictional mode that prevailed in Ireland in the aftermath of Joyce was a local variant of naturalism.[32] Mid- to late-twentieth-century Irish novelists such as Sean O'Faolain, John McGahern, and Edna O'Brien honed this bleak realism into a sharp-edged instrument of critique and then used it to lay bare the morbidity of the Irish Catholic Church. They targeted the sources of corruption that Joyce had previously anatomized: the Church's authoritarianism, its hypocritical betrayal of its own precepts, its insistence upon a childlike obedience from its members, its reduction of ritual to mindless routine, its fostering of a crippling scrupulosity, and, most significantly, its fear and loathing of sexuality. Because their narratives spotlighted the profound suffering of those entrapped within this malign system, the attack on Irish Catholicism enacted by these writers was devastating. But it was offset by a latent determinism that inhibited these works from ever advancing beyond critique to a transformation of Catholic practices and beliefs. They were capable of unraveling the imposing raiment of Irish Catholicism but not of fabricating anything new or more liberating from its filaments.

If one turns to Irish poetry, the most likely heirs to Joyce's aesthetic engagement with Catholicism would seem to be the loose coterie of modernist poets that arrived on the Irish literary scene in the 1930s. First identified as a group by Joyce's protégé Samuel Beckett, in his polemical review "Recent Irish Poetry" (1934), these poets—Thomas MacGreevy, Denis Devlin, and Brian Coffey—wore their Catholicism on their metaphorical sleeves. Their work addressed issues of faith with the mandarin subtlety that one would expect from epigones of modernism. In Beckett's formulation, what distinguished this group from their counterparts, the "antiquarians" still caught up in the vestiges of the Celtic Revival, was their awareness of the dissolution of traditional conceptions of reality, or what Beckett referred to as "the breakdown of the object."[33] Enabled by that recognition, these poets focused upon "the act . . . not the object of perception."[34] In the realm of faith, this resulted, as Beckett indicated in a separate review on Devlin, in a poetry that welcomed its severance from "social reality" in order to concentrate solely upon an interior spiritual quest. Beckett employed a familiar modern touchstone when he cast this poetry—this time referring specifically to MacGreevy—as being analogous to prayer.[35]

The qualities of this modernist verse adduced by Beckett—its intercessional nature as well as its abstraction from concrete social reality—are precisely what separates it from Joyce's irreverent delving into the communal experience of Irish Catholicism. The difference becomes apparent with even a cursory glance at the work of Denis Devlin, the most accomplished of these poets. Devlin (1908–1959) was born in Scotland to Irish emigrant parents but was educated primarily in Ireland, eventually receiving an MA in French from University College, Dublin, where he had a brief tenure as a lecturer. Most of his all too short adult life was spent away from Ireland in diplomatic service with the Irish government's Department of Foreign Affairs. That long "exile" from his cultural homeland is perhaps less a cause than an outgrowth of the deracinated cosmopolitanism evident even in the verse written prior to his diplomatic career. At its best, Devlin's poetry reprises the virtues of the early seventeenth-century metaphysical poets—John Donne, George Herbert, Richard Crashaw, Henry Vaughn—who were much in vogue when he began his poetic career, largely due to T. S. Eliot's promotion of them over the Romantics and Victorians in the English literary canon. The cultivation of the paradoxes inherent in Christianity, the playful exploitation of doctrinal niceties, the penchant for wrenched syntax and catachrestic metaphors—all of these qualities infused the religious poetry of the Metaphysicals with dramatic intensity of an authentic spiritual struggle. And they have a similar effect in Devlin's early poem, "Est Prodest," which Beckett highlighted in his review. At its outset, the poem evokes the remoteness of the divine through a symbolic geography that locates God as a polar terminus: "Tablelands of ice / Bastions of blocks of light / Are his identity."[36] That sense of spiritual alienation manifests itself internally in the poet's struggle to bridge the chasm between an incarnate God and an intrinsically corrupt humanity:

> If One they all say
> Shows himself in us
> Groups of men and women
> Mnemonic said of Eden
> That stink high in our nostrils
> Rich and poor and dead
> Then how darkly he
> Is broken among us
> In frosty slopes at hazard.[37]

Throughout its next dozen or so stanzas, "Est Prodest" spins forth from this crucial paradox of the incarnation an array, both abstruse and scintillating, of what the poem refers to as "frightened antinomies." In keeping with its Metaphysical precursors, the poem's resolution has the abruptness of an answered prayer, registered here in the sudden transformation of its initial glacial setting: "His cliffs of ice are melted, / Lord, thy wind with pollen! / Green land, be lilied with springs!"[38] As "Est Prodest" testifies, Devlin's devotional verse could never be accused, as Katharine Tynan's was, of neglecting "the profounder aspects of Catholicism." But for some readers, most notably Seamus Heaney, Devlin's poetry suffers under the "strain" of its scaffold of abstractions and its sedulousness. Even when Devlin anchored his poetry in a concrete religious practice as he did in "Lough Derg," named after the most popular pilgrimage site of Irish Catholicism, the result remained the same: a poem inhabited by the ghostly traces of a meditative mind rather than "the company of flesh and blood."[39] The gap between Devlin's aesthetic appropriation of Irish Catholicism and Joyce's is, ironically, perhaps best captured by T. S. Eliot's distinction between the self-consciousness of Metaphysical devotional poetry and a more authentic religious literature that would be "*un*consciously . . . Christian."[40] Eliot's exemplar of the latter is Dante, whose Catholic faith, in contrast to Joyce, remained indisputable. Yet for Joyce, as for Dante, the Catholicism that permeated his culture entered his work less by invitation than by osmosis.

While Devlin is often identified as Catholic poet, such a label could not be comfortably attached to any of the poets surveyed in this book. Their work lacks the devotional impetus and theological focus so strikingly evident not just in "Est Prodest" but even more so in Devlin's late poem, "The Passion of the Christ." Nonetheless, Catholicism seeps into their poetry as it did into Joyce's fiction. Its presence there, if not entirely unconscious as Eliot would have it, springs organically from their lived experience in a world inundated with Catholic ritual and doctrine. Their poetry does not forfeit the social reality of religious faith in favor of an interiorized spiritual struggle, as Beckett praises Devlin's for doing. Rather these poets consistently throw into relief the cultural substrate of the beliefs and practices of Irish Catholicism that impinge upon their psyches. Thus, for Austin Clarke (1896–1974), the earliest of the poets examined here, the trauma occasioned by an inquisitorial focus on masturbation in the confessional epitomized the Irish Catholic Church's large-scale effort to police and monopolize all discourse on sexuality. In the case of Patrick Kavanagh (1904–1967), the struggle to assert the value of the parochial, to concatenate the peripheral place with the Absolute, reflected the tensions that accompanied the Church's subsuming of localized nodes of the sacred, such as holy wells, within a centralized spiritual geography. The Northern Irish Catholic poet, John Montague (1929–), reveals how the scar of Partition etched so indelibly upon his psyche is also inscribed upon the sacrament of the Eucharist as it is appropriated by propagandists from both sides of the sectarian divide. Similarly, his more well-known Northern compatriot, Seamus Heaney (1939–) traces the guilt attending his poetic vocation to the sacrificial impetus that Irish Catholicism channels into mundane acts of self-denial as well as grander penitential exercises. When Eiléan Ní Chuilleanáin (1942–) interrogates the spectral figure of the nun haunting her imagination, she exposes the ambiguous legacy of Catholic women religious in Irish culture, the way in which they subverted the dominant patriarchal structure even as they were co-opted by it. Paul Durcan (1944–) links the psychological pain inflicted by a priestly standard of masculinity to the Catholic hierarchy's assertions of authority over the Irish body politic. For Paula Meehan (1955–), the youngest of the poets addressed here, the psychological and physical repression of women by the institutional Church culminates in the Marian cult that flourished among Irish Catholics.

While these poets are all sufficiently accomplished to generate aesthetic and intellectual interest on their own terms, their presence here derives from their colloquy with Irish Catholicism. In each case, that exchange is overt and far-reaching. It extends beyond the commonplace practice of the faith to its more sensational cultural manifestations—pilgrimages to holy wells, Croagh Patrick, and Lough Derg; the Eucharistic Congress of 1932; the outburst of Marian apparitions in the mid-1980s; the scandalous revelations concerning Magdalen asylums and clerical abuse in the 1990s; the enormously popular tour of Theresian relics in 2001. For some of these poets, the confrontation with Irish Catholicism is crystallized in a signature work, such as Clarke's *Mnemosyne Lay in Dust*, Kavanagh's *The Great Hunger*, Montague's "The Bread God," Heaney's "Station Island," and Meehan's "The Statue of the Virgin at Granard Speaks." Where that doesn't happen, as with Ní Chuilleanáin and Durcan, Catholic subject matter is dispersed throughout their oeuvres. For each of these poets, though, the struggle with their inherited faith constitutes a defining vector in the trajectory of their poetic careers.

The absence of these elements has led to the exclusion of several major poets of this period whose background is Irish Catholic. While the poetry of Eavan Boland (1944–) challenges the code of female domesticity sanctioned by the Irish Catholic Church, it is the critique of the nationalist mythos of Mother Ireland that ultimately drives her poetry. The ludic experimentation with form and language that has elevated Paul Muldoon

(1951–) to a position of prominence in both Irish and American poetic circles touches only tangentially upon Catholic themes. With Thomas Kinsella (1928–), the omission is perhaps more debatable. Allusions to Catholic doctrine and rituals recur periodically throughout his earlier poetry and have become increasingly prominent in recent Peppercanister volumes. But in my estimation, these references remain closer to the circumference than the center of a poetic imagination drawn by the magnetic pull of Jungian and ancient Irish myths of origin.

What sets the poetry examined in this book apart is the particularity with which it reconstitutes religious beliefs and principles. The distinctiveness of its constellation of poetry and religion derives from the asynchronous nature of twentieth-century Irish Catholicism. During a period when secular modernity had consolidated its cultural hold over the rest of the Western world, the hegemony of the Catholic Church in Ireland reached its apex. Even as late as the early 1960s, the sociologist C. K. Ward reported that the "proportions of Sunday church-goers and paschal communicants" probably included "ninety-five percent of urban Catholics and an even higher percentage of rural Catholics."[41] The establishment of the "free and neutral space" that, according to Taylor, characterizes modern secularity was achieved incrementally in Ireland, through a prolonged siege leveled by artistic and intellectual elites against the cultural and political authority of the Catholic Church. The barricade against modern culture that the Church hierarchy erected in the 1920s through censorship laws and hectoring encyclicals was breached early and often, but not without a price being exacted on the abettors of such intrusions. One need look no further than the abuse heaped upon W. B. Yeats in the early days of the Irish Free State by the *Catholic Bulletin* and other Church organs for his opposition to Church-sponsored legislative initiatives prohibiting divorce and expanding censorship. Inoculated by his "outsider" status as member of the Protestant ascendency and his worldwide renown, Yeats was not so much intimidated as energized by these attacks. He launched his counteroffensive against Irish Catholicism's rigid puritanism with the frontal assault of poems such as "Leda and the Swan" and "Crazy Jane Talks with the Bishop." By contrast, his younger and less established contemporary, the Irish Catholic poet Austin Clarke, masked similar critiques

it of any substantive content, preserving "emotions without the beliefs with which their history has been involved."[45] In contrast to Eliot, who insists that nothing can substitute for religious faith, Charles Taylor credits Arnold with establishing poetry's role as a viable option for those moderns inhabiting the borderland between belief and unbelief. Even more forcefully than Arnold, he insists upon the epiphanic power of romantic and post-romantic poetry, casting it as "the locus of a manifestation which brings us into the presence of something which is otherwise inaccessible, and which is of the highest moral and spiritual significance."[46] But since this poetry operates in the absence of any prevailing framework of transcendental truths, its epiphanies are always filtered through the poet's subjectivity, always "indexed to a personal vision."[47] As such, these poetic epiphanies come trailing clouds of hazy indeterminacy. They "open us to mystery," but having retreated from "ontic commitments," that is, determinate claims about the nature of ultimate reality, they too easily dissipate into amorphousness.[48]

The poetry discussed in this book is not immune to this condition. It does not aspire to creedal veridicality any more than its romantic and post-romantic precursors or modern counterparts do. But because of the uniquely liminal framework in which this poetry was produced, its spiritual manifestations are more definitive than those generated in societies where religion did not have the ubiquitous presence that it did in twentieth-century Ireland. Eiléan Ní Chuilleanáin's transference of the cloister's sacrality to the female body itself, John Montague's secular expansion of a eucharistic community founded on an all-inclusive charity, Paula Meehan's extrapolating of a more empowering visionary potential from Marian devotion, Seamus Heaney's exporting of grace from the religious superstructure of sacrifice to unsolicited experiences of givenness—these revelations as well as others garner authority not just from the poet's individual imagination but from the residue of traditional beliefs that still clings to them. Through their reverberations of a living—albeit precariously so—body of faith, they take on an additional cultural valence. Such a recognition is implicit in Heaney's defense of his own more modest cooptation of an indigenous Catholic tradition over against Yeats's magisterial creation of an uniquely syncretic mythos.

Regardless of Heaney's distinction, the syncretism so characteristic of modern poetry enters the poetry addressed here as well, whether in the form of Heaney's use of archaic Celtic and Germanic sacrificial myths or Montague's appropriations of chaos theory or Meehan's dabbling in Buddhism. But it is always complemented by the poets' reliance upon more culturally resonant Catholic matter. This will become increasingly rare as Catholicism recedes ever more rapidly to the margins of Irish social and cultural life. The poetry generated in that post-Catholic era will not register with the same urgency the threatening psychic and cultural potency of Irish Catholicism. As a consequence, while poets may still occasionally employ Catholic images and themes, they will not feel as compelled to work through this Catholic material. Whatever shards of Catholicism they choose to retrieve will already be pliable and, therefore, will not need to be deconstructed and refashioned. The value of that process will be clearer after we have surveyed the transfigurations that the poets in this book wring from their agonistic encounters with their inherited faith. Then perhaps we might be inclined to add a note of regret to the general celebratory chorus heralding the passing of Irish Catholicism.

1

Austin Clarke's (Anti-)Confessional Poetics

No modern Irish writer was more traumatized by Catholicism than the poet Austin Clarke (1896–1974). The specific cause of this psychic wounding emerges in his poetry only after decades of evasive disclosures and silence. But if Clarke's autobiography is to be believed, that early and distinctively Catholic trauma fashioned his imagination. He opens the first volume of his memoirs, *Twice Round the Black Church*, by recalling the guilty fear aroused in him as a young child by the apparently moving eyes of a portrait of Shakespeare. Clarke invests this seemingly trivial episode with a status akin to that of the boat-stealing passage in the opening book of Wordsworth's *The Prelude*: it is the moment that marks the poet's birth into the sublimity of his own imagination. Against the obsessive hold that the painting exerts over his imagination, the young Clarke finds that the conscious exertions of his will are futile. It is only when his imagination is guided by unconscious forces, when an act of somnambulism brings him unexpectedly into the painting's presence, that the fear it inspired suddenly dissolves. This episode, positioned at the outset of Clarke's autobiography, serves as an apt synecdoche for a poetic career defined by the imagination's co-optation by and resistance to the experience of panoptic surveillance institutionalized in the Catholic ritual of confession.

Later in the memoir, it becomes apparent that Shakespeare's portrait, with its seemingly omniscient gaze, is a surrogate for the actual agent of surveillance that imprinted itself upon the poet's nascent consciousness. When he was seven, Clarke made his first confession. After he had disclosed his "little tale of fibs, disobedience and loss of temper," the priest asked him a "strange question" that he found incomprehensible. When he demurred, the priest questioned him more rigorously until he finally "in fear and desperation . . . admitted to the unknown sin."[1] The question that the priest asked concerned the act of taking pleasure in touching oneself. In pursuing such a line of inquiry, if not in his overly zealous persistence, Clarke's confessor was following the recommendations of the standard manuals concerning the administration of confession. The young Clarke's subsequent experiences of confession confirmed this. His family, like many Catholics in Ireland at this time, believed confession to be a necessary prerequisite for the reception of the Eucharist at Sunday mass. Because of the incessant questioning about his sexual urges and his guilt-inducing attempts at evasion, confession became "a weekly ordeal."[2] It was only later in young adulthood that he fully realized how deleterious "the effects of this tampering" with his psyche were.[3] In both his autobiographical verse and prose, Clarke obliquely links the psychic wounds induced by this early interrogation of his sexuality to his failure to consummate his love relationship with Geraldine Cummins (referred to in both his memoir and poetry under the pseudonym Margaret), an artistically inclined young woman whose early religious life was, like his own, shaped by "insidious questioning in the confessional."[4] The sexual difficulties associated with this relationship were a catalyst for a mental breakdown that confined Clarke to a mental hospital for a thirteen-month period from 1919 to 1920. Eventually, after his release from the asylum and the collapse of his short-lived and apparently unconsummated marriage to Cummins, Clarke began the arduous process of addressing the trauma that lay at the root of these personal catastrophes.

Critics have often designated Clarke's poetry as "confessional," largely on the basis of his long autobiographical poem *Mnemosyne Lay in Dust*, which described in detail his confinement in St. Patrick's Hospital, the mental asylum located in the center of Dublin. But only rarely do they register the full significance of this term as it applies to Clarke's work. The exception is John Goodby, who adumbrates this chapter's line of argument by briefly linking Clarke's confessional poetics to Michel Foucault's analysis of the disciplinary power of the Catholic ritual of confession.[5] In its typical literary usage, the term "confessional" encompasses a subgenre of poetry inaugurated by American poets of the 1950s and '60s (most notably, Robert Lowell, John Berryman, Sylvia Plath, and Anne Sexton) that foregrounds the intimate and, occasionally, sordid details of the poet's private life. As the term implies, such poetry was seen as analogous to the sacrament of confession and its secular counterpart, the "talking cure" of modern psychoanalysis. Thus, Robert Phillips, writing in one of the first scholarly studies of this group of poets, asserts that "these new confessional poets give to the public those outpourings previously reserved for the Father Confessor or the analyst."[6] In Austin Clarke's case, though, this label takes on a highly charged and ironic valence, for the personal traumas that his poetry divulges are presented as having been initiated by the very act of sacramental confession. Far from being an extension of this ritual, the confessional dimension of Clarke's poetry is predicated upon his critical scrutiny and radical revision of the Catholic sacrament of confession. Indeed, the overall trajectory of Austin Clarke's poetic career is distinguished by his development of a paradoxical (anti-)confessional poetics in which a therapeutic imperative to confess unfolds in tandem with the exposure of the ecclesiastical deformation of that act. This deconstruction of the Catholic ritual of auricular confession eventuates in a healing gesture that moves far beyond the effort of other confessional poets to annul their worst depredations by transforming them into art. The ultimate outcome of Clarke's poetry, like that of the ritual it usurps, is absolution, an act of liberation rather than commutation. Purged of the scrutinizing judgment and penitential discipline of the confessional, the absolution that Clarke offers is absolute rather than conditional. Its promise of freedom from guilt is comprehensive, extending beyond the poet's self to all of humanity, opening itself to even the most profound forms of alterity.

1

While the provenance of the private auricular mode of confession that has characterized the Catholic sacrament of penance throughout the last millennium is uncertain, no place has a better claim to being the site of its origin than Ireland. In the first centuries of the Church, penance was a matter of public display rather than a private exchange.[7] Those who had committed the most egregious sins—apostasy or murder—were consigned by the local bishop to an order of penitents who were removed from ordinary communal life and subjected to spectacular forms of penitence that included shaving heads for males and veiling faces for females, wearing sackcloth and ashes, and arduous fasting. In this formation, penance was a lengthy ordeal undertaken once in a lifetime and then only by a very few among the community of believers.[8] During the sixth and seventh centuries, an alternative mode of repentance arose in the monastic orders. There the expectation that the monk reveal his sins on a regular basis to the abbot or an elder inaugurated a roughhewn version of auricular confession. This practice was first formalized via penitential manuals that provided exhaustive lists of sins and corresponding penances, the first and most significant of which were produced by Irish monastics. In the penitentials of Irish saints such as Finnian (c. 590) and Columbanus (c. 608), this auricular mode of penance was interwoven with the Celtic tradition of soliciting spiritual guidance from an *anamchara* or "soul-friend."[9] The first of these manuals, "The Penitential of Finnian," reveals through its distinct classifying of sins of clergy and of laity that this new form of private confession was intended not just for those who had taken religious vows but for laity as well.[10] Even more significantly, the confessions mandated by these penitentials were not the one-time generic declaration of sinfulness that those entering the earlier order of penitents had made. They involved instead a frequent and thoroughgoing articulation of specific sins, including even such seemingly trivial matters as mental lapses.[11]

If the Irish penitentials provided the template for the modern ritual of private confession, its full-scale implementation was not realized until the fourth Lateran Council in the early thirteenth century, which obliged all laity to confess their sins to a priest annually and required clergy themselves to confess even more frequently. It was at this time that confession acquired the disciplinary power attributed to it by the French philosopher Michel Foucault. According to Foucault, in the Christian era the classical injunction to "know oneself" was transmuted into an imperative to confess the "truth about oneself," a duty to scrutinize the deepest recesses of the self in order to first discover and then articulate the truths hidden there.[12] In Foucault's genealogy, while the Lateran council represented "a formidable extension" of the sacrament, the sixteenth-century Council of Trent's intensification and refinement of its disciplinary power was even more significant.[13] In its Tridentine formulation, the practice of confession was augmented through the development of the private confessional box and rigorous discursive strategies for the examination of penitents. These innovations immeasurably strengthened the capacity of confession to effect the "continual management of souls, conducts, and finally, bodies."[14] The last of these—the exertion of mastery over the flesh—was, according to Foucault, the ultimate aim of this expansion of the techniques associated with confession. During this early modern period, confession centered upon the sins of lust generally associated with the Sixth Commandment. Whereas previously such sins had been defined primarily in terms of improper external relationships, they were now internalized, regarded as intrinsic to the individual's corporeal nature.[15] Under this new regime, both penitent and confessor were faced with a seemingly impossible obligation, the duty to expose the first traces of concupiscent desire in the individual, to bring under the purview of confession "all the insinuations of the flesh: thoughts, desires, voluptuous imaginings, delectations, combined movements of the body and the soul."[16] The guiding assumption of this inquisitorial process was that lust has its provenance in the desire for oneself. Indeed, Foucault goes so far as to claim that the Council of Trent rendered "the discourse of confession" into "the discourse of shame and of the control and correction of sexuality [that] essentially begins with masturbation."[17] However tendentious such an assertion may be, Austin Clarke's experience offers powerful confirmation of the core of truth embedded within it.

Perhaps even more pertinent for understanding of the impact of confession upon Clarke's poetry are Foucault's insights concerning the discursive structure of the practice of confession. The disciplinary power of confession derives in large part, according to Foucault, from the dialectic of "enunciation" and "silence" that it imposes upon discourse about sexuality.[18] On the one hand, the practice of confession demands that the individual give voice to sexual desire, articulate the most minute arousals of the flesh. Yet even while confession compels speech about sexuality, it imposes stringent restrictions upon the circumstances in which such speech is allowed. In the confession box, one must speak about sexuality, but outside of that narrow zone, one is expected to remain silent. This dynamic would have been even more acute for those who like Austin Clarke lived in a society that aggressively enforced this injunction against speech about sexuality through rigid censorship laws and a repressive moral code. The effect of such an arrangement was to ensure that speech about sexuality occurred within a highly imbalanced discursive situation, where the power resides not with the speaker but entirely with the auditor, who judges and directs.[19] More than anything else, it was this conjoining of the articulation of sexuality to its judgment by an institutional authority that invested the practice of confession with such extraordinary regulatory power over the individual psyche.

Austin Clarke was hardly the only Irish writer whose youth was marked by the shame and angst that accompanied the obligation to confess one's sins in detail to a stranger. One of the more distressing scenes in James Joyce's *A Portrait of the Artist as Young Man* involves Stephen Dedalus's confession of his manifold acts of sexual immorality to a Capuchin priest in the Church Street Chapel, an episode drawn directly from Joyce's own life.[20] But in the case of Stephen Dedalus (and of his creator as well), this experience in the confessional caps a temporary period of religious renewal that is quickly superseded by a commitment to an aesthetic vocation rooted in the pains and pleasures of temporal life. Tellingly, Joyce's first published story, "The Sisters" from *Dubliners*, registers not only his awareness of the insidious power of confession but his ability to master it through his art. Near the end of story, one of the sisters reveals that her brother Fr. Flynn was relieved of his priestly duties after being found alone and laughing madly in the confession box. By showing the confessor rather than the penitent as the one enervated by the onerous obligations of confession, Joyce reverses the power dynamics of the ritual. It is a different matter altogether with Austin Clarke, who, lacking his predecessor's confidence and resilience, struggled throughout both his personal and artistic life to redress the ill effects of his early confessions.

The disciplinary regime of confession to which both Joyce and Clarke were subjected was not an isolated feature of Irish life but was instead a widespread cultural phenomenon from the late nineteenth through much of the twentieth century. In contrast to other sacraments, detailed evidence concerning the extent and frequency of confession among Catholics is hard to come by since the aura of secrecy surrounding the ritual prohibits the keeping of any official records.[21] Nonetheless, the prevalence of confession among Irish Catholics in the last century is supported both by anecdotal observation as well as more formal sociological data. Louise Fuller, the preeminent historian of Irish Catholicism in the second half of the twentieth century, points out that in the 1950s "on Saturday nights, there were long queues for confession throughout the length and breadth of the country."[22] Her assertion correlates with the results of a comprehensive national survey from 1974 that showed that 70 percent of Irish Catholics went to confession on a bimonthly basis.[23] Given the slippage in such practices in the aftermath of the Second Vatican Council, it seems reasonable to extrapolate similar, if not even higher, rates of participation for confession in early twentieth-century Ireland.

Frequent private confession on such a mass scale was, however, anomalous in the larger schema of Irish Catholicism, an outgrowth of modernizing reforms and the sharp increase in the number of clergy and churches that occurred throughout the latter half of the nineteenth century. Prior to that time, the disciplinary power of confession was limited. According to S. J. Connolly, Irish Catholics in the late eighteenth and early nineteenth century were concerned about confession "only in the context of not dying without absolution" and conceived of it "not in terms of the theology of repentance and amendment, but as a wiping of the slate to be accomplished before death." For most, participation in the sacrament was "confined to the canonical minimum of once or twice a year, and in many cases attendance fell below even this minimum standard."[24] At the same time, though, priests of this period were trained, in keeping with the Tridentine intensification of confession, to subject penitents to an exacting process of examination. A manual used for the instruction of seminarians in Maynooth in the early nineteenth century presented the confessor's role as relentlessly inquisitorial:

> Since the confessor acts the part both of judge and a physician, he ought to become acquainted with the diseases and the offences of the penitent,

> in order that he may be able to apply suitable remedies, and impose due penance, and lest a sin that is mortal should be accounted as venial, or the foul viper lurking in the deep recesses of the heart should not venture to put itself forth to view, he ought to therefore sometimes to question the penitents on the subject of the 6th . . . commandment, where he suspects that they are not altogether pure, especially if they be rude, ignorant, bashful or agitated . . . A prudent confessor will, as far as in his power, advance from more general statements to more particular: from the less shameful to those which are more so; nor will he take his commencement from the external acts, but from the thoughts. Has not the penitent revolved some improper ones in his or her mind? Was this done advertently? What kind of desire was it? Has he or she felt unlawful passions?[25]

Such confessional rigorism was, however, more a matter of theory than common practice. In the pre-Famine period, most Catholics fulfilled their canonical obligation of annual confession through "stations of confession," a customary practice in which biannually "in preparation for Christmas and Easter, the priest went to a number of designated houses in his extensive parish to hear confessions and say Mass."[26] In such circumstances, confession was a perfunctory matter, a quick sotto voce declaration of one's sins in the adjacency of a crowd of one's neighbors. William Carleton, who as a Catholic peasant in the early nineteenth century had certainly participated in such stations, describes in his story "The Station" how the priest in his eagerness to get to the feast that culminated the station "contrived to unsin . . . [the parishioners] with an alacrity that was really surprising."[27]

Whatever Carleton's penchant for exaggerating abuses in Catholic practice, the basic accuracy of his description is confirmed by the considerable efforts that the Catholic hierarchy took to delimit confession to churches and, thereby, eradicate a custom they regarded as barbarous and ineffectual. Resistance to this new and more private form of confession was so strong though that the practice of holding "stations of confession" persisted well after the Dublin provincial decrees of 1831 called for their abolition. It was only gradually throughout the latter half of the nineteenth century that stations gave way to confession held at scheduled times in churches.[28] The ordeal of being regularly scrutinized in the privacy of the confession box that Austin Clarke endured as a young boy was then a relatively new phenomenon in Irish culture. It is not surprising, therefore, that in his initial reaction against this modern instrument of ecclesiastical control Clarke turned to the distant cultural past for aid.

2

Austin Clarke began his poetic career with redactions of the foundational myths of the Gaelic past, *The Vengeance of Fionn* (1917) and *The Sword of the West* (1921). This belated attempt to align his work with the previous generation's grand project of cultural renascence reflects both the young poet's insecurity and his ambition. With his next books, *The Cattledrive in Connaught* (1925) and *Pilgrimage and Other Poems* (1929), Clarke managed more successfully to differentiate his work from that of his Revivalist precursors as he increasingly employed the material gleaned from the Celtic past to address, however obliquely, the personal traumas triggered by his early subjection to a sexually repressive Church. Such a maneuver, Clarke suggested, was less a matter of personal than cultural authenticity. In a note appended a few years later to what is perhaps the most noteworthy poem from *Pilgrimage*, "The Young Woman of Beare," Clarke indicated that "the drama of racial conscience" evinced in this poem's overt conflict between sexual desire and ecclesiastical authority is one that "particularizes" or distinguishes Irish poetry and that it was ignored by the "elder poets of the Celtic Twilight" because, he implies, they lacked firsthand experience of that conflict. He further emphasized this poem's present-day relevance in a newly independent Ireland where "the immodesty of present-day female dress is denounced in virile Pastorals, and our Parliament passes laws against temptations."[29] It is widely recognized that in this first phase of his poetic career, Clarke strategically culled material from the Celtic past, especially from the early medieval Celtic Church, in an effort to illuminate his struggle against the Irish Catholic orthodoxy of his own day. Gregory Schirmer articulates the consensual view regarding the nature of this complex act of cultural refraction: "Medieval Ireland served Clarke as an extended metaphoric vehicle, then, in two ways—as a time when religion, in contrast to that of the present day, was devoted to learning and art, and as a time when religion, in a sorry parallel to modern Ireland, worked against natural human instincts."[30] Expanding upon the second of these points, Maurice Harmon suggests that Clarke found validation for his own suffering in "certain historical figures" of this period who exhibited "the same kind of mental uncertainty that Clarke himself had been educated into and which was the consequence of the modern Church's insistence on rules and regulations."[31] Such assessments, accurate enough at a surface level, fail to adequately register the specific strategic function that animates Clarke's most potent appropriations from this cultural depository. What is missing here is a recognition of the way in which Clarke in these early poems positions the treatment of sexual desire in the medieval period as a counter to the process of intensive surveillance that characterized the modern ritual of confession. In several key poems from *The Cattledrive in Connaught* and *Pilgrimage and Other Poems*, Clarke shows how the practices and accomplishments of the Celtic-Romanesque Church as well as the actions of its pagan opponents not only countenance but even sanction those "insinuations of the flesh" that the practice of confession in early twentieth-century Ireland ruthlessly sought to extirpate.

In the delicately wrought "Secrecy," from *The Cattledrive in Connaught*, Clarke casts what is perhaps the greatest cultural achievement of the early medieval Irish Church, the Book of Kells, as a bower in which erotic desire is both protected from the judgmental gaze of ecclesiastical authority and transmuted into timeless art:

> Had we been only lovers from a book
> That holy men who had a hand in heaven
> Illuminated: in a yellow wood,
> Where crimson beast and bird are clawed with gold
> And, wound in branches, hunt or hawk themselves,
> Sun-woman, I would hide you as the ring
> Of his own shining fetters that the snake,
> Who is the wood itself, can never find.[32]

This poem's sanctioning of desire is strengthened when it is contrasted to the situation described in an earlier piece from this volume, "Scandal," where the speaker laments the public exposure and condemnation of his love affair by a priest to whom his lover has ostensibly confessed her sin. In "Secrecy," the lovers' preying upon one another's flesh is not rudely exposed but artfully concealed.

The poet envisions concupiscent desire as being protected and preserved through its literal insinuation into the zoomorphic letters of the illuminated manuscript, a condition that the poetic text itself replicates with its convolved syntax and intricately interwoven patterns of oblique rhyme and alliteration. Secrecy, the poem implies, fosters sublimation. When erotic desire is not cancelled out by the censorious gaze of authority, its energy is held in reserve and made available for higher purposes, such as the production of works of art like the Book of Kells.

In "The Young Woman of Beare," from *Pilgrimage and Other Poems*, concupiscent desire is exonerated not by its incorporation into the high cultural treasures of the church but rather through its affiliation with a mythic figure drawn from popular folkloric tradition. The speaker of Clarke's poem is, as Maurice Harmon notes, a younger variant of the mythic Old Woman of Beare, the *caillech Bhéire Buí*, a sovereignty goddess and a precursor of latter-day Mother Ireland figures whose love affairs, as recorded in an Old Irish poem, served primarily to legitimate the political authority of a succession of west Munster kings.[33] What is most telling for our purposes is the way in which Clarke uses this personification of the "bright temptation" of the flesh to transvalue key aspects of the modern practice of confession:

> Half in dream I lie there
> Until *bad thoughts* have bloomed
> In flushes of desire.
> Drowsy with *indulgence*,
> I please a secret eye
> That opens at the *Judgment*. (*CPC*, 161; emphasis added)

Rather than being flushed out, condemned, and subjected to remission, the "bad thoughts" that the young woman of Beare induces in herself and others foster a sensual reverie that animates the inner eye of the spirit. The recounting of her various sexual exploits offers further justification for the concupiscent desire that she embodies by linking this force to the politically powerful families that governed Ireland in its late medieval florescence—the de Burghs, Ormands, Fitzgeralds, and MacWilliams.[34] In Clarke's revision of this traditional material, the sexual exchange between these political figures and the woman of Beare serves not to confirm their political authority so much as the potency of her desire.[35] Although she offers warnings to young women not to follow her model and expresses fear of the clergy who condemn her, Clarke's young woman of Beare ultimately remains unrepentant and concludes by affirming her power over the strictures imposed by religious practice:

> The men and women murmur;
> They came back from Devotions.
> Half-wakened by the tide,
> Ships rise along the quay
> As though they were unloading.
> I turn a drowsy side—
> That dreams, the eye has known,
> May trouble souls to-night. (*CPC*, 166)

The contrast between the Tridentine ritual of confession that so traumatized Clarke in his youth and the practices of the Celtic Church is rendered even more acutely in the title poem of *Pilgrimage and Other Poems*. The pilgrimage envisioned here encompasses many of the most significant sites and artifacts associated with the golden age of the Celtic Church: Clonmacnoise, Cormac's Chapel at Cashel, Croagh Patrick, the hermitages of the ascetics on Skellig Michael, the Ardagh chalice, the Annals and illuminated manuscripts produced by monks. With its panoramic scope, its quick cuts between scenes, its foreshortening of spatial and temporal distance, the poem evokes the experience of moving alongside a museum diorama more than an actual pilgrimage route. However, "Pilgrimage" does include at least one scene that accurately reflects what would have occurred at the site of one of Ireland's most well-known pilgrimages. The poem's penultimate stanza describes the actual penitential exercises that pilgrims at Croagh Patrick—St. Patrick's "holy mountain"—performed. By incorporating St. Patrick into the scene, Clarke identifies these practices (which were, according to at least one historian, post-medieval) with the mythic origins of the Celtic Church.

Beyond a rocky townland
And that last tower where ocean
Is dim as haze, a sound
Of wild confession rose:
Black congregations moved
Around the booths of prayer
To hear a saint reprove them;
And from his boat he raised a blessing
To souls that had come down
The holy mountain of the west
Or wailed still in the cloud. (*CPC*, 152)

According to Michael Carroll, evidence indicates that by the early twelfth century, Croagh Patrick was "an established pilgrimage site" and that pilgrims there engaged in penitential fasting. At some later point, presumably after the medieval period since reports from that period fail to mention this expansion, the penitential dimension of the pilgrimage to Croagh Patrick incorporated the traditional ritual of circling around a sacred cairn while reciting prayers, a practice also designated by the term "station."[36] Since the pilgrims to Croagh Patrick often enhanced the penitential force of this ritual by conducting it in bare feet, the exercise would have been accompanied quite literally by wailing and gnashing of the teeth. Indeed, the nineteenth-century English novelist William Thackery caustically observed during his visit to Croagh Patrick in 1843 that female penitents were "shrieking with the pain of their wounds."[37] Repentance, as experienced in this traditional context, is not a matter of private scrutiny, but of public performance. Instead of a solitary psychological trauma, it involves a physical ordeal undertaken by a crowd. Because of its ecstatic, almost Dionysian nature, which the poet signals by his designation of it as "wild," this confessional ritual does not seek to regulate erotic desire so much as to provide it with a compensatory outlet.

In his next book, *Night and Morning and Other Poems* (1938), Clarke forcefully exposes the deleterious consequences that arise when communal penitential practices such as this are superseded by the intensive self-discipline of private confession. Here, Clarke less frequently examines the present through the refracting lens of the Celtic past and focuses instead on transitions within the interior life of the individual. For that reason, this book has frequently been hailed as marking the onset of Clarke's confessional poetry, where that term is understood in its more standard generic sense as referring to frank articulations of the depredations of the poet's personal life. But one has only to contrast the poems in this book with those written in the aftermath of Clarke's long hiatus from poetry to recognize the prematurity of this designation. None of the poems in *Night and Morning and Other Poems* exhibit the kind of autobiographical detail, the specific and concrete personal references that pervade "Ancient Lights," the title poem of Clarke's next book of poetry, published seventeen years after its predecessor. The anguish provoked by Clarke's early experience in the confessional undergirds *Night and Morning and Other Poems*, but it is addressed in an abstract manner that focuses less on the individualized nature of the suffering involved and more on the essential features of the phenomenon that provoked it. This is evinced by the fact that, as Vivian Mercier notes, the signature word of this book is "thought," which is used fourteen times in the eleven poems that constitute the short volume. While Mercier identifies the range of references associated with this word—from "intellectual activity" to "painful, almost obsessive recapitulation of familiar dilemmas"—he as well as other critics fail to recognize its connection to the regimen of self-examination instituted in the confession box.[38] Clarke foregrounds this connection in the opening lines of "Mortal Pride," the book's second poem:

> When thought of all our thought has crossed
> The mind in pain, God only knows
> What we must suffer to be lost,
> What soul is called our own. (*CPC*, 182)

The angst-ridden process of self-reflection described here is precisely what Tridentine confession demanded from penitents, who were expected to register even the subtlest "insinuations of the flesh" and submit them to the judgment of the confessor. The psychological strain produced by such internal surveillance runs like a fault line through most of the poems in this volume.

Clarke represents this juridical regime of self-scrutiny as a primal transgression that desecrates a prior state of innocence. In these poems, confession in its modern formulation appears to be less an event of absolution than an occasion of sin in itself. For instance, in the opening of the volume's title poem, the casuistical habit of mind that reduces "confession to despair" is identified with the persecution of Christ during his passion.

I know the injured pride of sleep,
The strippers at the mocking post,
The insult in the house of Caesar
And every moment that can hold
In brief the miserable act
Of centuries. Thought can but share
Belief—and the tormented soul,
Changing confession to despair,
Must wear a borrowed robe. (*CPC*, 181)

A similar connection is evoked, albeit more obliquely, in the description in "Mortal Pride" of how "thought of all our thought" has "*crossed* / the mind in pain" (emphasis added). This notion of confession as violation of the incarnation is intensified in this poem's second and final stanza, which alludes in a coded manner to Clarke's unconsummated and abortive first marriage:

Pray, how shall any bride discover
A husband in the state of bliss,
Learn in the curious arms of love
The ancient catechism
Man must obey? She never fears
He will forget the sacrament.
But thought is older than the years:
Before our doom, it came and went. (*CPC*, 182)

Far from describing how a husband's lapses as a confessant inhibit his marriage, as G. Craig Tapping implies, this passage suggests precisely the reverse.[39] What thwarts the sacramental union of body and soul in marriage is the relentless interrogation of sexual desire elicited by the practice of confession and the resulting tendency toward "overindulgence in continence," which Clarke in the second volume of his memoir implicitly identified as the root cause of his mental breakdown and his failed relationship with Geraldine Cummins.[40]

To the degree that a solution to the dilemma of an overscrupulous conscience is intimated in this volume, it is found in the aptly named "Repentance." The key to understanding the solution hinted at in this poem lies in the connection that Clarke posits between it and the traditional Irish literary form of the confession or repentance poem.[41] As the label suggests, such poems enumerated the poet's sins and appealed to God or Mary for forgiveness. On the basis of this brief description, the repentance poem might seem to be little more than a literary gesture of submission to religious orthodoxy. Commenting on the early nineteenth-century Irish poet Antaine Raiftearaí's (Anthony Raferty) religious poetry, including his version of the *aithri* or traditional repentance poem, Gearóid Denvir goes even further. He identifies it with an "almost Jansenistic attitude of fatalism" that "portrays man as unfree, sinful, and in need of the grace of God to achieve redemption."[42] Nonetheless, there is evidence even in the Confession poem of the aura of authority associated with the ancient role of the Irish poet or *file*. Instead of submitting himself to a priestly mediator in a private confession, the poet writing in this form publically proclaims his sins, pronounces judgment himself upon them, and solicits on his own for their absolution.

In "Repentance," as in many of his early poems, Clarke appropriates both thematic material and stylistic techniques employed by the Irish poets of the past in an effort to position himself as the modern-day heir to their cultural authority. But in this case, the poet's attempt to don the spiritual mantle of his precursors is marked by a special urgency, motivated, as it is, by a desire to resolve the deep-seated psychological trauma brought about by his experiences in the confessional. Here for the first time, Clarke describes those experiences directly: "For I had made a bad confession / Once, feared to name in ugly box / The growing pains of flesh" (*CPC*, 186). The sense of guilt-ridden doom triggered by that experience pervades the poem. To mitigate that, the persona seemingly adopts a posture of "submission [that] is explicitly fearful" although whether the poet himself endorses or ridicules this response is a matter on which critics disagree.[43] In either case, such a reading unduly privileges the poem's penultimate stanza, with its stark description of the speaker at mass "cupping . . . [his] heart with prayer" (*CPC*, 186), over its more tentative conclusion. That last stanza finds the speaker drawing solace from the legendary story of St. Patrick's casting out of demons on Croagh Patrick and envisioning the possibility of a salvific act of self-exorcism:

> No story handed down in Connaught
> Can cheat a man, nor any learning
> Keep that fire in, turn his folly
> From thinking of that book in Heaven.
> Could I unbutton mad thought, quick-save
> My skin, if I were caught at last
> Without my soul and dragged to torment,
> Ear-drumming in that dreadful place
> Where the sun hides in the waters? (*CPC*, 187)

This passage exemplifies how Clarke, through his intricate use of slant and cross rhymes, successfully translates traditional Irish poetry's complex patterns of assonance and rhyme into modern English.[44] Consider in that regard the chiasmic interplay of rhyme in this stanza's first three lines: where the phrase that opens the first line "no story" is echoed by the medial "nor any" in the next line; the phrase that begins the second, "can cheat," is an off rhyme of the word "Connaught" that concludes the first line; and the phrase straddling the caesura in the third line—"in, turn"—is an echoic inversion of "learning," the terminal word from the prior line. Masterfully accomplished at the level of style, Clarke's effort at cultural appropriation remains only partly fulfilled at the deeper level of speech act. There the poet modernizes the prayer of the traditional Confession poem by envisioning a more autonomous act of absolution, but the fact that this is posed only as a hypothetical possibility indicates his deep uncertainty about its efficacy.

The unusual verb ("unbutton") that Clarke uses to describe this hypothesized gesture of self-forgiveness links deliverance to disclosure. It is not surprising then that in the penultimate poem of this volume, "Summer Lightning," Clarke describes for the first time the darkest experience of his life, his thirteen-month-long confinement in a Dublin mental asylum. But as the title suggests, this poem offers only the briefest glimpse into this darkness. It is a snapshot that must be placed within a larger sequence to be fully understood, which only occurred twenty-eight years later when "Summer Lightning" was incorporated as section 8 of *Mnemosyne Lay in Dust*, the late confessional poem that describes in excruciating detail Clarke's hospitalization and recovery. As in "Repentance," in "Summer Lightning" the confessional act initiated by the poem remains truncated. Both poems expose the terrifying power of those ostensibly authoritative judgments imposed upon the self, but neither can muster the spiritual and imaginative resources necessary to counter those judgments. Inaugurated by a Jovian thunderbolt, "Summer Lightning" concludes its first and final stanzas with a damning appraisal of the asylum's inmates as men in whom "God's likeness died" (*CPC*, 190). The inability to check such a judgment is marked most powerfully in the diptych of delusional inmates that constitutes the third and medial stanza of "Summer Lightning":

> James Dunn leaped down the dormitory,
> Thought has no stopping-place,
> His bright bed was a corner shop,
> Opening, closing, late.
> Behind a grille, the unfrocked priest
> Had told his own confession:
> Accident in every street
> Rang the Angelus. (*CPC*, 191)

Here, as in Joyce's "The Sisters," the failure to absolve oneself is implicitly linked to paralysis, which in this case takes the form of a Sisyphean cycle of recriminating thought and compulsive action. That Clarke continued to experience a measure of psychic paralysis long after his confinement is evinced by the fact that the act of absolution left unfinished in "Repentance" and "Summer Lightning" only occurred after a seventeen-year hiatus from poetry. During that period, he occupied himself by writing prose fiction and drama that once again displaced his trauma back into the Celtic past.

3

Long acknowledged as a "pivotal" poem in Clarke's career, "Ancient Lights," the title poem of the volume that Clarke published in 1955, is the first of his poems that is confessional in the full sense of that term.[45] Not only does this poem reveal in explicit autobiographical detail the trauma that inaugurated Clarke's agonizing self-scrutiny and debilitating attitude toward sexuality, but even more significantly, it completes the act of self-absolution that was forecast in the earlier poems. After grounding itself in the north Dublin neighborhoods of the poet's childhood and foreshadowing the loss of innocence to follow, the poem proceeds in its second and third stanzas to recount for the first time in Clarke's published writings his torturous experience as a young boy in the confessional.

> Being sent to penance, come Saturday,
> I shuffled slower than my sins should.
> My fears were candle-spiked at side-shrines,
> Rays lengthened them in stained-glass. Confided
> To night again, my grief bowed down,
> Heard hand on shutter-knob. Did I
> Take pleasure, when alone—how much—
> In a bad thought, immodest look
> Or worse, unnecessary touch?
>
> Closeted in the confessional,
> I put on flesh. (*CPC*, 199)

Clarke's description here of confession in early twentieth-century Ireland parallels in striking ways Foucault's analysis of the Tridentine formation of this sacramental ritual. First, there is the focus on masturbation as the primal sin, the root from which all subsequent sins of the flesh spring. This is followed by the call for a rigorous self-monitoring that would carefully calibrate the extent of one's concupiscence, a point highlighted by the way in which the poet skews normal syntactical order to locate the adverbial phrase—"how much"—in a position of greater emphasis at the end of the line. Finally, there is the way in which the practice of confession, far from repressing sexuality, cultivates a heightened awareness of it.

The speaker's premature assumption of the responsibilities associated with corporeality, together with the guilt precipitated by his failure to acknowledge the full extent of his investment in fleshly desire, evoke that sense of persecution, self-loathing, and fear of damnation that earlier poems such as "Night and Morning," "Mortal Pride," and "Repentance" associated with the experience of confession. But in this case the poem describes, albeit with some obliquity, the process of moving beyond this psychologically constrictive condition. It does so initially via an overt bit of symbolism. The speaker, leaving the church after confession, witnesses "a cage-bird," released into the open air, attacked and torn to pieces by a group of sparrows. In this parabolic episode, an emblem of the young poet's own entrapment within a sexually inhibited consciousness is destroyed by a sparrow, a traditional figure of sexual licentiousness. The fact that the killing of the bird is described in musical terms—"Plucked, roof-mired, all in mad bits. O / The pizzicato of its wires!" (*CPC*, 200)—provides a telling reminder of the confessional poet's quest to render his own psychic turmoil into song.

The difficult process of loosening the hold of a constrictive disciplinary regime over one's psyche and poetry culminates in the final three stanzas. In the first of these, Clarke refuses the injunction to be true to the orthodox religious identity epitomized by his namesake, St. Augustine, and accepts that his role as poet is necessarily heretical—"Poetry burns at a different stake" (*CPC*, 200). What follows is the act of self-absolution that releases him from his debasement and restores him to the fullness of life. By projecting this scene back into the Protestant church (the Black Church of his memoir's title) that bordered his childhood home, Clarke stresses the break with Catholic tradition inherent in this unmediated absolution that the penitent bestows upon himself:

> Still, still I remember awful downpour
> Cabbing Mountjoy Street, spun loneliness
> Veiling almost the Protestant church,

Two backyards from my very home,
I dared to shelter at locked door.
There, walled by heresy, my fears
Were solved. I had absolved myself. (*CPC*, 200)

The revitalizing effects of this act are signaled through terms and images that ironically invoke both aspects of Catholic penitential practice as well as the physiological domain against which its disciplinary techniques were primarily directed. In his memoir *Twice Round the Black Church*, Clarke describes how a priest, employing the linguistic discretion recommended by the standard manuals for confessors, queried him about masturbation by asking, "Did you let your nature flow?"[46] In the poem's concluding description, an ecumenical cloudburst in which the heavens and the sewers are conjoined repudiates the premise underlying the priest's question—that one's natural sexual impulses should be dammed/damned:

Feast-day effulgence, as though I gained
For life a *plenary indulgence.*

. . . . Waste water mocked
The *ballcocks*: down-pipes sparrowing,
And all around the spires of Dublin
Such swallowing in the air, such cowling
To keep high offices pure: I heard
From shore to shore, the iron gratings
Take half our heavens with a roar. (*CPC*, 200–201; emphasis added)

Clarke's identification here of effluence as the mark of a newly absolved consciousness offers an implicit justification for the shift in poetic style that characterized the second half of his career. While the best of his earlier work, *Pilgrimage and Other Poems* and *Night and Morning*, had been distinguished by its carefully wrought verbal artistry and concentrated thematic unity, Clarke's later poetry exhibits a looseness of style, a penchant for prolixity, digressiveness, and obscurity that at times irritates more than it interests. Such extemporizing is compensated for by a correlative broadening of the material incorporated into the poetry. It is not just that Clarke in his confessional mode openly addresses previously occluded traumas of the psyche but that he, more than any Irish poet of his time period, engaged directly with topical matters of social and political life, especially as they affected those most oppressed by the collusion of church and state. In epigrammatic satires scattered throughout the four books of poetry published in the first ten years after Clarke began writing poetry again, *Ancient Lights* (1955), *Too Great a Vine* (1957), *The Horse-Eaters* (1960), and *Flight to Africa* (1963), he spotlighted a range of scandalous policies and practices: the ban on contraception ("Marriage," "The Choice"), the physical abuse of children at industrial schools and reformatories run by the Christian Brothers ("Corporeal Punishment"), and the exploitation of young unmarried women at mother and baby homes and Magdalen asylums ("Living in Sin," "Unmarried Mothers").

The uninhibited outspokenness characteristic of both Clarke's confessional and satiric poetry resonates with even more significance when it is considered in light of the discursive habits inculcated by auricular confession. As we noted previously, according to Foucault's analysis, confession imposed a complex dialectic of "enunciation" and "silence" upon the discourse of sexuality whereby the penitent was required to disclose even the most nebulous intimations of sexuality to the confessor but not say anything to anyone else. Much of the disciplinary power of the ritual lay in these discursive constraints. That the Catholic hierarchy in Ireland was deeply concerned with preserving that power is evident from its strong opposition to the Mother and Child scheme of 1950, the subject of one of Clarke's most pointed satirical poems. A central component of the bishops' resistance to this policy advocating free health care for poor mothers was the concern that physicians would infringe upon the confessor's monopoly with regards to the discussion of matters of sexuality. In this context, Clarke's open references in his later poetry to forbidden sexual practices such as contraception and masturbation subvert the Church's attempt to control the discourse of sexuality.

Equally telling is the way in which Clarke's anticlerical satires reverse the power relations inherent in the speech act of confession. In the confessional, the penitent abashedly declares his own wrongdoings to an ecclesiastical authority who appraises them. Clarke's satirical poems, on the other hand, invert this by exercising judgments upon the sinful actions perpetrated and concealed by the Church and its representatives. Frequently, the accusation leveled in the poem condemns the Irish Catholic Church for its hypocritical materialism. To cite one of the most potent examples, in "Three Poems about Children," Clarke blames the Church's miserly stinginess, its negligent desire to avoid "vain expense" (*CPC*, 197), for the death in a fire of thirty-five girls at a Poor Clare orphanage that lacked a fire escape.[47] The obvious disparity in the harm done by such acts of institutional corruption and that effected by individual sins of concupiscence reveals the absurdity of the relentless focus upon the latter in the confessional.

The explicitly satiric mode that Clarke cultivated when he returned to writing poetry defused the Church's juridical authority by exposing its serious moral lapses. It also fostered a broader social perspective that allowed him to locate the Church's disciplining of the body within a larger cultural project of technological mastery over nature. Thus, in "The Loss of Strength" from *Too Great a Vine*, he extrapolates upon the aforementioned metaphor of masturbation as natural effluence to establish a link between the Church's attempt to constrain and regulate the flow of his bodily fluids and the construction of a massive hydroelectric station that severely curtailed the Shannon's natural current: "Now engineering / Machinery destroys the weirs, / Directs, monk-like, our natural flow" (*CPC*, 215). Similarly, in the more loosely structured "The Hippophagi" from *The Horse-Eaters*, Clarke depicts the present-day slaughtering of horses for meat as the natural outcome of decades of technological development. He tangentially associates this brutally utilitarian appropriation of the horses' bodies to the way in which the Catholic Church's inculcation of repressive attitudes toward sexuality "circumscribed" (*CPC*, 233) his own body.[48]

As these poems illustrate, there was a profound symbiosis between the satiric and confessional strains in Clarke's later poetry. The personal suffering revisited in the latter fostered an acutely empathetic sensibility that was attuned to forms of oppression and exploitation overlooked by the society at large. At the same time, the satire's canalizing of criticism away from the self and toward the public sphere alleviated the poet's deeply embedded sense of guilt, allowing him to grant his imagination freer access to the most prohibited areas of his life. The most significant result of this poetic infiltration into the forbidden zones of the psyche is *Mnemosyne Lay in Dust* (1966), the long poetic sequence that is the apotheosis of Clarke's confessional poetry.

As the classical allusion in its title suggests, Clarke's poetic reconstruction of his mental breakdown and year-long confinement in an asylum centers upon a psychosis involving a catastrophic loss of memory. *Mnemosyne* exposes this radical disassociation of the self from its past as a regressive response to an underlying psychological trauma, a defense mechanism that has badly backfired. Against this, the poem proffers a more authentic form of absolution based upon an act of re-membering that integrates the forbidden "insinuations of the flesh" within the conscious self. No poem of Clarke's has received more critical attention than this one. And much of that commentary has focused, appropriately enough, on the linguistic techniques that Clarke employs to evoke the disorienting terror of both his madness and its treatment. As the lines from the second section of the poem quoted below illustrate, Clarke's odd transformation of nouns to gerunds, syntactical elision of subjects and objects, dropping of articles, perfunctory lists of things and actions all work to powerfully convey the experience of what happens when madness and its institutional corrective "unself him" (*CPC*, 325):

> Straight-jacketing sprang to every lock
> And bolt, shadowy figures shocked,
> Wall, ceiling; hat, coat, trousers flung
> From him, vest, woollens. (*CPC*, 326)

My focus though will be on examining how this confessional poem operates at a narrative and figurative level to redress the damage produced by the sacramental ritual of confession. In that regard, I want to begin by briefly delineating the ways in which *Mnemosyne* presents the poet's mental illness and confinement as an amplification of the experience of being "closeted in the confessional."

We have already seen how in "Summer Lightning," incorporated here as section 8 of this eighteen-part sequence, Clarke characterizes madness as being caught up in a seemingly endless cycle of guilt-inducing and self-recriminating thought: "Thought has no stopping-place // . . . Forever, sinning without end" (*CPC*, 336). These lines expose the earlier injunction to "Think . . . Think" (*CPC*, 332) that concludes section 5 as more a symptom than a cure. As far back as the early poem "Mortal Pride," Clarke had identified oppressive self-reflection as a deleterious consequence of confession; here he anatomizes the pathology latent in this habit of mind. This interminable self-scrutiny results, as Foucault reminds us, from an internalization of the surveillance that governs the ritual of auricular confession. As presented in *Mnemosyne*, confinement in the mental asylum is characterized more than anything else by the maximization of such surveillance. Epitomizing the principle of Bentham's Panopticon, the asylum is structured so as to make possible the "uninterrupted assessment . . . [and] transcription of individual behavior."[49] As such, it functions as the confessional writ large. In the following passage from the poem's second section, Maurice Devane, Clarke's pseudonymous counterpart, finds himself under incessant observation:

> Maurice had wakened up. He saw a
> Circular peep-hole rimmed with polished
> Brass within the door. It gloomed.
> A face was glaring into the bed-room
> With bulging eyes and fierce moustache. (*CPC*, 327)

The ominous disciplinary power of such surveillance is laid bare by Maurice's delusional belief in section 5 that he is in "an Exhibition Hall" under the constant gaze of a uniformed and frowning "Watcher," who casts "the shadow of a policeman" (*CPC*, 331). Despite his sense of the malignancy of this surveillance—"Evil was peering through the peep-hole" (*CPC*, 333)—Maurice is himself interpolated into the process through his anxious self-observation: "Often he stared into the mirror / Beside the window, hand-drawn by fear" (*CPC*, 330).

This intensive scrutiny functions in the asylum as it does in the confessional as a mechanism for regulating a body rendered unruly by madness or sin. In the first part of *Mnemosyne*, Devane finds his body being forcibly placed in a steam bath, constrained by a straitjacket, and isolated in a padded cell. David Wheatley aptly characterizes this dimension of the poem: "Where the body makes an appearance in the poem, it is as something to be disciplined and controlled; loss of control over bodily functions is treated with horror by the narrator and punished harshly."[50] In this context, Devane's refusal to eat should be seen not just as an indicator of his suicidal despair but as a desperate act of resistance to the institutional power being exerted over his body, an attempt to evade this harsh governance of the flesh through a process of "*dis*carnation."[51] When a feeding tube is inserted in Maurice, his ejection of this device is described in a manner that forecasts the act that subsequently reconciles Maurice to his bodily existence: "Choking, he saw a sudden rill / Dazzling as baby-seed. It spilled // In air" (*CPC*, 334).

Since Clarke's psychological struggles began with a confessor's censorious focus on masturbation, it is altogether fitting that his healing, as configured in the poem, involves a transvaluation of that "sin." This occurs at the midway point of the sequence in section 10, which is in every sense of the word the seminal segment of the poem. It is here that Mnemosyne, who as the poem's title predicted "lay in dust" (*CPC*, 332) at the end of section 5, reappears and initiates a curative process of remembering. In the first part of this section, the memories are collective, fleeting, and jumbled—epitomized by the image at the end of the first stanza of a jettisoned history book. They incorporate discrete events, such as the general elections of 1919 and the ending of World War I, that were roughly contemporaneous with Clarke's confinement as well as more diffuse intimations of the threatening presence of colonial power. The political tenor of these memories, together with Devane's prior delusion that he was a guerrilla fighting the Black and Tans, establishes a correlation between the poet's private trauma and the public ordeal of the nation as it struggled for independence. However resonant such a connection may be, and many critics have found it to be so, these hallucinatory historical allusions serve a more evasive than heuristic function here. They are part of that fitful dialectic of resistance and realization that therapeutic acts of remembering always involve and that Clarke brilliantly replicates in this section. Of these avoidance strategies, the most potent is madness itself, where the razing of consciousness seemingly provides a refuge from judgment:

The scales are broken.
Justice cannot reach them:
All the uproar of the senses,
All the torment of conscience,
All that twists and breaks,
Without memory or insight,
The soul is out of sight
And all things out of sight
And being half gone they are happy. (*CPC*, 339)

The illusory nature of this retreat, signaled by the Yeatsian flourish of these last lines, is established by the delusion that soon follows. Imagining a severed head lying on the bed next to him, Maurice is wracked by an undifferentiated guilt.

Appropriately, this exposure of the inability of psychically induced amnesia to safeguard against culpability triggers the reappearance of Mnemosyne, who returns the poet to the age of seven when confession marked him with the indelible taint of guilt. That experience, like all deeply repressed psychic material, manifests itself indirectly: first in the displaced form of a childhood bogeyman and then, more significantly, through a mythic figure that condenses the putative offense that elicited his guilt and the authority who condemned it. Thus Onan, the biblical character who epitomizes the sin of masturbation, enters the poem in the form of a priest:

Often in priestly robe on a
Night of full moon, out of the waste,
A solitary figure, self-wasted,
Stole from the encampments—Onan,
Consoler of the young, the timid,
The captive. Administering, he passed down
The ward. Balsam was in his hand.
The self-sufficer, the anonym. (*CPC*, 340)

There are enough of the traditional connotations associated with onanism in this passage to lead an astute reader of this poem such as David

Wheatley to declare that Maurice Devane's "self-absorption reaches its sterile climax at the end of the section with a description of masturbation."[52] Against this, Neil Corcoran stresses the healing power of this act of bodily release, a point accentuated by the passage's ironic undercutting of the priest, the deliverer of the guilt-inducing judgment upon it.[53] The positive valence of masturbation in this passage becomes all the more evident when it is considered in light of the larger narrative trajectory of the poem. The identification of semen as salubrious here contrasts sharply with an episode in section 6 where Maurice's dream alludes to the catastrophic collapse of Clarke's romantic relationship with Geraldine Cummins due to the sudden arrival of "unwanted semen" (*CPC*, 333) during one of their encounters. As noted previously, evidence suggests that couple's failure to consummate their relationship, apparently due to a fear of sexuality inculcated in both parties by their experiences of confession, was a significant factor in Clarke's mental breakdown. By reversing the attitude that precipitated Maurice's collapse, this passage marks a dramatic and potentially curative realignment in his psyche. This cure begins in section 11, where Maurice abandons his attempt at self-starvation and eats the "ripe, ruddy, delicious" (*CPC*, 341) strawberries placed before him. This act, which is described not in terms of mere subsistence but as a sensual indulgence, parallels the preceding gesture of sexual self-satisfaction in that both are solitary and elemental forms of physical pleasure. Through the conjunction of these actions at this pivotal moment in Maurice's recovery, Clarke transmutes masturbation from the primal sin into a rudimentary benison. In doing so, he finally consummates the process of self-absolution that defines so much of his poetic career, recognizing at last that where there is no sin, there is no need for forgiveness. The fact that Maurice struggles in the remaining sections of *Mnemosyne* before finally completing his recovery is a fitting reminder of the difficulty involved in overcoming such deep-rooted trauma. As such it serves as a synecdoche for the many years that it took Clarke to produce a poetry that fully nullified the disciplinary power of the confessional, that made something ameliorating rather than shameful out of the secret of the body's most intimate secretions.

In the aftermath of *Mnemosyne Lay in Dust*, Clarke extrapolates its act of self-absolution in a way that distinguishes his Catholic-inflected confessional poetry from its more secular counterparts. Instead of merely superseding the sacrament of penance, Clarke's poetry defuses and then reappropriates its power. Whereas the confessional poetry of his American contemporaries strove, often futilely, for self-forgiveness, Clarke amplified the absolution of the Catholic ritual into a more authentically catholic principle. He did so in poems such as "The Disestablished Church" and "A Sermon on Swift," from a volume named after the latter poem and published in 1968, by once again tapping into the forgotten resources of the Celtic Romanesque tradition. In this case, it was the thought of the largely ignored ninth-century Irish monk and philosopher John Scottus Erigena. Clarke distills a notion of universal absolution from Erigena's complex Neoplatonic vision of the eventual return of all existent things, including even those that are ostensibly irredeemable, back to their divine source.[54] Here is how he puts it in the conclusion of the Swift poem, which is cast as an address from the pulpit of St. Patrick's Cathedral on the 300th anniversary of Swift's birth:

> In his sudden poem *The Day of Judgment*
> Swift borrowed the allegoric bolt of Jove,
> Damned and forgave the human race, dismissed
> The jest of life. Here is his secret belief
> For sure: the doctrine of Erigena,
> Scribing his way from West to East, from bang
> Of monastery door, click o' the latch,
> His sandals worn out, unsoled, a voice proclaiming
> The World's mad business—Eternal Absolution. (CPC, 460)

By attaching this principle to the savage indignation of Swift, Clarke purges it of any tincture of negligent complaisance. Instead, through his mélange of Swift and Erigena, he formulates an act of judgment that is doubly absolute—absolving precisely because it is totalizing. While Clarke realized, as we have noted above, that judgment could not be mitigated by individual madness, such is no longer the case when irrationality is seen as endemic. Through his Swiftian declaration that the world is a madhouse, Clarke condemns history as a nightmare even as he acquits those trapped within it. This realization might have easily led Clarke to follow his nemesis Samuel Beckett along the familiar path of a downtrodden nihilism, yet it does not. When Erigena is described as "unsoled," Clarke's pun intimates that he is not swallowed by the void but brought into contact with the ground of his being.

Clarke's assertion via Erigena of "Eternal Absolution" eventuates neither in Swift's lacerating rage nor in Beckett's interminable despair, but instead becomes the springboard for a Rabelaisian affirmation of the vagaries of human corporeality. Thus, in "Tiresias" (1971), his penultimate poem, and its shorter and earlier counterpart, "The Dilemma of Iphis" (1970), Clarke employs hermaphroditic figures from Greek mythology to advocate for a polymorphous sexuality that circumvents gender, the most basic of the disciplinary principles that govern the human body. While there is an echo here of Erigena's notion that the resurrected human body passes beyond the division of gender, Clarke differs from his monastic precursor in that the transgendered bodies of his late poems retain and exercise their full carnality.[55] Strangely, or perhaps not so strangely, this poet who suffered intensely from the Catholic Church's effort to police human corporality ultimately surpassed all of his Irish contemporaries in celebrating the body's irrepressible heterogeneity. Forty years later, Clarke's poetic vision in this regard, as in so many others, seems remarkably proleptic.[56]

2

Kavanagh's Parochialism

A Catholic Poetics of Place

While Austin Clarke's conflict with Catholicism centered upon control over the inner terrain of his psyche, for Patrick Kavanagh, the countryman, the contested ground was external. Kavanagh's effort to negotiate the tensions inherent in Catholicism's attitude toward the landscape ultimately led him to fashion a spiritual cartography that drew upon Catholic principles and practices but transcended the institutional church's efforts to regulate the sacredness of place. The tutelary spirit of Kavanagh's poetic imagination was primarily a genius loci that, depending upon his location and perspective, manifested itself either as a beneficent or malign presence. Such attention to the charisma of place has been a central feature of Irish poetry as far back as the *dinnseanchas* or place-lore poems composed by the Irish *fili*. But what distinguishes Kavanagh from his precursors in this tradition is his acute awareness of the challenges awaiting the modern writer whose efforts to conjure up the spirit of the landscape must compete with the Catholic Church's appropriation of that power. Indeed, Kavanagh's quest to formulate a poetics of place that registers the complex dynamics of its spirituality invests his poetry with a significance that more than compensates for its occasional formal deficiencies.

It also gives rise to his most important contribution to Irish literary and cultural criticism—the concept of parochialism. For Kavanagh, parochialism designates a dialectical sense of place based upon the reciprocal interplay of the local and universal, a spatial variant of the familiar hermeneutical circle whereby the understanding of part and whole mutually anticipate and reinforce each other. This principle was famously exemplified in Kavanagh's mid-career poem "Epic," where a seemingly trivial land dispute between small farmers in his home parish of Inniskeen garners a wider significance when it is paralleled with Homer's *Iliad;* in turn, Homer's ancient epic becomes more readily accessible to a modern audience as we realize that Homer "made the *Iliad* from such / A local row."[1] That this notion of parochialism constitutes an important step in the fashioning of a truly postcolonial consciousness has been frequently acknowledged. But what has been neglected is an understanding of the extent to which Kavanagh's parochialism reflects a particularly Irish Catholic sensibility with regards to place, one that is rooted both in deeply embedded theological principles as well as in the cultural struggle between localized folk variants of the faith and the ecclesiastical center.

Kavanagh first fashioned this concept in 1952 as a weapon in his battle against the hegemonic nationalism that he believed was corrupting Irish culture. Seeking to distinguish his artistic cultivation of his rural County Monaghan homeland from the romantic primitivism of the fin-de-siècle Celtic Revival and the mid-century neo-Revival, Kavanagh followed Coleridge's principle of concept formation via desynonymization—the synonyms differentiated in this case being the words "parochial" and "provincial."[2] "The provincial," Kavanagh averred, "has no mind of his own; he does not trust what his eyes see until he has heard what the metropolis—towards which his eyes are turned—has to say on any subject . . . The parochial mentality on the other hand is never in any doubt about the social and artistic validity of his parish."[3] With this distinction, Kavanagh sought to evade one of the most dangerous legacies of colonialism, the insidious dynamic by which the colonized province and the imperial metropolis define themselves against each other. In doing so, he became, in the words of Declan Kiberd, "a genuinely postcolonial thinker, one who had emptied his mind of the categories devised by colonialist and anti-colonialist alike."[4] Contrarily, provincial writers such as the Celtic revivalist J. M. Synge and the neo-Revivalist poet F. R. Higgins, according to Kavanagh, remain entrapped within these categories. Eager to do their part in fashioning a national consciousness but lacking an insider's knowledge of the actual lives of the Irish peasantry, these writers short-circuit the complex dialectic of local and universal, substituting the metropolis for the universal and the metropolitan simulacra of the local for its actuality. In the crucible of provincial imaginations such as theirs, the local is always steeped in the elixir of the national or imperial. On the other hand, parochial writers, such as James Joyce and George Moore, possess the courage to value the local for its own sake and thereby produce works that, paradoxically, transcend national boundaries. When rendered in the brush strokes of authentically parochial writers such as these, local color is not single-hued but prismatic. Or as Kavanagh more bluntly puts it: "Parochialism is universal; it deals with the fundamentals."[5]

It would be a mistake, though, to delimit Kavanagh's parochialism to an apologia for literary regionalism in the face of an essentializing nationalism. If this term merely designates an effort to bolster the status of a marginalized area through a geographically particularized verisimilitude, then Antoinette Quinn would be correct in her assertion that "very little of Kavanagh's own work is parochial."[6] But Kavanagh's choice of the term "parochial" (which in its primary meaning refers to the parish) to denominate this concept suggests that there is a religious dimension to this idea that extends beyond its polemical role in postcolonial cultural politics. That Kavanagh associated "parochialism" with Catholicism is evinced by his most direct statement on the relation between his poetry and his religious faith: "The subject matter of the poet is the Universal and in this he is one with Catholicism. By a peculiar paradox the pursuit of the Universal and fundamental produces the most exciting local colour as well."[7] This passage, despite its inversion of Kavanagh's other formulations of parochialism, follows them in emphasizing the reciprocal interchange of the local and the universal. Even more significantly, in doing so, it tacitly identifies this process with the spiritual quest for the Absolute. Kavanagh's intimations here concerning the relationship of spatiality and spirituality bear a resemblance to the thought of Philip Sheldrake, a theologian who trained as a Jesuit and whose work reflects the strong influence of that great Jesuit theorist of spatiality, Michel de Certeau. Sheldrake argues that there is an "inevitable tension," intrinsic to Christianity but especially heightened in the case of Catholicism, "between the local and universal dimensions of place."[8] The Catholic understanding of place, according to Sheldrake, oscillates back and forth between a perspective that emphasizes the placement of the divine in the here and now, its mediation "through place, local particularities and the sacramental space of community," and a counter-recognition that "the divine presence cannot be imprisoned in any contracted place or series of places . . . [but] is to be sought throughout the *oikumene*, the whole inhabited world."[9] The spirituality of place that Sheldrake advocates is one that reconciles these countervailing impulses, one that seeks the Absolute through both "a particular 'placement' *and* a continual movement beyond each place in search of an 'elsewhere,' a 'further,' an ever greater."[10] Such a synthesis of a localized piety with an awareness of the boundless horizon of the universal is what Kavanagh's notion of parochialism implicitly demands as well. It is his struggle to fashion a response to this imperative, a struggle first articulated in the later part of his career but latently present from its outset, that animates the patchwork corpus of Kavanagh's poetry and justifies its designation as parochial in his heightened sense of this term.

In the first phase of his career, which more or less concluded with his departure in 1939 from his rural Monaghan home, Kavanagh's poetry was distinguished by a sacramental vision that saw the local landscape as encompassing a divine presence and by the intermittent intrusion of a more disillusioned perspective that registered the spiritual and material desolation of his isolated rural homeland. Most commentators interpret this discordancy primarily in literary terms, casting it as evidence of the poet's shifting allegiances between a pastoral neo-romanticism and an anti-pastoral realism.[11] To the extent that they acknowledge the religious dimension of this early verse, it is usually in an attenuated manner, characterizing it in terms of a nebulous "Catholic transcendentalism" or a generalized sacramentality.[12] What is missing here is an awareness of the actual social processes that undergird the interplay of belief and skepticism in Kavanagh's early poetry concerning the spirituality of place. In the absence of such a context, it is easy to mischaracterize the "Christian pantheism" that appears in many of these poems as "highly untraditional" when precisely the opposite is the case.[13] In fact, a similar amalgam of Christian doctrine and iconography and pagan animism manifested itself in the localized folk variants of Catholicism that pervaded medieval and early modern Catholic Europe. These popular, colloquial religious practices primarily took the form of festivals celebrating local saints, pilgrimages to nearby shrines, and other cultic activities that blended Catholicism with an animistic faith in the enchantment of the local landscape.[14] Such practices were resisted in the aftermath of the Council of Trent with increasing vigor but varying degrees of success by the ecclesiastical hierarchy of the Church, which sought to eradicate or, when that was not possible, co-opt these folk rituals.

In an Irish context, the shorthand label for this struggle between localized variants of the faith and the ecclesiastical center is the Devotional Revolution.[15] According to the anthropologist Lawrence Taylor, Ireland's long-deferred Tridentine reformation, which reached its apex in the late nineteenth century, was at its core a battle for control over "the geography of power" in which the bishops sought "to replace one set of central places with another."[16] The fact that the front line of this conflict was the parish and that its antagonists are reflected in the competing meanings of this word establishes an intriguing symmetry between this cultural struggle and Kavanagh's notion of parochialism. At one level, parish (which is etymologically derived from the Greek word for neighborhood) designates a loosely bounded physical region and the closely knit community that inhabits it—or as Kavanagh put it, a "cultural parochial entity" whose boundaries were the "distance a man could walk in a day in any direction."[17] Understood in this manner, the parish was throughout Catholic Europe the site of a localized rural religious *mentalité*, a *"religion du terroir"* that the philosopher Charles Taylor, who borrows the term from the French scholar Philippe Boutry, describes as a "religion 'of the soil' . . . lived in each village as a collective norm" and rooted in "the customs of a particular community."[18] While this "religion 'of the soil'" was often directed toward the fulfillment of basic material needs, such as curing or preventing illness, fostering fertility, or protecting crops from various external threats, its functional purpose arose from a deep-seated belief in the spiritual potency of the local landscape that resisted the disenchantment and homogenizing of place fostered by modernity.[19] This notion exists in tension with the counter-designation of parishes as the foundational "ecclesiastical administrative units" of the Catholic Church. Formalized in the aftermath of the late sixteenth-century Council of Trent, "the parish system" was developed as a mechanism for strengthening the cohesiveness and uniformity of Catholicism.[20] Understood in this second sense of the term, the parish no longer constituted sacred ground in its own right; instead, its spiritual potency was defined and delimited by its incorporation within a tightly organized, hierarchical system. What is ultimately at stake in these differing meanings of the word "parish" is the relation of the local and the universal: the former hypostatizes the universal in the local while the latter subsumes the local within an ostensibly universal structure. As we shall see, in his fullest realizations of parochialism, Kavanagh evokes a spatiality in which the dynamic interplay of the local and universal transcends the limitations of each of these alternatives.

In Ireland, this conflict between these two competing senses of the parish—between the parish as the site of a localized "religion 'of the soil'" and the parish as a branch office of the central ecclesiastical authority—was crystallized in what Lawrence Taylor refers to as the "contest between the chapel and the well."[21] The latter was the nearby holy well, of which there are estimated to have been some three thousand in Ireland, dedicated to a local saint or, in some cases, to a more central Catholic figure.[22] It was also the site of a ritual known variously as the "pattern" or *turas*. Of uncertain origin, the *turas* to the local holy well followed a typical structure. On the feast day or holy day associated with the well's patron, the local community would gather at the well. The pilgrims would often engage in stations, the ritual of praying while walking, often in bare feet or on knees, in circles around the well or some nearby cairn. Aside from the penitential station, the activities at the holy well centered upon the amelioration of the harsh realities of peasant life. Participants in the *turas* frequently washed themselves with or drank the water from the well or collected it to be used at home for blessing their animals or fields. In acknowledgment of the well's power, they would leave as a mark of appreciation small items such as pieces of cloth attached to a nearby tree.[23] As is the case with many localized religious rituals, the holy well *turas* blurred the boundary that modernity interposes between religious and secular activities. Penitential stations and the solicitation of cures occurred side by side with various social festivities. The presence of such merrymaking at an ostensibly religious event drew the ire of the episcopal authorities of the Catholic Church, who worked assiduously from the late eighteenth and early nineteenth century onwards to squelch or co-opt the holy well *turas*.[24]

The primary outpost of ecclesiastical control was the chapel, the construction of which was the linchpin for the formation of villages and towns throughout nineteenth-century Ireland.[25] Through the liturgical rituals and devotional practices that were centered upon the chapel, the Church sought to extirpate the sacred from the landscape and enclose it within an institutional framework, where access to it could be more carefully supervised. While the Church was generally successful in establishing the hegemony of the chapel over the well, breaches remained in its effort to establish a *cordon sanitaire* around the sacred, or so Lawrence Taylor's fieldwork in western Donegal suggests. There as late as the 1980s, "the notion of a different sort of power, and perhaps a different sort of social world . . . [was] kept alive at the wells and in the discourse of the wells."[26] Extrapolating the beliefs implicit in the local inhabitants' stories about the wells, Taylor concludes that "for them, the local geography 'signifies' in a way that links rather than separates 'sacred' and 'profane' knowledge—joining the mundanely practical to the morally or magically instructive."[27]

Additional confirmation for the persistence of the holy well *turas* in the face of official ecclesiastical opposition can be found in Kavanagh's autobiographical novel *The Green Fool* (1939), where he recounts the pattern at the local holy well—Lady Well, located near Dundalk, about fifteen miles from his home near the village of Mucker in County Monaghan.[28] Lady Well, as its name suggests, was identified with the Virgin Mary, and the date of the *turas* there was, appropriately, the eve of the Feast of the Assumption. But in noting the significance of that feast, which he describes as being even greater in that part of Ireland than St. Patrick's Day, Kavanagh emphasizes its place in the seasonal cycle, specifically its concurrence with the harvest. Kavanagh's description of the *turas* to Lady Well reveals how closely it corresponded to the "patterns" of the prior century, incorporating both penitential and protective rituals and interfusing the sacred with the secular.

> Every year all the neighbours around me went there and carried home with them bottles of its sacred waters. These waters were used in times of sickness whether of human or beast. Some folk went barefoot and many went wearing in their boots the traditional pea or pebble of self-torture . . . In about three hours we arrived at Lady Well. The road in the vicinity was like a rowdy bazaar-ground. There was singing, not of hymns, but of comic songs that had nothing to do with piety . . . All the vicinity of the Well was packed with pilgrims. Like the medieval pilgrims very probably; some were going round on their bare knees making the stations, some others were doing a bit of courting under the pilgrim cloak. There was a rowdy element, too, pegging clods at the prayers and shouting. A few knots of men were arguing politics. I overheard two fellows making a deal over a horse.[29]

Another point of consonance between Lady Well *turas* and the traditional "pattern" was clerical opposition to the ritual. But while the "priests didn't like the Well and tried to discourage the pilgrimages," which they condemned as pagan, the "peasant folk" remained firm in their belief that the power of Lady Well was authentically religious.[30] In his concluding remarks on this event, Kavanagh validates the spiritual potency of the pattern without necessarily crediting its more magical elements. Despite having forgotten to bring the water from the well and being "weary in body and mind," Kavanagh proclaims himself renewed in spirit in the aftermath of the pilgrimage, his "soul . . . fresh as rain-green grass." A visit to Lady Well is salutary because, like its namesake, it is an entry point into the mystery of the incarnation, an axis where a variegated humanity comes into intimate proximity with the divine: "Our Lady was a real lady and human; she was not displeased, I knew, because some who pilgrimed in Her name were doubters and some cynics and a lot of vulgar sightseers. She is kind and no doubt she enjoyed the comic twists in the pageant round Lady Well."[31]

1

This folk religious belief in the sacred power of local geography, evident in Kavanagh's remarks on the Lady Well *turas*, pervades his early poetry. But that poetry also registers the impact of the Catholic Church's efforts to contract and contain that power. As a result, Kavanagh vacillates between a faith that his homeland is a "sacred charismatic landscape" and a desolating sense that the ground on which he dwells is mere clay bereft of any animating presence.[32] It is the former attitude that characterizes "Ploughman," the title poem of his first book, where Kavanagh casts the farmer's fields as a sanctuary and the plough's opening of the soil as a hierophantic act:

> I find a star-lovely art
> In a dark sod.
> Joy that is timeless! O heart
> That knows God! (*CPKK*, 7)

Such Christian-inflected animism recurs through this book and in the poems written in its immediate aftermath. Consider "April," for instance, where the verdant fields are seen as impregnated with the divine, or "To the Man After the Harrow," where the spring planting is equated with the primordial act of creation, or "Primrose," where the rural scene appears to a child's eyes as "Christ transfigured" (*CPK*, 31). If many of these poems suffer from stylistic slackness and amorphous rural settings, that is not the case with Kavanagh's best poems in this vein, "Christmas Eve Remembered" and "A Christmas Childhood," published in 1939 and 1940 respectively. In each of these, but especially the latter, the arrival of Christmas marks a ceremonial interlude in which temporal and spatial distinctions between the sacred and profane are erased. The poet's tiny Monaghan parish of Inniskeen and his family's farm become the epicenter of Christian geography—Bethlehem at the moment of the incarnation. The stable where his mother is milking is the manger where the Christ child lies; the "three whin bushes" on the horizon are "the Three Wise Kings" (*CPK*, 41); the music from his father's melodeon is the celestial choir that moves the stars.

Kavanagh's growing distance from this Christianized animism is evinced by his adoption in this poem of a retrospective framework and a child's perspective. To emphasize this point, in 1943 he added a preliminary section to "A Christmas Childhood" that overtly indicates his alienation from this belief and attributes the loss to a more conscious awareness of his native ground, or, as he puts it, to his having eaten "the knowledge that grew in clay" (*CPK*, 39).[33] The nature and impact of that desecrating knowledge are revealed more fully in "Stony Grey Soil," a poem contemporaneous with the original version of "A Christmas Childhood." Here Kavanagh's parish is no longer presented as a sacred precinct but as a barren wasteland incapable of sustaining poetry, love, or anything else that might ennoble existence. In the poem's conclusion, the speaker reveals his loss of faith in the enchantment of the nearby landscape, forsaking the "peasant's prayer" in which, as he puts it, "The first gay flight of my lyric / Got caught" (*CPK*, 39). Instead of paying homage to the sanctity of the local, he renders the parish place-names into bywords for a way of life that is stunted and stillborn:

> Mullahinsha, Drummeril, Black Shanco—
> Wherever I turn I see
> In the stony grey soil of Monaghan
> Dead loves that were born for me. (*CPK*, 39)

"Shancoduff," written about the last of the aforementioned places when Kavanagh was still in situ, lacks the harshness of its successors. It registers the topographical details of the eponymous black hills of the poem's title with a loving exactitude even as it invests them with a quasi-mythic grandeur: "They are my Alps and I have climbed the Matterhorn / With a sheaf of hay for three perishing calves / In the field under the Big Forth of Rocksavage" (*CPK*, 21). But the poem ends on a note of disenchantment as a group of cattle-drovers, whose status as outsiders immunizes them to the strange charisma of the place, expose its dereliction:

> The sleety winds fondle the rushy beards of Shancoduff
> While the cattle-drovers sheltering in the Featherna Bush
> Look up and say: "Who owns them hungry hills
> That the water-hen and snipe must have forsaken?
> A poet? Then by heavens he must be poor."
> I hear and is my heart not badly shaken? (*CPK*, 21)

The tension between the attitudes manifested in "A Christmas Childhood" and "The Stony Grey Soil" is internalized and explicitly located within an ecclesiastical context in "Why Sorrow?" (1940), the first of the three long poems—the others being *The Great Hunger* and *Lough Derg*—written in the aftermath of Kavanagh's move to Dublin in 1939. Rejected for publication by the Cuala Press, this poem remained unpublished during Kavanagh's lifetime.[34] The inconsistency of the verse, which varies widely from near doggerel to passages of considerable lyric intensity, and the inconclusiveness of the poem's overall narrative, certainly validate the decision not to publish this work. But for all of its flaws, the poem provides an invaluable lens into the cultural dynamics affecting the spirituality of place in Irish Catholicism in general and Kavanagh's poetry in particular. Kavanagh's decision to center this poem around the consciousness of the parish priest, Father Mat, is especially telling since that figure played a central role in the debate over spiritual cartography set in motion by the Devotional Revolution. It was the parish priest who was charged by the church hierarchy with the task of eradicating or appropriating the localized folk religion.[35] In the case of Father Mat, that task is exacerbated by the fact that his status is more liminal than the typical parish priest in early twentieth-century rural Ireland.

A product of the peasantry himself, he is identified in the poem as a man of the people, who is thoroughly integrated with the parish—"a part of the place, as natural as / The stones in grazing fields" (*CPK*, 46)—and who intermingles freely with his parishioners, discussing the everyday affairs of rural life: "fairs, / The price of pigs and store-cattle" (*CPK*, 54). As such, he differs sharply from his curate Father Ned, who combines doctrinal rigor with the deference to authority and punctiliousness typical of the shopkeeping middle-class from which he, like many of his real-life clerical counterparts, originates. But while Father Mat is more attuned to the rhythms of peasant life than his curate, both his clerical status and reflective temperament establish him as someone set apart: "So like mere earth and yet not one of us" (*CPK*, 54). This ambivalent position as both insider and outsider in the local community identifies Father Mat as a surrogate for Kavanagh himself, whose literary talents and ambitions placed him in a similarly intermediate situation in his parish of Inniskeen.

Given this linkage, it is not surprising then that Father Mat's animism is ascribed in the poem to his "pagan" poetic sensibility. The tendency of the few commentators who discuss this poem has been to leave matters there and to treat Father Mat's belief in the enchantment of the world around him as being, like that of Kavanagh himself, a purely literary phenomenon. This reductive sense of the provenance of Father Mat's (and by extension Kavanagh's) animism leads Antoinette Quinn to ascribe to the poem a "rootless, non-indigenous aesthetic" that is "not only unparochial but anti-parochial."[36] Such a claim ignores the fact that the "god-in-landscape" faith that Father Mat espouses at the outset of this poem correlates to a central component of folk-based religious practices.[37] The literary inflection given to this belief is not so much a mark of deracination as it is an indication of an attempt to preserve a waning sense of the spiritual potency of the local landscape. Father Mat's inability to sustain the traditional rural amalgam of Christianity and animism reflects Kavanagh's historically grounded understanding of the parish priest's pivotal role in the suppressing of such folk-based religious practices. Even more significantly, it reveals Kavanagh's growing difficulty in reconciling a belief in the charisma of the local landscape with an awareness of the suffering of the humans who dwell there, his recognition that there is a hollowness at the heart of even the most hallowed place, a lack that ultimately compels us to look elsewhere in our search for the Absolute.

In a manner similar to "A Christmas Childhood," Father Mat's "pagan" mythologizing of nature is presented as an extension of childhood reverie, exemplified, in particular, by his vision of a "long garden between a railway and a road" as a sacred grove—"the Garden of the Golden Apples" or Hesperides (*CPK*, 47). This animistic perspective continues unabated through adolescence where his prayers are disrupted by his awareness that "the Gospel was printed over an older writing / And its damnation was crawling under the Host" (*CPK*, 51). As an adult, his ability to fulfill his priestly vocation is marred by his ongoing commitment to this "earth-love," which an orthodox Catholicism centered on the Crucifixion would leave "all flattened out" (*CPK*, 45). Eventually, he is driven to a desperate act of renunciation:

> The whitethorns are drenched,
> The dripping branches on the carts going home

Is a holy-water blessing this hour.
But this that was once a miracle is now
To Father Mat the abominable symbol of
The Golden Calf. (*CPK*, 59)

This apostasy is triggered by Father Mat's repeated exposure in the confessional to the desolation of his parishioners' lives. After hearing a young man confess the verbal and physical abuse of his parents, the priest sees the beloved local landscape as despoiled rather than enchanted, more like Gethsemane than the Hesperides: "All that was / His heart when he was happy must not be; / The Way of Christ's Sorrow is shaded by no tree" (*CPK*, 52). Father Mat's attunement to the human misery that surrounds him shatters any vestige of his faith in the "god-in-landscape" and leaves him struggling to cope with a profound sense of displacement: "O Fear, / When consciousness blows through the debris / We are unhomed" (*CPK*, 57).[38]

As a remedy for the dislocation brought about by this stripping of the sacred from the local landscape, Kavanagh resorts to one of Catholicism's most privileged rituals—the pilgrimage to a remote and officially designated sacred site, in this case the penitential Station Island of Lough Derg. Such a pilgrimage deepens the experience of dislocation by acknowledging its underlying existential truth: that at a fundamental level, the Christian's earthly condition is one of "exile" and the search for a lost home.[39] But after evoking this primordial loss, the pilgrimage resolves it by leading its participants to a site where a sacred power has been consolidated and sanctioned by Church authorities. As such, the Catholic ritual of pilgrimage constitutes a particularly rich imbrication of spatiality and spirituality. It accommodates the divine with an act of passage as well as a particular emplacement and thereby simultaneously acknowledges both its distance and its proximity. But when considered in terms of the struggle between "official" Catholicism and its localized folk variants, a pilgrimage such as Lough Derg also represents an effective form of co-optation. It dislodges the sacred from the local vicinity to a more distant and somewhat defamiliarized location, one that is seemingly more autonomous, less constrictive than the parish chapel but that is in fact still a tentacle of the centralized structure of the institutional Church. Such co-optation is even more striking in the case of the Lough Derg pilgrimage, which likely began as a *turas* to a holy well dedicated to a local saint but from the twelfth century onwards was appropriated by ecclesiastical authorities and given a more expansive focus, one that was first international and then in the modern period national in scope.[40]

As a strategy for ameliorating the displacement occasioned by the conflict between Father Mat's devotion to the local landscape and his role as an agent of a central episcopal authority, the Lough Derg pilgrimage fails. What Father Mat discovers among his fellow pilgrims at Lough Derg is not the generalized aspiration for holiness and comprehensive asceticism of the early monastic penitents but rather a narrow concentration on their own specific material needs—marriage for the lovelorn Dublin shopkeeper and the lonely unattractive countrywoman, a painless death for an old man. The realization that the pilgrims to Lough Derg are no different from his own parishioners, that they respond to the universal valence of the site by dissipating it into particularized forms of immanent human longing, leaves Father Mat prone to a cynical dismissal of the entire pilgrimage: "The Cynic whispered to Father Mat . . ." (*CPK*, 63). The fact that the poem concludes abruptly with this unfinished statement reflects Kavanagh's profound ambivalence toward the pilgrimage: his unwillingness to give himself over to a full-blown rejection of it, but his inability to discern any authentic spiritual significance in it.

2

Kavanagh's response to his own sense of displacement, echoed in Father Mat's dilemma, was to engage in the secular counterpart to the pilgrimage—migration from the marginalized countryside to the metropolitan center. His greatest achievement with regards to the poetics of place was his eventual transfiguration of this migrant's journey into his own version of a pilgrimage, a "hegira," as he puts it, that culminated on the banks of the Grand Canal in Dublin.[41] The process of doing that was both personally and artistically difficult and took Kavanagh more than a decade to accomplish. It began with an act of poetic exorcism in which Kavanagh attempted to free his imagination from its possession by the genius loci of his rural homeland. The resulting work, *The Great Hunger,* the first major one that he completed while living in Dublin, has long been recognized as a masterpiece of demythologizing, but the myth that it deconstructs has usually been presented as something external to the poet's consciousness and therefore easily dismissed—specifically, the idyllic pastoral vision of rural Ireland promulgated first by the Celtic Revival and reiterated later by Eamon de Valera. Both the poem's power and its significance are enhanced, though, if we recognize that it is primarily an act of self-critique, a comprehensive questioning of Kavanagh's lingering religious devotion to his place of origin.

To understand more precisely the attitude that Kavanagh subjects to such rigorous scrutiny in *The Great Hunger,* we need to turn briefly to "Art McCooey," a poem that precedes its longer counterpart by a few months. Written in homage to the eponymous eighteenth-century Irish poet and farm laborer from nearby Creggan in County Armagh, "Art McCooey" incorporates many of the same quotidian details of rural peasant life that are presented more expansively in Kavanagh's saga of the small farmer Patrick Maguire in *The Great Hunger.* But here the local place, despite the stultifying routine of work and idle chatter that characterizes the lives of those who dwell there, is invested at the poem's conclusion with a demiurgic power: "Unlearnedly and unreasonably poetry is shaped, / Awkwardly but alive in the unmeasured womb" (*CPK,* 43). The idea that one's natal place, no matter how paltry seeming, holds within it a vast spiritual magnitude is, as we have seen, the premise that underlies the folk-based "religion 'of the soil'" practiced throughout Ireland well into the twentieth century. In *The Great Hunger,* this belief is reduced to a regressive illusion. The poem correlates the attachment to the local homeland with a failure to de-cathect from a maternal presence, casting it as an Oedipalized form of spatiality. In that regard, Kavanagh's poem anticipates one of the central insights of Michel de Certeau, who argues that the creative engagement with place, as opposed to a habituated immersion in it, arises from the "decisive and originary experience . . . of the child's differentiation from the mother's body."[42]

The notion of the local as an intimate matrix resonated deeply with Kavanagh. Even the essay in which he most fully articulates his notion of parochialism concludes with a clichéd paean to the idea of the motherland: "Why do we always need to go back? What is it we want to return to? Freud says, the womb, and there is something in it too. We are never happy from the moment we leave the womb. The Mother is the roots. The Mother is the thing which gives us a world of our own."[43] *The Great Hunger* similarly acknowledges the magnetic power of the maternal, but it presents that power as mortifying rather than creative. Here the womb of the motherland is not an empyreal space but rather a narrow ambit in which one is immured—in short, a tomb. Nowhere is this made more explicit than in the following passage from section 13 of the poem, which summarizes the harsh spatial reality of Maguire's life:

> But the peasant in his little acres is tied
> To a mother's womb by the wind-toughened navel-cord
> Like a goat tethered to the stump of a tree—
> He circles around and around wondering why it should be.
> . . . .
> A sick horse nosing around the meadow for a clean place to die. (*CPK*, 86)

This figure of one's homeplace as a constrictive maternal space is bolstered by the central role that Maguire's mother plays in the poem's overarching narrative. By eliminating the father from the scene, Kavanagh was able to foreground Maguire's oedipal fixation with the woman who becomes "wife and mother in one" (*CPK*, 66). One of the poem's strengths is its exposure of the malign synergy of psychological neurosis and economic necessity in post-famine rural Ireland. Motivated by the pragmatics of economic survival as well as a concern for her status in the household, Maguire's mother counsels him to displace his erotic energy onto the maternal surrogate of the land: "she praised the man who made a field his bride" (*CPK*, 65). This displacement is graphically illustrated in the poem's sexualized scenes of planting in which "men are spanging across wide furrows, / Lost in the passion that never needs a wife— / The pricks that pricked were the pointed pins of harrows" (*CPK*, 64). The hyper-alliteration of that last line not only stresses Maguire's erotic connection to the land but aurally evokes the perverse solipsism of that relationship. This is brought out even more forcefully in the pathetic scene that concludes the poem's second section, where Maguire's weekly masturbation is placed in contiguity with his fieldwork:

So Maguire got tired
Of the no-target gun fired
And returned to his headlands of carrots and cabbage,
To the fields once again
Where eunuchs can be men
And life is more lousy than savage. (*CPK*, 67)

Of course, the poem lays the blame for Maguire's sexual frustration and his claustrophobic existence not only on his actual mother but on Holy Mother Church. That *The Great Hunger* indicts the Catholic Church for its attenuation of Ireland into "that metaphysical land / Where flesh was a thought more spiritual than music" (*CPK*, 73) is now a critical commonplace. What has been not been noted is how the poem links the Church's repression of sexuality to its constriction of the local landscape's sacrality. As we have seen, the peasant's rootedness is portrayed here as a kind of entombment. That condition is not alleviated but exacerbated when Maguire and his fellow parishioners enter the Church and find "the chapel pressing its low ceiling over them" (*CPK*, 76). This deadening sense of enclosure reflects the Church's rupture from the folk religious animism that infused the natural world with spiritual significance and thereby provided these peasant farmers with an occasional epiphanic moment: "Yet sometimes when the sun comes through a gap / These men know God the Father in a tree" (*CPK*, 68).

In *The Great Hunger*, Kavanagh deepens his analysis of this conflict by suggesting that both combatants in the "contest between the chapel and the well"—the ecclesiastical authorities as well as the peasant practitioners of the localized folk religion—manifest a constrictive sacramentality that circumvents the dynamic interplay of universal and particular.

But he dreamt of the
    Absolute envased bouquet—
All or nothing. And it was nothing. For God is not all
In one place, complete and labelled like a case in a railway store

Till Hope comes in and takes it on his shoulder—
O Christ, that is what you have done for us:
In a crumb of bread the whole mystery is. (*CPK*, 72)

The obliquity of the passage requires careful parsing. Maguire's dilemma is that he believes that either the Absolute is encompassed within a particular place or else that place is abysmal in every sense of that word, either the local motherland is a vessel harboring the divine or it is a black hole. What thwarts the first of these possibilities and leaves Maguire stranded in a place of desolation is the ecclesiastical dogmatism that restricts the divine presence not just to the chapel but even more narrowly to the consecrated host. The passage, however, holds out another option in its strange metaphor of a portmanteau God. On one level, the image in its comic absurdity mocks the notion that God can be contained "all / In one place," suggesting instead a more dispersive incarnation in which, as subsequent line puts it, "God is in the bits and pieces of Everyday" (*CPK*, 72). At the same time, it evokes the prospect of a divine presence that is mobile, an Absolute that is in transit, that can be concretized only within a horizon that opens hopefully towards "an 'elsewhere.'"[44] These lines, however inchoately, convey one of Kavanagh's most profound elaborations of the dialectic of local and universal that constitutes parochialism. But it was not until later, in the "urban hymns" written after nearly fifteen years of life in the city, that this insight was fully realized in poetic form.[45]

Through their exposure of the underlying causes of Kavanagh's displacement from his rural homeland, "Why Sorrow?" and *The Great Hunger* provided a coda to this phase of the poet's life. In contrast, the last of the three long poems that Kavanagh wrote during his first years in Dublin, *Lough Derg* (1942), is a more forward-looking work. While this poem sought to complete the assessment of the traditional religious practice of pilgrimage that was left unfinished in "Why Sorrow?," in doing so it indirectly addressed the anxieties and aspirations that marked Kavanagh's analysis of the cultural and spatial dynamics of his newfound urban existence. Lough Derg, as it is presented in this poem, is in crucial ways a miniaturized version of the metropolis. Like Dublin, it is a site in which a mélange of strangers from diverse regions and classes are thrown together in close quarters. As Antoinette Quinn notes, in the poem "men and women from town and country and from twelve of the thirty-two counties are represented: priests and laity, the professional classes, civil servants, shopkeepers, farmers, the urban and rural poor."[46] The poem's opening description of the pilgrims' progress could just as easily serve to describe the migration of the peasantry to Dublin. The homonymic equation of "parish" and "perish" highlights the moribundity of the countryside from which pilgrims and migrants alike are seeking a reprieve:

> From Cavan and from Leitrim and from Mayo,
> From all the thin-faced parishes where hills
> Are perished noses running peaty water
> They came to Lough Derg. (*CPK*, 90)

Moreover, through its critical exposure of the ways in which the Lough Derg pilgrimage manifests the standardizing impetus of post-famine Irish Catholicism, Kavanagh's poem reflects his suspicion of the hegemonic power of the metropolis. At the same time, the poem holds out the hope that like the pilgrimage, the city might also generate from the conglomeration of strangers ad-hoc communities more egalitarian and sustaining than their established counterparts.

An offshoot of a projected book on Irish pilgrimages that Kavanagh researched but never finished,[47] *Lough Derg* bears the traces of that provenance in its rich repertoire of circumstantial detail documenting the experience of the Lough Derg pilgrimage: the "black tea, dry bread" (*CPK*, 96) served to the fasting pilgrims, the vigil prayers and hymns, "the bell [that] brought the sleepers from their cubicles" (*CPK*, 100), the idle chatter of the pilgrims at the hostel, their singing of "O Fare Thee Well, Lough Derg" as they depart the penitential island. But Kavanagh's attention to this surface aspect of the Lough Derg experience does not distract him from the deeper purposes of the pilgrimage as a spatial practice. Thus, near the poem's beginning he identifies the common goal that, at an intuitive level at least, animates the pilgrims, the belief that Lough Derg might "encave in the rubble / Of these rocks the Real" (*CPK*, 91), that in this sanctioned place the Absolute has been given a local habitation.

Having foregrounded the premise that underlies this as well as other pilgrimages, Kavanagh focuses upon the ways in which this principle is distorted by the ecclesiastical framework in which Lough Derg is circumscribed. What catches the poet's attention in that regard is the extent to which the Lough Derg pilgrimage reflects the consolidation of Catholicism in post-famine Ireland. As with the practices prescribed by the so-called Devotional Revolution and the celebrations associated with the triumphalist Eucharistic Congress of 1932, the rituals that occupy the pilgrims at Lough Derg emanate from a centralized authority. Local particularities are swallowed up in an omnivorous and specious uniformity:

> The rosary is said and Benediction.
> The Sacramental sun turns round and "Holy, Holy, Holy"
> The pilgrims cry, striking their breasts in Purgatory.
>
> The same routine and ritual now
> As serves for street processions or Congresses
> That take all shapes of souls as a living theme
> In a novel refuses nothing. No truth oppresses. (*CPK*, 91)

Epitomized by the new basilica of St. Patrick, "where everything is ordered and correct" (*CPK*, 92), the process of standardization imposed upon the pilgrimage is metaphorically linked to other forms of regulation by which the metropolitan center asserts its control over the periphery: "Like young police recruits being measured / Each pilgrim flattened backwards to the wall / And stretched his arms wide" (*CPK*, 92). Indeed, from Kavanagh's perspective, even the physical features of Lough Derg manifest the centripetal power of the emergent nation-state, rendering it into a virtual national heritage site, a simulacrum of a deserted Irish village that encapsulates the nation's traumatic history of famine and emigration:

> The middle of the island looked like the memory
> Of some village evicted by the Famine,
> Some corner of a field beside a well,
> Old stumps of walls where a stunted boortree is growing.

These were the holy cells of saintly men—
O that was the place where Mickey Fehan lived
And the Reillys before they went to America in the Fifties.
No, this is Lough Derg in County Donegal. (*CPK*, 93)

Kavanagh's emphasis on the nationalist character of Lough Derg resonates with the most well-known anthropological analysis of the pilgrimage. In their comprehensive study of Christian pilgrimages, Victor and Edith Turner assert that the Lough Derg pilgrimage functions on an ideological level to solidify Ireland's identity as Catholic nation: "At Lough Derg, it is entirely probable that Catholic ideas and doctrines become impregnated with Irish experiences . . . while the specific symbols and ideas of Irishness, including that of being a persecuted people, are correspondingly Catholicized, 'elevated to the altars of the Church,' so to speak, where Ireland becomes 'the martyr nation.'"[48] As we have seen, Kavanagh was suspicious of precisely this kind of blanket assignation of national traits. What he objected to was the way in which a hegemonic nationalism, in contrast to the interplay of the local and universal that characterized parochialism, nullified distinctive particularities in favor of a formulaic national ideal. In *Lough Derg*, however, Kavanagh seems at times willing to forgo this objection and to identify the elusive universal at the heart of this pilgrimage with the all too familiar "spirit of Ireland": "But something that is Ireland's secret leads / These petty mean people" (*CPK*, 92).[49] More commonly, though, he subjected the nationalist aura projected onto the Lough Derg pilgrimage to critical scrutiny and, at times, withering mockery, as in the following hyperbolic assertion of Ireland's martyr status from an old Leitrim man who claims,

Servant girls bred my servility:
When I stoop
It is my mother's mother's mother's mother
Each one in turn being called in to spread—
"Wider with your legs," the master of the house said.
Domestic servants taken back and front.
That's why I'm servile. (*CPK*, 103)

In lieu of this kind of meretricious nationalism, Kavanagh seeks to discern in the Lough Derg pilgrimage a universal dimension that acknowledges rather than abrogates singularities, one based not in the standardization of the rituals but in the constellation of the individualized experiences of the pilgrims. In theological terms, what he wants to reveal is the way in which at Lough Derg "the Communion of Saints / Is a Communion of individuals" (*CPK*, 101). To make this principle tangible, he spotlights three particular pilgrims: Robert Fitzsimons, a literarily inclined farmer; an unnamed, defrocked Franciscan from Dublin; and Aggie Meegan, a young countrywoman with a tragic secret. The male characters suffer from Kavanagh's tendency to project himself onto his creations while his hackneyed descriptions of Aggie reflect his difficulty in investing the women of his imagination with the texture of real life. For Kavanagh's purposes, however, even the limited verisimilitude of these characters is sufficient. It is in the interaction between these people, not in the depths of their individual psyches, that the authentic meaning of the Lough Derg pilgrimage will be found. The confessional exchanges that both Aggie and the anonymous ex-monk have with Robert Fitzsimons crystallize the pain of human experience and the concomitant need for loving kindness. These "confessions" fulfill the pilgrimage's penitential purpose but in a heterodox manner. Moreover, the sins confessed expose fissures in the ecclesiastical structure of Irish Catholicism that have widened over the decades and now threaten its stability. The Franciscan had sexually abused a convent schoolgirl while Aggie tells an even sadder story of "birth, bastardy and murder" (*CPK*, 102).

In "Why Sorrow?," such revelations of sin and loss had a desolating impact upon Father Mat that left him feeling "unhomed," displaced. That is not the case, however, in *Lough Derg*. In that poem, the hard "centre" of the Lough Derg pilgrimage, the source of that place's sacred power, is associated with the communal sharing of "the secret of pain" (*CPK*, 109). The nature of that communal experience deserves fuller elaboration. In the interactions between the three aforementioned pilgrims, Kavanagh adumbrates something akin to what the anthropologists Victor and Edith Turner referred to as *communitas*. By this, the Turners referred to the kind of informal, ad-hoc community fashioned by liminal experiences such as pilgrimages.[50] Opposed to the established social structures that organize and define everyday life, *communitas* is "spontaneous, immediate, concrete, not abstract." Generating "bonds [that] . . . are undifferentiated, egalitarian, direct, extant, nonrational, existential, I-Thou," it exhibits an incipient utopianism in its striving "toward universalism and openness."[51] One of the primary purposes of the officially sanctioned religious rituals and services at Lough Derg, according to the Turners, is to normalize this informal community and consolidate its energy into a coherent ideology.[52] However, in spite of those standardizing efforts, the more contingent, existentially based *communitas* percolates below the surface, liable to crop up at any time. When it does so, it opens a space that renders the ordinary social boundaries between self and other porous. In Kavanagh's poem, the utopian potential of that space is most fully realized in Robert Fitzsimmon's internalization of Aggie's pain and his bestowal of forgiveness upon her. When placed in contiguity with this exchange even the banal pleas for marriage and jobs expressed by other pilgrims are elevated and made worthy of the Shakespearean sonnet form in which they are expressed. Near the beginning of the poem as Kavanagh articulated the congruencies between the Lough Derg pilgrimage and the fashioning of the nation, he declaimed that,

> So much alike is our historical
> And spiritual pattern, a heap
> Of stones anywhere is consecrated
> By love's terrible need. (*CPK*, 93–94)

The poem in its entirety deepens this glib overstatement. What consecrates the "heap / Of stones" that is Lough Derg is not its correspondence to the elusive spirit of the nation. It is instead the way in which the space opened by the pilgrimage engenders its own extemporaneous parish, a "Communion of Individuals" that concretizes universal principles of love and forgiveness.

3

Lough Derg expresses, albeit indirectly, Kavanagh's hope that the contingency and contiguity of city life might foster in a manner analogous to the pilgrimage the formation of a sacramental bond between strangers. But he soon discovered that such a *communitas* was not easily recaptured within quotidian urban reality. Indeed, many of the poems that Kavanagh wrote in the aftermath of *Lough Derg* present his new place of residence, the city of Dublin, as the antithesis of that sacred site. Rather than sympathy and forgiveness, this urban domain is characterized by mutual recrimination and mockery. During his first decade and a half in Dublin, Kavanagh struggled, as many migrants from the countryside did, to establish an economic and social position for himself in the alien environment of the city. He lived a penurious existence, surviving through freelance journalistic work as well as handouts scrounged from family and friends. His efforts to find a supportive community of fellow artists in the literary milieu of Dublin were even more frustrating. The pubs and salons frequented by the literati constituted the kind of liminal space that might be expected to generate some form of *communitas*, but to Kavanagh, Dublin's bohemia was a district characterized by malign mediocrity, unconducive to fellowship of any type and particularly inhospitable to a rural interloper. What distinguishes Kavanagh's experience of urban displacement from that of other rural migrants is that he does not just indict the city for its anomie but continues to sift through the fluctuating welter of the metropolis until he eventually succeeds in locating the numinous in its midst.

Like many migrants to the city, Kavanagh initially tried to negotiate its unsettling foreignness by finding traces in it of the rural world that he had left. He offered a tongue-in-cheek description of this mind-set in one of his essays: "I remember, when I came to Dublin for the first time, being disappointed with the façade of Trinity and wondering why they didn't get a good plasterer to float and pebbledash it."[53] If Dublin architecture disappointed him in his search for the familiar, on occasions at least, the scenes that he witnessed on its streets echoed Monaghan village life. That is evinced by the following passage, first incorporated in "The Wake of the Books," a tedious diatribe against censorship, and then excerpted with several subsequent stanzas as a separate poem:[54]

Sometimes I can see in these poor streets
A little village, and hear in the women's gossip

The talk of country women at a well
Echoing in the valleys. (*CPK*, 147)

But such episodes were anomalous, and Kavanagh soon discovered the futility of his efforts to regard the city as an extension of his country home. He voiced the reaction of many other migrants when he used the timeworn image of the urban jungle to evoke the disorientation that characterized his first years in Dublin. Thus, in "Jungle," the bourgeois precinct of Pembroke Road, where he lived from 1943 to 1958, is transmuted into the heart of darkness. As T. S. Eliot had done before him, Kavanagh reveals how the ostensible urbanity of the urban middle class masks an underlying barbarism fueled by the insatiable consumption and competition that drive city life.

If this poem begins by asserting the poet's bewilderment in his new home, it ends by contrasting that place against one of the countryside's most privileged sites, the holy well.

On Baggot Street Bridge they screeched,
Then dived out of my sight
Into the pools of blackest porter—
Till half-past ten of the jungle night
The bubbles came up with toxic smell
From Frustration's holy well. (*CPK*, 149)

The allusion here to the scene from canto 22 of Dante's *Inferno* where the poet-pilgrim witnesses the grafters diving into bubbling tar pits underscores the fraudulent and debased nature of the city. Left unmoored by the materialism of Dublin and his difficulty in gaining access to it, Kavanagh reverses the perspective adopted in *The Great Hunger.* His Monaghan home, seen through the roseate lens of nostalgia, becomes once more a sacred place against which his Pembroke Road residence is measured and found wanting. This is especially apparent in "Antenatal Dream," one of his best poems from this period. There nostalgia becomes a form of spiritual possession, with the obsessive presence of the rural landscape in his consciousness rendered ambivalently as both blessing and curse:

For we are all you'll know
No matter where you go—
Every insect, weed,
Kept singing in my head. (*CPK*, 168)

These primal memories could not, however, block out the hellishness of the urban scene, which is even more overtly foregrounded in "Adventures in the Bohemian Jungle," a heavy-handed satire that uses as the vehicle for its mockery a fictionalized civic festival honoring the Dublin theater world. Following in the footsteps of Dryden's *MacFlecknoe* and Pope's *Dunciad*, this poem, like several others from this period, critiques the city's corrupting influence upon the arts. Like its Augustan counterparts, Kavanagh's poem relies on geography to reinforce its satire. The fact that "the entrance to the bohemian jungle . . . lies on the perimeter of Commerce" highlights the avarice of the Dublin literati while a procession of the "Catholic Cultural League" into the theater district signals the artists' obsequious collaboration with those who wield power in the society (*CPK*, 159). Lastly, the presence of a group of American tourists, frustrated by the apparent absence of sex from the festival, reveals Kavanagh's prescient anxiety that the metropolis is a nodule infected by the homogenizing plague of globalization.

No matter how infernal the city seemed to him, Kavanagh recognized that a retreat back to the life of a peasant farmer in Monaghan would have meant his death as an artist. Whatever doubts he had about that assumption were quickly put to rest whenever he visited the family farm in Mucker for more than a few days. Alienated from his present urban environment, separated irrevocably from the rural homeland of his past, Kavanagh was left dangling, his deracinated imagination withering. The only pathway out of this dead end seemed to lead inward, towards the cultivation of a geography of the mind detached from any actual topographical site. The remedy for the hellish urban place was to be found in what he referred to as a "placeless Heaven." That at least is the course that he charted for himself in "Auditors In," a poem written in the immediate aftermath of his bitter urban satires:

Somewhere to stay
Doesn't matter. What is distressing
Is waking eagerly to go nowhere in particular.

From the sour soil of a town where all roots canker
I turn away to where the Self reposes,
The placeless Heaven that's under all our noses. (*CPK*, 182)

In a brilliant gloss on this passage, Seamus Heaney identifies this "placeless Heaven" as the terminal point in Kavanagh's poetic pilgrimage: "When he writes about places now, they are luminous spaces within his mind. They have been evacuated of their status as background, as documentary geography, and exist instead as transfigured images, sites where the mind projects its own force. In this later poetry, place is included within the horizon of Kavanagh's mind rather than the other way around. The country he visits is inside himself."[55] The posture that Heaney assigns to Kavanagh here is perfectly apt with regards to "Auditors In" and several other well-known poems included in Kavanagh's magisterial final volume *Come Dance with Kitty Stobling and Other Poems* (1960). What troubles me is Heaney's suggestion that Kavanagh in his last poetic efflorescence never ventures out from this inner terrain. If Kavanagh's ultimate triumph is the transmutation of the charisma of place into a "placeless Heaven," then he must be seen as forsaking his lifelong negotiation of the concrete complexities of place in favor of a retreat into a disembodied subjectivity. When the local is vaporized and sublimated into a purely inner space, parochialism dissipates into an assertion of the imagination's appropriative power, and the aura of a particular place, its genius loci, is reduced to the penumbra of a solitary consciousness. But such an account overlooks the fact that several of Kavanagh's greatest poems from this period are very specifically located.

"The Hospital" is an interesting case in point. Written shortly after the operation for lung cancer that Kavanagh himself identified as the catalyst for his poetic rebirth, this poem would seem on the surface to support Heaney's claim that Kavanagh's later poetry primarily celebrates the transfiguring power of his own imagination, for it shows how in the alembic of the poet's consciousness even the most "common and banal" things are rendered into spiritual treasure (CPK, 217). But the poem is far from being "placeless." Spatiality, pace Heaney, is crucial to the zen-like attentiveness that characterizes this first of what Kavanagh called his "noo pomes,"[56] a label that humorously links his newfound poetic posture to the spiritual concentration and composure of Japanese noh drama. The hospital ward, with its bland functionality and prison-like enclosure, forces the poet into a heightened state of awareness in which even concrete walls, wash basins, a gravel driveway, and a bent gate can be seen as numinous. The hospital is the site of a poetic epiphany in large part because it is an anomalous place that is set apart and sealed off from the surrounding urban environment, what Michel Foucault called a "heterotopia."[57] Such spatial sequestration fosters the poet's belief that its temporal equivalent might be established within his consciousness, that loving attention might make it possible to "snatch out of time the passionate transitory" (*CPK*, 217). But it is precisely the fact that the hospital is of restricted and temporary access that limits its usefulness as site for parochialism. For this spatial practice to be fully realized in the city, Kavanagh needed an open public space.

Ironically, he finally found it on the bank of the Grand Canal near Baggot Street Bridge, the very spot that he had previously described as Stygian. The two sonnets that celebrate this discovery and represent Kavanagh's greatest contribution to the poetics of place derive their power from the physical and cultural geography of this site. The border region inhabited by these poems is characterized by Joe Cleary as "suburban," where that term refers not to "the new residential tracts on the perimeter of the city," but to a "landscape where the country and the city are merged and mutually divested" of their conventional associations.[58] The way in which this suburban space hybridizes city and country is central to these poems' dynamic implementation of parochialism. Like the landscape of Kavanagh's rural parish of Inniskeen, this stretch of the Grand Canal is also seen as enchanted, animated with a spiritual presence, as the opening of the first of the Canal Bank sonnets reveals: "Leafy-with-love banks and the green waters of the canal / Pouring redemption for me"

(*CPK*, 224). But the spirituality associated with Kavanagh's newly consecrated urban parish differs from the local folk religion of the countryside. No settled "religion of the soil," it incorporates the fluidity and welter of the city. Instead of a holy well, its sacred spot is the Grand Canal, where the heavenly waters are purifying despite bearing the detritus of the city, are neither contained nor stationary but expansive and in constant flux. Similarly, in contrast to the established pattern of the holy well *turas*, the religious activity elicited by this site is infused with the improvisational nature of city life, a point stressed near the conclusion of the first sonnet when the poet proclaims "give me ad lib / To pray unselfconsciously with overflowing speech" (*CPK*, 224).

In a prose recapitulation of the first Canal Bank sonnet, Kavanagh stressed the exclusive and idiosyncratic nature of this experience: "And because that grass and sun and canal were good to me they were a particular, personal grass, sun and canal. Nobody anywhere else in the world knew that place as I knew it."[59] But this privatizing claim is belied by the latter of these two poems, "Lines Written on a Seat on the Grand Canal, Dublin," which culminates in the opening of this space to others: "O commemorate me with no hero-courageous / Tomb—just a canal-bank seat for the passer-by" (*CPK*, 227). Even more so than its precursor, this sonnet emphasizes the canal's status as an intermediate zone, signaled here by its metonymic affiliation with islands and bridges. Kavanagh labels the interstitial space carved out by this poem as "Parnassian," a term that for him designates not so much an aloof aestheticism as a sense of sovereignty that, like parochialism, releases one from obeisance to the sanctioned attitudes of the metropolis: "The poet teaches man worried about his position and his validity to cease to worry and then he will have a valid position. Parnassus is a point of view. In the presence of the Parnassian authority we are provincials nowhere."[60] The Parnassian posture evoked in this Canal Bank sonnet operates in a manner similar to what Michel de Certeau refers to as "local authority." According to de Certeau, local authority is what spatial discourse asserts when it provides "supererogatory semantic overlays that insert themselves 'over and above' and 'in excess,' and annex to a past or poetic realm a part of the land the promoters of technical rationalities and financial profitabilities had reserved for themselves."[61] The annexation effected by this poem takes the form of a proleptic act of commemoration that does not so much dedicate this space to the past as inaugurate it for the future. It carves out a clearing "within a system of defined places" that offers passersby at least a temporary liberation from the prescribed and sanctioned itineraries of urban life.[62] By the time that Kavanagh wrote this poem in the late 1950s, the Grand Canal had largely lost its functional purpose as a system for transporting goods back and forth from the countryside to the city. Such barges as enter the city in this poem bear only the "mythologies" of the rural hinterland. But Kavanagh wants to maintain the Canal as a site of transportation, albeit of a more intangible nature. In opening this space on the canal bank, Kavanagh seeks to conjure up a spectral counterpart to the *communitas* that he found lacking in contemporary urban reality. He provides future denizens of the city an opportunity to join him and traffic in mythologies, to transact a spiritual exchange that would offload the sacral into the quotidian, allowing the universal to flow for a moment at least through the local. It is here more than anywhere else that Kavanagh realizes the deep truth about the geography of the spirit that is implicit in his notion of parochialism: that the Absolute can never be firmly fixed in one spot but only glimpsed in the wake of its passage through a particular place.

3

Partition and Communion in John Montague's Poetry

For poets raised in Protestant-dominated Northern Ireland such as John Montague, Catholicism was not just an instrument of oppression, as it was for Austin Clarke and, to a lesser degree, Patrick Kavanagh. It was itself an object of persecution. In the northern state, Catholics were discriminated against politically and economically, and their religious beliefs were openly mocked. In the face of this sectarianism, Montague found in Catholicism's central ritual of the Eucharist a construct for transcending this division, but one that first had to be purged of its own traces of tribalism.

Montague's work was born out of the primal wound of the Partition of Ireland in 1922, which ensured the independence of the southern twenty-six counties but truncated Ulster into a six-county semiautonomous province of the United Kingdom. The imposition of this artificial border left Ulster an atrophied and broken province—"the creaking branch . . . the stricken limb" of the Irish body politic.[1] Nowhere was this more apparent than in Montague's homeland, the border county of Tyrone, which, having been "severed" from the Free State counties of Donegal and Monaghan, became "a stranded community / . . . neither Irish, nor British" (*CPM*, 178). There is, as Montague's poetic reportage reveals, something intrinsically absurd about the act of political partition. The sudden shearing and makeshift suturing of the warp and woof of a culture generates a disjunctive social space, where one repeatedly encounters, *"the impossible as normal, / lunacy made local, / surrealism made risk"* (*CPM*, 346). If such jarring discordancies can from a distance seem energizing, their impact on those who live under their sway is more likely to be crippling. In "The Same Fault," a poem from his magisterial sequence *The Rough Field*, Montague reveals how the Partition leaves its dark mark on the bodies and psyches of those whose lives it fissures—first in the form of a scar etched on both the poet and his father's foreheads and then as a dispositional defect passed down from father to son:

> My father had the same scar
> In the same place, as if
> The same fault ran through
> Us both: anger, impatience,
> A stress born of violence. (*CPM*, 42)

The dilemma that such an inheritance poses for Montague as a poet is made evident in the next poem from this sequence, "Sound of a Wound." In response to a self-reflexive inquiry into the nature of an art occasioned by such trauma, he posits two possible answers to the question of "what sound a wound makes": the first is a retreat into nostalgic lamentation, a poetry that evokes "the pain of / a lost . . . / pastoral rhythm"; the second a bitter venting that, like republican folk songs, releases "the vomit surge / of race hatred" (*CPM*, 42–43). Montague's achievement as a poet was to give voice to this personal and communal trauma without succumbing to such reactionary measures. His counter-strategy was to probe more deeply into the wound itself, to incorporate its cleaving into his poetry. To fashion a poetry that assimilated rather than evaded such fracturing, he turned to the modernist poets whom he encountered in America in the 1950s and '60s. The influence of William Carlos Williams was especially notable in this regard, providing a model of lyrics based upon curt, sharply enjambed lines as well as of longer poems composed from disjunctive sequences that organize the shards of quotidian experience, ancient myth, and historical reality into mosaic-like arrangements.[2] However, in the poetic sequences—*The Rough Field* (1972), *The Dead Kingdom* (1984), *Border Sick Call* (1995)—that are his greatest achievement, Montague is never content merely to dwell on division but is ultimately driven by the quest for what he calls "an unpartitioned sensibility," or what Seamus Deane refers to as "a reconciled community."[3] Deane contends that this goal is never realized, that ultimately "nothing can dislodge the spear of isolation" from Montague's psyche or poetry.[4] Yet Montague does find some assuagement, if not a cure, for the wound of the Partition. This salve is derived in part from the Catholic sacrament of communion, which enters his poetry most directly in the seminal section of *The Rough Field*—"The Bread God." The title, drawn from a scurrilous attack on the Eucharist by Protestant extremists, establishes that ritual as a focal point for the sectarian divisions afflicting Northern Ireland. But Montague discerns in communion a template for a more inclusive communal relation rooted in our shared corporeality.

1

Montague's poetic appropriation of the sacrament of communion is surprising given his general disdain for the doctrinal Catholicism imposed upon him in his youth.[5] To understand why Montague would want to recuperate this element of a seemingly outmoded religious heritage, we need first to consider his assaying of the forces that divided his homeland and the various means by which they might be countered. The poet's investment in this etiological analysis is not just cultural but deeply personal. His father, James Montague, was a republican activist whose participation in what his son referred to as "the holy war to restore our country" led to his exile to the United States (*CPM*, 40). When he was unable to support his wife and family, he remained in New York while the rest of the family returned to Ireland, except the youngest son, John, who was separated from his mother and eventually sent to his father's family home in Garvaghy, County Tyrone, to be raised by his paternal aunts. The "primal hurt" of this early sundering of family ties lingered well into Montague's adulthood, manifesting itself most tangibly in a stutter induced by a teacher's mockery of his American accent (*CPM*, 181).

In tracing the genealogy and trajectory of the fault line that fractured his own family as well as his community of origin, Montague exhibits an expansive historical perspective. Thus, in the section of *A Rough Field* titled "A Severed Head," he casts the Partition as the culmination of an act of political betrayal that began when Hugh O'Neill and his fellow Gaelic chieftains self-servingly capitulated to the English invaders in the aftermath of the Battle of Kinsale, thereby setting in motion the severing of Gaelic Ulster. Similarly, in poems such as "Balance Sheet" and "Roseland" from later in *A Rough Field,* Montague reveals how the accoutrements of capitalist modernity—an expanded motorway, a shabby concrete dance hall—intensify the sundering of this community from its past. But the depth of the trauma afflicting his divided homeland is such that Montague ultimately feels compelled to supplement history with myth.

In contrast to his fellow countryman Seamus Heaney, Montague's recourse to myth in his analysis of the sectarian violence of Northern Ireland comes with considerable ambivalence. Nowhere is this more apparent than in the medial section of *The Dead Kingdom*, appropriately entitled "The Black Pig." The reference here is to the Black Pig's Dyke, a series of prehistoric defensive trenches strewn along the ancient border of Ulster and Connaught, but also, as the title poem of this section indicates, to the "mythic bristled beast" whose angry burrowing "first threw up . . . [this] bloody border" (*CPM*, 152). Having evoked this archaic provenance for the tribal conflict in his homeland, Montague overtly rejects it in a subsequent poem, "The Plain of Blood." Again, the poem takes its title from ancient Irish myth, in this case from Mag Slecht, a plain in present-day County Cavan where blood sacrifices were ostensibly made to appease the corn god, Crom Cruach.[6] Neither Nordic sagas like those Heaney alluded to in *North* nor this indigenous myth, Montague proceeds to suggest, can illuminate the "malevolence" contaminating contemporary Ulster. Instead, that must be seen as the outgrowth, as he sardonically puts it, of "wise imperial policy" that intentionally pitted "small peoples / against each other, Orange / Order against Defender" (*CPM*, 155). Substantiating this assessment is the epigraph that introduces this section, an actual quote from a British military commander in Ulster prior to the 1798 insurrection in which he proudly announces his plans to "increase the animosity between Orangemen and the United Irish" (*CPM*, 151). This is precisely the kind of shrewd historical analysis of sectarian violence that critics have excoriated Heaney for failing to provide. But after foregrounding this critically sanctioned explanation, Montague finds that he cannot sustain it. Indeed, the final three poems of this section, "The Web of Man (*A Curse*)," "Red Branch (*A Blessing*)," and "Deities," each resort back to a mythic context in their assessment of the political conflict in the North. The rapid-fire, two-beat line employed in the last of these poems infuses it with a tone of blunt truth-telling. But what initially appears to be an exercise in demystification *("From our needs / we create them")* eventually gives way to a reassertion of the authority of the autochthonic gods of the pagan Greeks and Celts (*CPM*, 158). The poem concludes by starkly asserting that modern humanity, despite its pretensions to an enlightened rationalism, remains in thrall to these dark subterranean powers:

left to himself
stripped of creed,
man still faces
the old powers:

violence fuming
from some crater. (CPM, 159)

There is a symbiotic relationship between Montague's stenciling of the Partition upon these archaic rifts and his skepticism concerning any attempt to orchestrate history through mass political action. No political quietist, Montague has always been sympathetic to the revolutionary impetus: hence, his dedication of the penultimate section of *The Rough Field*, "A New Siege," to the Irish republican firebrand Bernadette Devlin and his empathetic response to the Parisian student radicals of 1968 whose ersatz attempt at revolution he witnessed firsthand. However, he sanctioned these attacks against the established order, not so much because he believed that their visionary goals were realizable but rather because he regarded them as socially invigorating, as infusing the body politic with a necessary surge of "Blakean energy."[7] This is not to suggest that Montague is in any way inimical to the aspirations of northern Irish Catholics to establish a politically unified Ireland, but only that he is acutely aware of the extent to which such nationalist movements can betray their inaugurating motives. It is for that reason that he once suggested that nationhood is "something to forget once you have achieved it."[8]

This viewpoint finds validation in his critical appraisal of the revolution that resulted in Ireland's partial independence, the ideals of which he sees as first having been co-opted by a puritanical Catholic Church and then superseded altogether by the tidal surge of global capitalism. His most extensive analysis of the society that ultimately arose from the seeds of the Easter Rising occurs in section 8 of *The Rough Field,* "A Patriotic Suite," titled after the Irish composer Sean O'Riada's symphonic masterpiece. If O'Riada's plaintive harmonies envelope the emergent nation-state in a melancholic, nostalgic haze, Montague's jarring dissonances bring its contradictions into relief. This is perhaps most apparent in the last of this section's ten parts, which recapitulates several of the leitmotifs that give "A Patriotic Suite" a measure of coherence. The reference at this section's outset to "the gloomy images of a provincial catholicism" is juxtaposed a few lines later with a conclusion that encompasses the utopia of traditional Irish myth, Hy Brasil, within the framework of capitalist modernity, signaled by an allusion to the spike in the gross national product in the early 1960s and the appearance at the poem's end of a rental car (*CPM,* 68). This conclusion gives a particularly ironic valence to the fourth part of "A Patriotic Suite," where Montague reflects on the radical utopianism that James Connolly, in particular, ascribed to the Easter Rising:

Christ and socialism—
Wheatfield and factory
Vivid in the sun:
Connolly's dream, if any one's. (*CPM,* 63)

The naïveté that underlies Connolly's revolutionary vision is evoked by the reversion in these last two lines to the pat rhyme of doggerel while the precise nature of his oversimplification is laid bare in the subsequent and final stanza:

All revolutions are interior
The displacement of spirit;
By the arrival of fact,
Ceaseless as cloud across sky,
Sudden as sun.
Tremor of a butterfly
Modifies everything. (*CPM,* 63)

Crucial here is Montague's allusion to the "butterfly effect," a linchpin of contemporary chaos theory. This principle was formulated in the early 1960s by the meteorologist Edward Lorenz to explain the extraordinary effect that slight variations in seemingly trivial initial factors could have upon the weather. In more general scientific terms, the butterfly effect refers to the way in which complex natural systems display "sensitive dependence upon initial conditions" and are, therefore, characterized by "aperiodicity" and "unpredictability."[9] Montague in this passage posits that history operates in a similar manner. He supports this claim, ironically, with an epigram from Fredrich Engels, the co-formulator of perhaps the most influential determinist theory of human history. Shorn of its original context, Engels' remark confirms the impossibility of predetermining the outcome of political action *("The real aims of a revolution, those which are not illusions, are always to be realized after that revolution")* and sanctions the poet's assertion that the vicissitudes of history summon spiritual transformations, the only kind of revolution that one can truly effect (*CPM*, 62).

Montague's enfolding of historical events within the fluxions of a more comprehensive cosmic process calls to mind the example of W. B. Yeats, whose systematizing of history he both mimics and modifies. According to Steven Matthews, "the closest that Montague comes to Yeats" is in the penultimate section of *The Rough Field*, "A New Siege," where he attempts "to see contemporary history against the background of cosmic change."[10] This section, like others throughout *The Rough Field*, focuses upon the iterations of sectarian violence that have defined so much of Irish history. In this case, the attacks by Protestant paramilitaries on peace marchers near Burntollet, County Derry, in 1969 are counterpoised with the siege of Derry by the Catholic forces of James II in 1698. The parallels are spatial as well as temporal as the border dividing Ireland is replicated on a smaller scale in the meandering walls that separate Catholic and Protestant sections of Derry and Belfast, encasing hatred in "a hygienic honeycomb" (*CPM*, 73). Montague, however, does not just expose this metastasized partitioning but transmutes these lines of division into dynamic vectors. This transformation is highlighted in the anaphoric dyads that begin almost half of the poem's sixteen stanzas: "Lines of history / lines of power // . . . Lines of defiance / lines of discord" (*CPM*, 70). And it is evident as well in the way in which the poem infuses the "hemistich" of Anglo-Saxon verse with the accelerated tempo of William Carlos Williams's offset triadic stanzas.[11]

Montague's deployment of this charged "zigzagging" (*CPM*, 72) line reaches an apotheosis with its conversion of the "rough field" of his divided homeland—Garvaghey, the name of his paternal townland, is an Anglicization of the Irish for "rough field" (*CPM*, 5)—into a cosmic field of energy:

> the rough field
>   of the universe
> growing, changing
>   a net of energies
> crossing patterns
>   weaving towards
> a new order
>   a new anarchy
> always different
>   always the same. (*CPM*, 73)

In this telescoped snapshot of the universe, Montague redacts Yeats's totalizing system in light of chaos theory. Instead of the steady-state oscillations between *primary* and *antithetical* cycles so precisely charted in *A Vision*, "the rough field" of Montague's universe is radically indeterminate. Its unfathomable fusion of order and chaos, design and chance, evades the governing categories of human consciousness and, as such, can only be endured, not comprehended. This subsuming of history within an all-encompassing but unpredictable process prohibits Montague from reviving the role of poetic magus that Yeats perfected. Indeed, *The Rough Field* is structured around the failure of the imagination to superimpose an overarching pattern upon history.[12] Both the opening and concluding movements of this poetic sequence culminate with the poet acknowledging the futility of the gyre-like perspective he has adopted: "with all my circling a failure to return" (*CPM*, 81). When he does claim in "The Source," a poem from the middle part of this sequence, to have closed this magic circle, his assertion is exposed as a drunken illusion. Believing that while his "neighbours sleep" he has discerned "the pattern history weaves / From one small backward place," his flight of fancy is abruptly ended when he encounters a herd of cows and faces the sobering realization that all such schemas are rendered absurd by the slaughterhouse of history: *"Store cattle: / The abattoirs of old England / Will soon put paid to them"* (51–52). From this earthbound perspective, the "rough field / of the universe" seems little more than a rapacious maw.

In "Process," a crucial poem from his later sequence *The Dead Kingdom,* Montague elaborates on this dark truth:

> The structure of process
> time's gullet devouring
> parents whose children
> are swallowed in turn,
> families, houses, towns,
> built or battered down,
> only the earth and sky
> unchanging in change,
> everything else fragile
> as a wild bird's wing;
> bulldozer and butterfly,
> dogrose and snowflake
> climb the unending stair
> into God's golden eye. (*CPM,* 132)

This poem consolidates the universalizing maneuver whereby Montague discerns in the specific wounds of history traces of the omnivorous power of mutability. Against this leveling force, it posits contrasting forms of redress. The first involves a Yeats-like fatalism and Olympian detachment, evident here in the rapid ascent to a seemingly imperturbable celestial framework. But the poem's second section forgoes the distanced solitude of this transcendental perspective for mundane acts of communion, abandoning the stairway to heaven for the tenuous ligatures that humans cast over the abyss.

Each close in his own
world of sense & memory,
races, nations locked
in their dream of history,
only love or friendship,
an absorbing discipline
(the healing harmony
of music, painting, poem)
as swaying ropeladders
across fuming oblivion
while the globe turns,
and the stars turn. (*CPM*, 132)

Especially noteworthy here is Montague's foregrounding of intersubjective relationships against opposing forms of solipsism—the isolated individual consciousness and the exclusionary collectives of tribe and nation-state. The basis for a more authentic community, Montague suggests, lies in the small-scale acts of interpersonal bonding (love, friendship, the shared pleasure of the artwork) that arise from and seek to assuage the inexorable toll exacted by the "structure of process" upon individual bodies. Undergirding this recognition of the salvific potential elicited by the common burden of corporeality is Montague's experience of the Catholic sacrament of the Eucharist and its revelation of what he refers to as "the flesh-graced Word" (*CPM*, 24).

2

The Eucharist enters Montague's poetry most prominently in a context that highlights the interfusion of theology and politics in Northern Ireland. In "The Bread God," which was originally published as a Dolmen Press chapbook in 1968, Montague juxtaposes excerpts of anti-Catholic propaganda disseminated by Protestant extremists in Northern Ireland with a series of lyric poems and prose passages drawn from family letters and the fiction of the nineteenth-century lapsed Catholic and Tyrone native William Carleton, each describing the place of the Eucharist in the lives of the native Irish peasantry. This complex experimental work, which eventually became the third section of *The Rough Field*, has been cited by Montague himself as the catalyst that revived his flagging efforts to complete this decade-long poetic project. As he puts it in the preface to *The Rough Field*: "I managed to draft the opening and the close, but soon realized that I did not have the technique for so varied a task . . . At intervals during the decade I returned to it, when the signs seemed right. An extreme Protestant organization put me on its mailing list, for instance, and the only antidote I could find against such hatred was to absorb it into 'The Bread God'" (*CPM*, 5).

By incorporating these Protestant polemics into "The Bread God," Montague counterpoises the sacrament of communion with the divisive sectarianism that generated the fault line of the Partition. At once a sign and agent of unity, the Eucharist celebrates the real presence of the body of Christ not only in the sacramental bread and wine but also in the gathering of his followers. It manifests, in the words of a post–Vatican II commentary contemporaneous with Montague's poem, the reparation of a broken human community through "the redemptive love of God" which "unites men [*sic*] with each other and with God . . . opening individuals out into fully developed personal relationships of mutual trust, knowledge, and love."[13] Against this, the poem sets the fissiparous posture of evangelical Protestantism, specifically Ian Paisley's Free Presbyterian Church of Ulster, whose ceremonies Montague occasionally attended in an effort to understand the hatred spawned by its presiding minister.[14] Yet the absorption (as Montague puts it) of this hateful propaganda into "The Bread God" involves something more complex than an act of abrogation. Ultimately, Montague employs these vitriolic tracts as an astringent. By assimilating their indictment of the Eucharist for its idolatry and tribalism, his poem distills a more authentic vision of communion from which these corrupting elements have been purged.

Prior to his recent reincarnation as a minister in a coalition government, Paisley was known as a promulgator of aggressive anti-Catholicism and thus as one of the primary fomenters of the political turmoil of Northern Ireland. According to Steve Bruce, the preeminent scholar of Paisley's career, his ideology was defined by a fierce separatism—"an ill-tempered refusal to accept the humanity of those with whom one differs on matters of substance"—and a quasi-paranoiac suspicion of ecumenical movements.[15] These beliefs were, in turn, grounded in a narrow eschatology that regarded the present era as the end times and cast the Catholic Church in the role of apocalyptic anti-Christ.[16] While never overtly identified as Paisleyite, the tracts that Montague cites in "The Bread God" advocate positions that closely parallel those associated with Paisley and his sympathizers. The following, which appears in the middle of the poem's six lyrics, is a particularly salient example, noteworthy for both its shrill tone and the extremity of its assertions:

DEAR BROTHER!
ECUMENISM *is* THE NEW NAME *of the* WHORE OF BABLYON
SHE *who* SHITS *on the* SEVEN HILLS
ONE CHURCH, ONE STATE
WITH THE POPE THE HEAD OF THE STATE: BY RE-UNION
ROME MEANS ABSORPTION
UNIFORMITY MEANS TYRANNY
APISTS = PAPISTS
But GOD DELIGHTS IN VARIETY
NO *two leaves are* EXACTLY *alike*! (*CPM*, 25)

Reprising the traditional Ulster Protestant slogan, "Home Rule means Pope Rule," in the more incendiary rhetoric promoted by Paisley, this passage reduces the impetus towards unity to a drive for hegemonic power. Against the eucharistic insistence on the primacy of community, it advocates a narrow separatism under the guise of individual freedom. Similar fears are expressed, albeit less hysterically, in the poem's first piece of interpolated material, a letter from the Belfast Grand Lodge of the Orange Order to the British prime minister opposing the entry of the United Kingdom into the European Economic Community.[17] While the objections expressed in the letter focus on pragmatic constitutional issues, the repeated references to "The Treaty of Rome," the 1957 agreement that established the EEC, reflect the belief of Paisley and other fundamentalist Protestant leaders that the development of this international union was a diabolic enterprise and a sign of the impending apocalypse.[18]

Interposed between these attacks on secular and religious forms of ecumenism is the vicious mockery of the Eucharist that gives this poem its title:

> In a plain envelope marked: IMPORTANT
> THE BREAD GOD
> *the* DEVIL *has* CHRIST *where he wants* HIM
> A HELPLESS INFANT IN ARMS: A DEAD CHRIST ON THE
> CROSS
> ROME'S CENTRAL ACT OF WORSHIP IS THE EUCHARISTIC
> WAFER!
> IDOLATRY: THE WORST IDOL UNDER HEAVEN
> NOSELESS, EYELESS, EARLESS, HELPLESS, SPEECHLESS.
> (*CPM*, 24)

The charge of idolatry, made here in the most superficial fashion, has often been leveled against the Catholic ritual of Eucharist. It derives not only from bigoted hatred of the sort so amply manifested in this anonymous mailing but from misconceptions of the theological notion of real presence that lies at the heart of this sacrament. When the principle of transubstantiation is interpreted narrowly, as is sometimes done in Catholic commentary and practice, it gives rise to the assumption that the divine has been rendered into an objectified presence, susceptible of being manipulated and circumscribed by those who worship it. This is especially evident in the forms of eucharistic celebration—Adoration of the Blessed Sacrament, Corpus Christi processions—that occur outside the Mass. The Catholic phenomenologist Jean-Luc Marion aptly describes the sociopolitical implications of this reductive attitude towards transubstantiation:

> the community would seek to place "God" at its disposition like a thing, its thing, to reassure its identity . . . Of this "God" made thing, one would expect precisely nothing but *real* presence: presence reduced to the dimensions of a thing, a thing that is as much disposed to "honor by its presence" the liturgies where the community celebrates its own power.[19]

This tendency to reduce the transubstantiated host into a talisman of communal identity has a long provenance. In her astute analysis of medieval Corpus Christi processions, Sarah Beckwith shows how the body of Christ in the form of the host not only emblematized "the unity of the community" but also reinforced its internal and external boundaries, how these eucharistic celebrations functioned as "rituals of exclusion as much as rituals of inclusion."[20] Such chauvinistic conceptions of the Eucharist lurk in the background of "The Bread God," none more so than the the Eucharistic Congress held in Dublin in 1932, which employed the Eucharist in a triumphalist manner to consecrate the newly independent Irish Free State. Indeed, the subtlety and depth of Montague's treatment of the communal dimensions of the Eucharist becomes all the more apparent when it is contrasted with the political misappropriation of this sacrament during the Eucharistic Congress.

The Thirty-first Eucharistic Congress involved perhaps the largest public gatherings in Ireland since the monster rallies orchestrated by Daniel O'Connell in the 1840s, and it similarly interfused nationalist and religious fervor. During the last week of June in 1932, delegations from the Vatican and the Catholic Church throughout the world converged on Dublin. Hundreds of thousands attended each of the separate Masses for children, women, and men held throughout the Congress while the culminating Mass held at Phoenix Park on Sunday, June 26, attracted a crowd estimated at a million, close to a third of the nation's population.[21] The Cumann na nGaedheal government of W. T. Cosgrave saw the Congress not only as an occasion for celebrating the long-delayed attainment of national independence, but also as an opportunity for the nascent Irish Free State to demonstrate that it possessed the organizational infrastructure and civic order expected of the modern nation-state. On both fronts, Cosgrave's government and the Fianna Fáil government headed by Eamon de Valera that took power just prior to the Congress were successful. On an ideological level, many of the official pronouncements associated with the Congress as well as the ancillary publications inspired by it identified the spirit of the nation with the Eucharist. In the letter sent by the Irish Episcopate to prepare their congregations for this glorious event, the bishops asserted that the Eucharistic Congress would "be at once the celebration of God's glory and a nation's history." The letter went on to claim that "that the marvelous endurance of Catholic Ireland throughout the succession of prolonged and inhuman trials to which she was subjected . . . is rightly regarded as one of the miracles of history" and is attributable to "Our Lord Jesus Christ in the Blessed Eucharist—the Divine Mystery to which the soul of Ireland has clung throughout" its sufferings.[22] In *The Blessed Eucharist in Irish History*, a book published to coincide with the Eucharistic Congress, the prolific Catholic author Helena Concannon presents Ireland's devotion to the Eucharist as the cornerstone of its culture. Her lengthy examination of the role of the Eucharist in Irish history offers repeated confirmation of her belief that "everything of good that Ireland has won has come to her through the Blessed Eucharist and the Mass."[23] She was outdone, however, by the Irish American priest Fulton J. Sheen who presented a lecture at one of the many sectional meetings associated with the Congress. Sheen's metaphorical excursus paralleling Ireland with the eucharistic sacrifice fully displays the bombastic virtuosity that he later parlayed into a successful career on American television:

> Ireland's consecration was her persecution, for without the shedding of blood there is no remission of sins. Just as in the Holy Sacrifice of the Mass the grains of wheat coalesce to make the bread, and the grapes combine to make the wine . . . so too did the individual Irish hearts and minds and souls combine to make the national host on the paten of sacrifice and the national wine in the chalice of immolation.[24]

In sum, much of the rhetoric spawned by the Congress sought to obscure differences of class and region and to consolidate the sense of Ireland's national identity as univocally and exclusively Catholic.[25]

The lyrics as well as the excerpt from William Carleton's "The Midnight Mass" that appear at the outset of "The Bread God" seem at first glance to replicate the pious tribalism that accompanied the Eucharistic Congress. The poem begins with a brief four-line lyric recounting the Adoration of the Blessed Sacrament in Montague's home parish in Tyrone. This is followed, after the interruption of the letter from the Orange Lodge opposing the European Economic Cooperation, by a passage from Carleton describing the sublimity of Midnight Mass in early nineteenth-century Tyrone. With its central image of the torches carried by individual massgoers fusing together into "one wide surface of flame" (*CPM*, 23), the passage positions the Eucharist as an emblem of tribal unity. The subsequent lyric, "Christmas Morning," appears to be little more than an autobiographical addendum to Carleton's description. In a manner strongly redolent of Kavanagh, Montague recounts a Christmas Mass from his childhood in which the people from the nearby townlands came together as one to celebrate the feast of the Incarnation. But even in this overture, there are discordant notes that disrupt the reverential tone. The opening description of the eucharistic adoration provocatively calls to mind the worship of a zoomorphic pagan idol: *"And men with caps in hand kneel stiffly down / To see the many-fanged monstrance shine"* (*CPM*, 22). Moreover, the description of the parishioners in "Christmas Morning" attributes to this eucharistic community a bovine commonalty—"Grouped in the warmth / & cloud of their breath, / Along cattle paths" (*CPM*, 23).

Montague's critique deepens in the next two sections of the poem, consisting of an excerpt from a letter written by Montague's Jesuit uncle and the short lyric "Late-Comer." The priest's letter describes how in late nineteenth-century Tyrone the Eucharist had been reduced to an intermittent and tepid ritual and the practice of Catholicism, including even his decision to become a priest, had largely become a matter of convention. This aura of obsolescence is confirmed by the appropriately titled "Late-Comer." For the tardy mass-goer in this poem, the Eucharist has lost all its potency. Instead of entering through the sacrament into a deeper communion with others, he spends Mass marking his distinction from his fellow parishioners: "Studying the wen-marked heads / Of his neighbours, or gouging / His name in the soft wood / Of the choirloft" (*CPM*, 24). The lyrics that follow, "Crowd" and "After Mass," continue to present the eucharistic celebration in harshly realistic terms that contrast sharply with encomiastic discourse of the Eucharistic Congress. Bracketing the most vicious of the Paisleyite tracts, the one that casts the Catholic worship of communion as an act of apish conformity, these lyrics seem to substantiate that accusation. In "Crowd," the herd-like demeanor of the parishioners, evoked indirectly in "Christmas Morning," is overtly foregrounded: "The crowds for Communion, heavy coat and black shawl, / Surge in thick waves, cattle thronged in a fair, / To the oblong of altar rails" (*CPM*, 24). Similarly, "After Mass" shows how quickly the deeper communion celebrated in the Eucharist dissipates into a narrow tribalism as the mass-goers listen docilely to a politician and shift their focus to intergroup rivalries: "The notice of a football match: / Pearses *vs* Hibernians" (*CPM*, 25). The negative overtone of these lyrics resonates even more strongly when their correspondences to poems from later in *The Rough Field* are registered. Thus, the congruence between the image of the communicants as a herd of cattle and the "store cattle" being prepared for the slaughterhouse that the persona encounters at the end of "The Source" casts a shadow of futility over the eucharistic sacrifice. And the stultifying atmosphere of the after-mass gathering foreshadows the parody of the eucharistic meal that the persona and his neighbors enact in "The Last Sheaf," where an evening spent in "a brackish stour of stout / Paraffin, stale bread" in which "the current / Of community [is] revived to a near- / ly perfect round" quickly regresses into fruitless exchange of mutual self-pity and recrimination (*CPM*, 46–47).

It is precisely this nullifying context that renders the epithet for the Eucharist—"flesh-graced Word"—that appears at the end of "Crowd" so striking. Montague's redaction of the metaphorical description of the Incarnation that appears near the beginning of John's gospel ("And the Word became flesh and made his dwelling among us" I: 14) effects a critique of the scriptural literalism that grounds the Paisleyite tracts. If the Protestant hate mail reductively interprets the Eucharist as a form of mutilation that renders the Godhead "NOSELESS, EYELESS, EARLESS, HELPLESS, SPEECHLESS," Montague's appellation suggests that the Eucharist deepens rather than deforms the Incarnation. But the significance of this phrase supersedes doctrinal dogma. Its interweaving of flesh and word suggests that our common corporeality is the means by which communication occurs and the basis upon which community is formed. In turn, language, especially the poetic word, serves as a "surviving sign of grace" (*CPM*, 26), sustaining the bonds elicited by the flesh so that they linger long after the connective tissue has dissolved.

Yet even as Montague identifies the Eucharist as a "flesh-graced Word," a concrete manifestation of a spiritual presence, he resists the temptation to reduce this to something substantially present in the proximate here and now. As the culminating lyrics of "The Bread God" make clear, Montague acknowledges that the communal spirit generated by the Eucharist always involves a concomitant absence. This becomes more readily apparent when the temporality of the eucharistic sacrament is fully grasped. Because the Eucharist exists, to quote Jean-Luc Marion again, primarily as "as memorial . . . [and] eschatological announcement," in it the present is always perforated by the past and the future, the here and now riddled with the no longer and the not yet.[26] At its deepest level then, the community evoked through the Eucharist is promissory in nature. It comes into being only through the transmutation of past suffering into the possibility of a more redemptive future.

Montague implies something similar in the last two poems of "The Bread God"—"Penal Rock: Altamuskin" and "An Ulster Prophecy." The first of these is a sonnet that deftly echoes the commemorative dimension of the Eucharist by memorializing the sufferings of Irish Catholics during Penal times when they were forced to celebrate the Mass outdoors with only the barest protection from the elements. Like the sacrament that is its focus, the poem interfuses present and past, body and spirit. Upon entering this secluded spot, the contemporary bypasser discovers that it is haunted by the long-dead communicants of Penal times: "poor Tagues, folding the nap of their frieze / Under one knee, long suffering as beasts, / But parched for that surviving sign of grace" (*CPM*, 26). As in "Crowd," this poem foregrounds the tangible nature of the sacrament, identifying it as salve for the indigent corporeality of the peasant mass-goers. But any tendency to reduce the concrete materiality of Eucharist to an objective presence is thwarted in the sestet. There Montague juxtaposes contrasting acts of commemoration. Against the "crude, stone oratory, carved by a cousin" which seeks to monumentalize a past act of sacrifice, the poem sets a more ephemeral gesture of veneration: "A few flowers / Wither on the altar, so I melt a ball of snow / From the hedge into their rusty tin before I go" (*CPM*, 26). By transubstantiating this frozen matter into life-sustaining water and pouring it into this roughhewn chalice, the poet takes on, as Thomas Redshaw puts it, "a priestly role" and performs his own eucharistic ritual.[27] In doing so, he discloses the true nature of this sacrament: that it exists not as a "permanent present," a thing fixed in place before its worshippers, but only as a "gift, ceaselessly abandoned and taken up again."[28] This fugitive yet salutary act of remembrance contrasts sharply with the one endorsed in the preceding Paisleyite tract, where the opening injunction—"LOYALISTS REMEMBER! / MILLIONS *have been* MURDERED *for refusing to* GROVEL / *Before Rome's Mass-Idol*: THE HOST!" (*CPM*, 26)—emblazons the kind of bitter resentment that perpetuates the cycle of political violence.

A similar contrast is evident between the eschatological framework of the Protestant tracts and this section's final lyric, "An Ulster Prophecy." While the former remain immured in a narrow sectarianism that casts the Catholic Church as the anti-Christ ostensibly foretold in the Book of Revelations, Montague's concluding poem envisions the future possibility of a more inclusive Irish community. Montague's poetic prophecy draws its inspiration not from scripture but from Ulster Irish oral tradition refracted in light of the deeper dimensions of the sacrament of communion. As Liam Ó Dochartaigh has shown, Montague based "An Ulster Prophecy" on a translation published in 1957 in the journal *Ulster Folklife* of "Nonsense rhymes sung for Children," which were in turn "remnants" of the traditional Irish song type, known as "Song of Lies."[29] Montague's adaptations of and additions to this traditional material anchor its preposterous images within the context of the Partition and its attendant sectarian divisions. But his most telling redaction occurs in the conclusion, which changes the original reference from "a moor-hen in flight surveying all Ireland"[30] to "a curlew in flight / surveying / a United Ireland" (*CPM*, 27). Ó Dochartaigh emphasizes the dark undertones of this final image, asserting that it may refer less to "a bright Republican ideal" than "the reality of a land united in the nightmarish discords of the contemporary 'Troubles' or in the historical desolation of Tyrone after the Flight of the Earls."[31] To be sure, the absurdist tropes that form the basis of Montague's prophecy seemingly relegate this final vision to the status of a utopian pipe dream. This point is emphasized by the interpolated material that precedes this final lyric, an excerpt from a letter written by Montague's priest-uncle that concludes by hopefully asserting that *"perhaps this new man will find a way to resolve the old hatreds"* (*CPM*, 26). The reference here is to Terence O'Neill, the Protestant prime minister of Northern Ireland in the 1960s whose gestures toward political ecumenism were eventually shattered by Paisleyite opposition. By 1968 when the first version of "The Bread God" was published, O'Neill's vision of a more inclusive Northern Irish polity lay in shambles. Thus, Montague's foregrounding of his uncle's comment is profoundly ironic and reflective of the poet's deep suspicion about the political prospects for a "United Ireland."

However, if we consider "An Ulster Prophecy" in light of the eschatological features of the Eucharist, it takes on a more positive dimension. In its prefiguration of the *Parousia*, its solicitation of another kind of "new man," the Eucharist offers something akin to what Jacques Derrida, in another context, refers to as an "undetermined messianic hope,"[32] a belief in the possibility of the seemingly impossible: a community that would transcend the fixed divisions of the present. This form of eschatological hope, while not apolitical, resists encapsulation within any particularized political agenda. Thus, Montague's later poetry anchors this vision at the more basic level of intersubjective relationships: in gestures of "familial communion" (*CPM*, 162) that in the sequence *The Dead Kingdom* absolve, if only temporarily, the deadening psychic effects of the Partition; in the acts of charity performed by Montague's physician brother in *Border Sick Call* that eradicate the border separating north from south, Protestant from Catholic, self from other.

3

Occasioned by the death of the poet's mother and loosely organized in terms of the northward journey to her funeral, *The Dead Kingdom* ventures far afield into the domains of Irish myth, place-lore, and history. But in its last two sections, the sequence returns to its triggering event and culminates in Montague's most extensive exploration of his family of origin and the trauma of its division. As we have already noted, the travails of Montague's family mirrored those of their community. The dissolution of his parents' marriage was precipitated by the Partition and its aftereffects, specifically the father's exile as part of "the embittered diaspora of / dispossessed Northern Republicans" (*CPM*, 165) and his mother's subsequent inability to adjust to the immigrant's life in a Brooklyn tenement. Conceived during his parents' failed effort as reconciliation, Montague was sundered from his mother in infancy. After being suckled by wet nurses, he was eventually shipped back from America to Tyrone to be raised by his paternal aunts. It is not only the young poet who was cast adrift; both mother and father were similarly isolated, he in his Brooklyn boarding-house, she in the stultifying Tyrone village of Fintona. In "A Flowering Absence," the title poem of the penultimate section of *The Dead Kingdom*, the vacancy brought about by the dissolution of these primal bonds is cast as an inversion of the plentitude of the eucharistic community: "There is an absence, real as presence" (*CPM*, 181).

At times, Montague seems willing to bear "the spear of isolation" as the inevitable cost exacted by an authentic sense of self-identity, as in this stanza from "Northern Lights," the poem proceeding "A Flowering Absence":

> Each death is our own:
> a child of seven, as
> dawn drew in, I would
> lie awake, singing &
> sighing to myself, *I*
> *am I, and I must die;*
> recognising the self as
> I feared the end of it:
> the spirit fretting in-
> side the body's casket. (*CPM*, 179)

But even as this passage acknowledges the solitariness elicited by an awareness of mortality, the singsong childhood rhyme and the final strained enjambment expose such solipsism as a vestigial and factitious condition. The risk of such self-enclosure was exacerbated in Montague's case by his stutter, perhaps the most pernicious outgrowth of his traumatic early childhood. In such circumstances, the tendency to embrace solitude as the optimal condition for the poetic imagination would be strong. For Montague, this temptation is most clearly manifested in "Border Lake," a sonnet from the middle of the sequence. In the sestet, he employs Yeats's favored symbol for the unfettered soul—the swan—to evoke the possibility that an aloof and solitary aestheticism might protect the poet from the serrations of a sharply divided society. But the notion of poetry as an inner dialogue, an argument that one has with oneself as Yeats famously put it, while no doubt tempting to someone afflicted with a speech impediment, is overtly rejected by Montague. In the conclusion of "A Flowering Absence," poetry is instead figured as an act and agent of communion, a sacramental balm that frees the poet from the burden of "near speechlessness" and its attendant desolation:

> And not for two stumbling decades
> would I manage to speak straight again.
> Grounded for the second time
> my tongue became a rusted hinge
> until the sweet oils of poetry
>
> eased it and grace flooded in. (*CPM*, 181–82)

If *The Dead Kingdom* locates the family as the site where the dislocations of the Partition are most intimately registered, the sequence similarly envisions the quest for a "reconciled community" in terms of the reconstitution of familial bonds. Tellingly, the language used to describe this goal presents the family as a simulacrum of the mystical body that communicants ostensibly enter into through the Eucharist: "spirits exchanging / in familial communion" (*CPM*, 162). While this phrase appears in "Gravity," the first poem of the "The Silver Flask" section of the sequence, and refers specifically to the parallel relationship of the poet's still-gestating daughter and her dying grandmother, its implications are most fully realized in the title poem of this section. There, the temporary restoration of Montague's family of origin takes place in an explicitly eucharistic context. The family reunion occurs in the afterglow of midnight Mass in rural Tyrone, the simple solemnity of which recalls Carleton's description of a similar event in the passage cited in "The Bread God." Moreover, what specifically binds the family members together is their common partaking of the spirits in their father's silver flask, an obvious analogue for the chalice holding the consecrated wine. The eucharistic motifs associated with this experience are synopsized in the poem's penultimate stanza:

> Then driving slowly home,
> tongues crossed with the Communion

wafers, snowflakes melting in
the car's hungry headlights,
till we reach the warm kitchen
and the spirits round again. (*CPM*, 170)

But even as this image of "familial communion" is celebrated and its hopeful implications for the recovery of a lost community are evoked, its inadequacies as an exemplar are exposed. There is an aura of nostalgic speciousness that hangs about this scene, evident not only in the bathetic pun on "spirits" but in the declension from the sublimity of the opening to the tawdriness of the conclusion where the family is gathered under "the same tinsel of decorations" (*CPM*, 170) used long ago in Brooklyn. The regressive insularity of this family gathering becomes even more apparent when it is juxtaposed with "A Muddy Cup," a preceding poem that describes his mother's ill-fated time in America.

The parallel between the poems is foregrounded by their contrasting central symbols. If a draught from the father's silver cup marks one's participation in something private and integral, what the muddy cup of American life offers is amorphous and impure. The refusal of Montague's mother to drink from it reflects her abhorrence of a society that she sees as contaminated by its heterogeneity:

that muddy cup
my mother refused
to drink but kept
wrinkling her nose
in souvenir of

(cops and robbers
cigarstore Indians
& coal black niggers,
bathtub gin and
Jewish neighbours). (*CPM*, 167)

However, it is not just, as some readers suggest, the poet's mother who is being indicted here.[33] The poem also hints at the impediments to the formation of community—alienation and fragmentation—posed by

American urban life. This point is reinforced by the repeated references to his father's loneliness during his long sojourn in America. In "A Graveyard in Queens," a poem from an earlier volume, Montague even goes so far as to imply that in America the most authentic community is the cemetery, where the "avenues of the dead; / Greek, Puerto-Rican, / Italian, Irish" provide a semblance of "our true Catholic / world" (*CPM*, 284).

Between these extremes—the tightly circumscribed natal family and the inchoate agglomeration of American life—Montague posits the alternative of the communal bond established through marriage. In "A New Litany," the penultimate poem of *The Dead Kingdom*, his celebration of the family created through his second marriage provides a resolution of sorts to the dilemmas of isolation and dispossession so forcefully evoked throughout the sequence. As this poem's second section reveals, the marital family offers a richer image of community than the family of origin. It suggests that community is not just a matter of consanguinity or inheritance, but rather is fashioned through the complex interplay of chance and choice, receptivity and willed response. Or to paraphrase the poem, it is something that we make even as we are made by it. In the concluding lines of this section, Montague seems to follow, as he does throughout much of his love poetry, the time-honored tradition of casting the domain of the lovers as a private enclave set against a hostile world: "I place my hopes / besides yours, Evelyn, / frail rope-ladders / across fuming oblivion" (*CPM*, 184). The partial citation of the crucial passage from "Process" quoted earlier would seem to associate the marital couple with a makeshift transcendence too flimsy to support anything more than just the lovers. But the poem's last section suggests otherwise. Here the attractive power of the marriage bond emanates outward, consecrating the surrounding landscape and providing the footing for the formation of a larger community:

> A new love, a new
> litany of place names;
> . . . .
> the shrouded shapes
> of Mounts Brandon,
> Sybil Head and Gabriel;

powers made manifest,
amulets against loneliness,
talismans for work:
a flowering presence? (*CPM*, 184)

This final question holds out the prospect that marital love might incarnate a spiritual presence that, if properly cultivated, would flourish into a larger mystical body incorporating this particular place and its inhabitants. Such a vision, however, constitutes a retrenchment from the radical utopianism of the United Irishman and the eschatological dimension of the Eucharist evoked by "An Ulster Prophecy." It evades the dilemma of Partition by retreating from the border country of Tyrone to the southernmost reaches of Ireland. Whatever hopes for a united Ireland the earlier poem conveyed are either abandoned here or else collapsed into a kind of pre-Partition republican idyll.

Such a charge cannot be leveled against Montague's later poetic sequence, *Border Sick Call*. More cohesive than the longer earlier sequences, this work provides what is to this date Montague's last extensive probing of the wound of the Partition. It does so, appropriately enough, by recounting a journey in which the poet-narrator accompanies his physician brother Seamus as he treats the sick in the remote region along the border between County Fermanagh in Northern Ireland and County Donegal in the Republic of Ireland. The fact that the setting for the journey is a winter storm allows Montague to expand upon his earlier descriptions (see "Northern Lights" from *The Dead Kingdom*) of this northern border region as a domain of implacable coldness and frozen stasis. The acknowledgment, via this symbolic landscape, of the deadening effect of the Partition renders all the more powerful its overcoming through the reciprocal solicitude of the visitors and their hosts. In that regard, the ministrations of the physician and his poet-brother in this sequence realize on a small scale the deeper promise of the Eucharist—that it manifests a "charity [that] delivers itself body and soul" and that this charity must be extended to all forms of human brotherhood.[34]

This intersection of the spiritual and political is heightened by the poem's rendering of the brothers' journey as a Dantean pilgrimage, a connection overtly made by the poet-narrator at the end of the poem's second section:

And I remember how, in Fintona,
you devoured Dante by the fireside,
a small black World's Classic.
But no purgatorial journey
reads stranger than this,
our Ulster border pilgrimage. (*CPM*, 348)

Besides this passage, the poem incorporates citations from the opening lines of both the *Inferno* and the *Purgatorio* as well as allusions that cast the poet's brother as a Virgil-like mentor and guide, the denizens of the border region as "shades" (*CPM*, 347) and the landscape as a variant of the ice-covered inner circles of the Inferno.[35] In using Dante to describe the debilitating consequences of imperialism, Montague is following the precedent of Joseph Conrad, who recognized that the depredations of the Belgian conquest of the Congo could only be registered in terms of Dante's *Inferno.* But in contrast to the journey of Conrad's protagonist Marlow, the pilgrimage of physician and poet in *Border Sick Call* eventuates in something more salutary than a despairing acknowledgment of "the horror" of colonialism's aftereffects. The Dantean context is particularly appropriate for a domain such as the border region of Northern Ireland that has long been caught in the paralyzing grip of sectarian conflict, for the frozen depths of the *Inferno* are populated by the perpetrators (and sometimes simultaneously victims) of fratricidal violence and treachery. Dante's most famous emblem of such enmity and the hateful rumination it elicits is Ugolino's endless gnawing of his betrayer Ruggerio, an act of cannibalism that, like Ugolino's devouring of the dead bodies of his sons, travesties the eucharistic meal.[36] Contrarily, the central encounter in *Border Sick Call* involves an analogue to the ritual of communion, an exchange of fraternal care and hospitality that nullifies prevailing political divisions.

In this fourth section of the sequence, the poet and his physician brother are led by a gnome-like old man to the sickbed of his wife. The man acts like a "true host," reciprocating the doctor's charitable solicitude with a warm hearth and the gift of a "small prescription bottle of colourless poteen" (*CPM*, 350–51). Whereas previously in Montague's poetry such moments of communion occurred between members of the same family or tribal group, here its participants are near-strangers. The inclusivity of this impromptu community is intensified by the fact that the couple's ethnic status remains indeterminate.[37] For the denizens of this remote region, such sectarian distinctions are, according to the old man, as irrelevant as the border that would seek to consolidate them:

> "Border, did you say,
> how many miles to the border?
> Sure we don't know where it starts
> or ends up here." (*CPM*, 350)

To the degree that he acknowledges the border's presence, it is as a contrivance that has been exploited by both Catholics and Protestants alike for the profitable smuggling of contraband and cattle. The poet extrapolates the political implications of these acts of trespass by connecting them to the cattle raid celebrated in the foundational epic of Irish culture, the *Tain*. Like the modern-day cattle smugglers, the myth of Cúchulainn operates *"in defiance of human frontiers"* (*CPM*, 351). Embraced by both Ulster separatists and Irish republicans, it subverts the very sectarian divide that it ostensibly sanctions. The mythic allusion simply confirms what the old man had already acknowledged more matter-of-factly: "Have you ever noticed, cows have no religion?" (*CPM*, 351).

This perfunctory appeal to the unifying potential of an elemental corporeality is stated more explicitly two sections later in the physician's climactic epiphany. Inspired to a "near-vision" by a draught from the medicinal spirits that the old man gave to his visitors, the doctor declares to his brother that "the real border is not between / countries, but between life and death, / that's where the doctor comes in" (*CPM*, 353). From the physician's perspective, political barriers, such as those instituted by the Partition, dwindle in the face of the universal realities of our common bodily existence. Some might be inclined to castigate this position for its bad faith, seeing it as a retreat from the thorny particulars of political deliberation into a nebulous humanism. But the doctor's transcending of political divisions in the name of the charitable alleviation of bodily suffering is not an act of evasion. Or at least it is no more so than the activities of the international group *Médecins Sans Frontières* [Doctors Without Borders] whose organizational ethos he unknowingly echoes.

Such palliatives as the physician provides, however, offer at best a respite from a "pain [that] is endless" (*CPM*, 354). That's where the poet comes in:

> *But the poem is endless,*
> *the poem is strong as our weakness,*
> *strong in its weakness,*
> *it will never cease until it has said*
> *what cannot be said.* (*CPM*, 354)

In this passage, as throughout this entire sequence, Montague presents the poem's role as complementary to that of the physician's. It too seeks to provide succor from the agonies of the flesh. It does so not by addressing the physical pain of the body but by attending to the mystery of our embodiment. That mystery is, of course, what lies at the heart of the Eucharist. Set against the sacrament, the poem seems weak. Its flesh-graced word can never claim the status of the definitive, absolute Word. Whatever mystical body the poem conjures through its attention to the sorrowful mysteries of our corporeality remains fully human, lacking divine sanction, always suffused with doubt about its perdurability. That weakness might, however, as the passage notes, also be regarded as a strength. Thus, *Border Sick Call* itself addresses Montague's ongoing search for a "reconciled community" not by incorporating this border community into a political entity invested with the aura of national identity. What it offers is at once less and more; that is, the hope that if we acknowledge the vulnerability of the bodies that we inhabit in common, we may respond to one another more charitably and thereby mitigate the ills of the body politic. It is only by acknowledging the intertwining of one's own flesh with that of others, by accepting what the French philosopher, and former Catholic, Maurice Merleau-Ponty refers to as our "intercorporeality," that we can exhume the "ideal community of embodied subjects" that lies buried within existing human social arrangements.[38]

If there is a utopian element here, it is a utopianism that is chastened by both the stark realism of the poem's setting and narrative as well as its own doubts about the efficacy of its vision. As is often the case with Montague's poetic sequences, *Border Sick Call* concludes on an ambivalent note with a gesture of self-questioning: "Will a stubborn devotion suffice, / sustained by an ideal of service? / Will dogged goodwill solve anything?" (*CPM*, 357).

The subsequent question—"But in what country have we been?"—upon which both the sequence and the *Collected Poems* as a whole conclude, crystallizes Montague's vacillation between an abiding faith in the healing power of love and an equally persistent anxiety about the vacuity of all human endeavors. On the one hand, the question evokes the potency of the community fashioned by charity, its capacity to transcend and nullify deeply entrenched political divisions. But at the same time, it emphasizes the evanescence of these secular simulacra of the mystical body and leaves us wondering if they are only utopic—if they exist only in the vacancy of no man's land or if they are capable of transforming the spaces that we actually inhabit.

4

Transcending Sacrifice

How Heaney Makes Room for the Marvelous

No Irish writer since James Joyce has more openly acknowledged the influence of Catholicism upon his work than Seamus Heaney. Raised in a devout Catholic family in rural County Derry, Heaney grew up in an atmosphere thoroughly steeped in religion. He has frequently commented on the imaginative potency of this Catholic upbringing, which he says anchored his nascent consciousness within a "light-filled, Dantesque, shimmering order of being."[1] His poetic retrievals from this childhood reservoir range from familiar Catholic rituals to exotic accoutrements of the faith, such as the chasuble and ciborium, respectively, the outer vestment adorning the priest during Mass and the vessel that holds the consecrated eucharistic wafers.[2] What remains uncertain, as with Joyce, is Heaney's governing attitude toward Catholicism. Spurred on by the poet's own comments such as the one quoted above, some recent critics have cast Heaney as a Catholic fellow traveler, who no longer officially adheres to the faith but remains profoundly sympathetic to its beliefs. Thus John Desmond, while acknowledging Heaney's struggle to overcome the "narrow cultural Catholicism" of his upbringing, stresses his ongoing commitment to the metaphysical principle of "a vertical, transcendent dimension of reality [that] he learned in his early Catholic training."[3] A more nuanced version of this position comes from Peggy O'Brien, who emphasizes the impossibility and irrelevancy of determining the precise nature of Heaney's actual religious beliefs. What matters, she suggests, is his willingness, under the influence of the "intellectual Catholicism" exemplified by the great Polish poet Czeslaw Milosz, "to imbue poetry with a questioned but also felt religious impulse quite at odds with the metaphysics of modernism and postmodernism, ranging from agnosticism to atheism."[4] Against this position, there is the abiding view, articulated most forcefully by Henry Hart and Helen Vendler, that Heaney's poetry demythologizes and secularizes the essential elements of his inherited faith. According to Hart, "Heaney recollects Catholic spiritual exercises . . . to better focus on their hallowed assumptions, which now seem hollow, and attacks their methods even as he employs them."[5] This stance of demythologizing critique towards Irish Catholicism is, indeed, foundational in Heaney's poetics. As much as any twentieth-century Irish poet, with the possible exception of Austin Clarke, Heaney has committed his poetry to the task of dismantling the debilitating components of this cultural system. Foremost among these from his perspective is a sacrificial imperative sanctioned by a theology of atonement. But Heaney's undoing of this Catholic cult of sacrifice eventuates in something more than just divestiture. It opens space for the appearance of what Heaney refers to as the "marvelous"—the unforeseeable and seemingly impossible. In Heaney's poetry, this revelation is always tinged with the numinous. But the grace that accrues to it is elusive in nature, neither clearly supernal nor purely immanent, neither theistic in provenance nor fully desacralized. Heaney releases this epiphanic event from its theological bondage without handing it over to the forces of secular materialism. He sets it loose in the open territory between the zones of belief and unbelief, where it threatens the secure premises of each of these domains.

While sacrifice has long been recognized as a central component of Heaney's work, the commentary on this issue has mostly focused on his appropriation of Iron Age sacrificial devotions to a Mother Goddess in the bog body poems of *Wintering Out* (1972) and *North* (1975). The controversy triggered by Heaney's interfusing of these archaic ritualized sacrifices with the contemporary sectarian violence of Northern Ireland has been so strident that it has preempted critics from addressing the Catholic dimension of Heaney's obsession with sacrifice. Heaney himself has not been as reluctant to make such a connection. He has stressed how compelling he found the Catholic principle "that your own travails could earn grace for others, for the souls in purgatory" and how his mother epitomized for him "the whole theology of suffering, the centrality of sacrifice, of the cross, of losing your life to save it."[6] Elsewhere, Heaney cited this impetus toward self-sacrifice as the salient feature of Irish Catholicism. In a blurb describing *Station Island*, his poetic account of the Lough Derg pilgrimage, he identified this ritual as manifesting "those self-afflicting compulsions and obedient pieties which once lived in the very centre of the Irish Catholic psyche."[7] Similarly, in one of his first interviews, he describes how at a young age the sacrament of penance inaugurated him in the "negative dark . . . the gloom, the constriction, the sense of guilt, the self-abasement" that characterized Irish Catholicism as much as its assurances of a radiant overarching order.[8]

This distinctively Catholic belief in salvation via suffering and self-sacrifice springs from the traditional theology of atonement. Throughout his religious education, Heaney would have been instructed to regard Christ's death as compensation for human sinfulness and to see the Mass as a reiteration of this redemptive sacrifice. The crux of that dogma is succinctly described in Rev. Charles Hart's *The Student's Catholic Doctrine*, the catechetical manual through which Heaney received his religious instruction at St. Columb's College: "The great work which Jesus Christ came on earth to accomplish was that of man's Redemption, or that of reconciling man with an offended God. But to do this He had satisfy the Divine Justice for our sins . . . Thus, 'at a great price' indeed, Christ won for us Justification and eternal life."[9] Hart also emphasizes how this act of sacrificial atonement recurs in the eucharistic celebration of the Mass, where "Christ, under the appearances of bread and wine, continues to offer Himself in an unbloody manner on the altar through the ministry of His Priests, as He once offered Himself a bleeding Victim on the Cross to His Heavenly Father."[10] Irish Catholics were called to participate vicariously in Christ's sacrifice not just through the Mass but by offering up their everyday sufferings. John Charles McQuaid, archbishop of Dublin and perhaps the most influential Irish Catholic prelate in the twentieth century, asserted in a pastoral letter that every Catholic should aspire to "become in his tiny way, as one who expiates with the Divine Redeemer."[11] Such doctrine infiltrated the deepest levels of Heaney's consciousness. There it manifested itself in a sense of guilty indebtedness and a concomitant belief that his art ought to be an instrument of reparation. Indeed, according to Seamus Deane, the other great literary product of St. Columb's class of 1957, by the time of Heaney's early masterwork *North* (1975), poetry had become for him "a form of guilt and a form of expiation from it."[12] That guilt surfaces in the "note . . . of timorousness" that Deane hears reverberating throughout Heaney's poetry and prose.[13] Such an assessment strikes me as only partially accurate. For as this chapter will show, what distinguishes Heaney's work during the rich middle phase of his career is not timidity but rather a rigorous effort to excavate and expunge the root causes of that disposition—most notably, the toxic blend of self-abnegation and sacrifice cultivated by Irish Catholicism and exacerbated by colonial oppression.

Nowhere is this particular spiritual deformation more precisely x-rayed than in Nietzsche's tract *On the Genealogy of Morals,* where it is given the name of *ressentiment* and identified as a linchpin of Judeo-Christian moral theology. Ressentiment, according to Nietzsche, arises when those occupying the lower rungs of the social ladder allow their sense of inequity and deprivation to fester and turn rancorous. Instead of affirming life even in the face of its injustices, those afflicted with ressentiment convert their victimhood into a badge of moral superiority, transmuting the hallmarks of their powerless condition into virtues—meekness, humility, forbearance, self-denial. Through the promulgation of such values, ressentiment exacts revenge first against those who are more powerful but then in the asceticism that is its fullest efflorescence against life itself. Nietzsche's analysis of this internalization of revenge in ressentiment is particularly pertinent for our purposes. The anger fueled by ressentiment is redirected against the self primarily in the form of "bad conscience" or guilt.[14] It is the priest in Nietzsche's genealogy who offers those who see themselves as victimized both an explanation and a remedy for their suffering. He locates the cause of their pain in themselves, in some guilty act from their past, and identifies that pain itself as a cure, casting it as a sacrifice that must be embraced in order to redeem the debt incurred through past sins.[15] But as Nietzsche notes, "the feeling of guilty indebtedness" is not easily satisfied. Having taken hold in the psyche, it metastasizes, "spreading from within like a polyp, until at least the irredeemable debt gives rise to the conception of irredeemable penance, the idea that it cannot be discharged (*'eternal* punishment')."[16] To resolve this dilemma of an infinite and irredeemable debt incurred by humanity, Christianity, in what Nietzsche sardonically refers to as a "stroke of genius," sets forth the notion of Christ's crucifixion as a sacrificial act of atonement, whereby "God himself sacrifices himself for the guilt of mankind, God himself makes payment to himself."[17]

The guilt-laden diffidence that Deane identifies as the hallmark of Heaney's poetic personality bears a close family resemblance to Nietzschean ressentiment. Groups subjected to colonial oppression, such as the Irish Catholics of Northern Ireland, offer a particularly fertile breeding ground for this psycho-spiritual malady. For the cultural apparatus of colonialism—as Heaney himself notes in "The Ministry of Fear," a poem dedicated to his classmate and friend Seamus Deane—aggressively works to instill inferiority complexes in the subjugated population. And indeed, Nietzsche's description of the behavioral characteristics of ressentiment reads like an inventory of the traits displayed by the personae in many of Heaney's early and middle poems:

> the man of ressentiment is neither upright nor naïve nor honest and straightforward with him. His soul *squints,* his spirit loves hiding places, secret paths and back doors, everything covert entices him as *his* world, *his* security, *his* refreshment, he understands how to keep silent, how not to forget, how to wait, how to be provisionally self-deprecatory and humble.[18]

Heaney is himself acutely aware of this process of psychic warping, which he critiques in poems such as "Servant Boy" from *Wintering Out* and "Whatever You Say Say Nothing," "Freedman," and "Exposure" from part 2 of *North.* This dismantling of ressentiment intensifies throughout *Field Work* until it comes to a head in *Station Island,* where in the title sequence Heaney finally exorcises this self-abnegating dimension of his consciousness.

Heaney is much more attuned than Nietzsche to the realities of political oppression that fuel ressentiment, more willing, therefore, to lay the blame for this condition not just on the victims of colonialism but on their imperial masters. But what is remarkable about Heaney's critique is that he refuses to excuse himself or his community for acquiescing to the cult of victimhood fostered by both colonialism and Catholicism. In the last section of "Whatever You Say Say Nothing," for instance, the referencing of internment camps, fortified police stations, and bombings does not mitigate Heaney's harsh attack on his community's habitual nursing of its sufferings: "Competence with pain, / Coherent miseries, a bite and sup, / We hug our little destiny again."[19] Heaney recognizes, along with Nietzsche, that this resentful servility becomes more obdurate when the political realities of subjugation are reinforced by religious imperatives. This point is overtly made in "Freedman," a poem from the second half of *North* that exposes the Roman roots of Heaney's Catholicism. Through the guise of a slave "rescued" from barbarism by the Roman imperium, the poem addresses Heaney's education at St. Columb's, an opportunity made possible by the educational reforms instituted by the British government and then enacted by the Protestant-dominated Northern Irish government in 1947. This parallel highlights the traditional justification of imperial conquest as a civilizing process. In a manner reminiscent of Joyce, Heaney casts Catholicism as an insidious corollary of imperial power. In presenting the ashes applied to his forehead on Ash Wednesday as the mark of his vassalage, Heaney identifies the self-abasement cultivated by Catholicism as a central component of the slave mentality afflicting his own community. Tellingly, the poem concludes by endorsing poetry as an agent of liberation. As such, "Freedman" seems to mark a final jettisoning of all vestiges of *Incertus*, the Latin pseudonym, meaning "uncertain" or "unsure," under which Heaney wrote his first published poems. But, as we shall see, Heaney's residual self-doubt about his art could not be so easily erased. While he wants to believe that poetry is a "self-validating" endeavor, that the act of creation justifies itself through its own freedom, he is plagued by a lingering sense that the poet's freedom is not free but must be earned through sacrifice (*GT* 92). This struggle to envision poetry as not a determinate act of atonement but an incalculable gift pervades his prose writings. It defines many of his most prominent essays, including the introductory and title essays of *The Government of the Tongue* (1989) and *The Redress of Poetry* (1995) as well as his 1995 Nobel lecture, "Crediting Poetry." In delineating these opposing conceptions of poetry, we will be guided by the philosopher John Caputo's distinction—adapted from Jacques Derrida—between the phenomenon of the gift and the economic framework that governs almost all other human transactions, including the act of sacrifice. In this formulation, the economic is "the domain . . . of entities determined and exchanged, of calculation and balanced equations, of equity and sound reason, of laws and regularities" while the gift "'calls' . . . for an expenditure without reserve, for a giving that wants no payback, for distribution with no expectation of retribution, reciprocity, or reappropriation."[20]

1

Heaney's initial effort to conceive of art as gift rather than sacrificial reparation occurs in "The Interesting Case of Nero, Chekhov's Cognac and a Knocker," which opens *The Government of the Tongue*. This introductory essay focuses primarily on the second of the figures mentioned in its odd title—Chekhov and the gift bottle of cognac that he carried with him on a visit to the Siberian prison colony of Sakhalin—which, in Heaney's decoding of this episode, serves as an analogue for "the gift of his art" (*GT*, xviii). Extrapolating from this example, Heaney formulates a notion of lyric poetry as a "free gift . . . [that] always has an element of the untrammelled about it . . . a certain jubilation and truancy . . . a sensation of liberation and abundance which is the antithesis of every hampered and deprived condition" (*GT*, xviii). There is yet another element, though, to this Chekhovian anecdote that deepens its pertinence for Heaney's own struggles as an artist. In Chekhov's "unconsciousness identification of something in himself with his serf grandfather," Heaney sees a reflection of his own entrapment within a legacy of subjugation. He realizes that, like the Russian writer, he will gain access to the free gift of his art only after having "squeezed the final drop of slave's blood out of himself." The path to "psychic and artistic freedom" lies, in other words, in the surmounting of ressentiment and its unappeasable sense of guilt (*GT*, xvii).

Heaney's struggle to extricate his understanding of poetry from the bonds of obligation and indebtedness comes to a head in the title essay of *The Redress of Poetry*, a selection of the lectures that Heaney delivered while he held the position of Oxford Professor of Poetry from 1989 to 1994.

The essay itself is an extended parsing of the various implications of its ambiguous title. The primary meaning of redress is, as Heaney acknowledges in quoting the OED, a form of "reparation . . . or compensation for, a wrong sustained or a loss resulting from this."[21] Heaney initially seems quite willing to place poetry within this metaphorical framework of economic exchange, citing with approval in the preface to the volume the American poet Robert Pinsky's assertion that the poet must answer to an obligation that is "as firm as a borrowed object or a cash debt" (*RP*, xiv). But he chafes against this economic trope and subverts it through an act of etymological scavenging that recovers a radically different meaning of "redress." Derived from hunting, this archaic use of redress refers to "a matter of finding a course for the breakaway of innate capacity, a course where something unhindered, yet directed, can sweep ahead into its full potential" (*RP*, 15). When applied to poetry, this usage allows Heaney "to profess the surprise of poetry as well as its reliability; . . . to celebrate its given, unforeseeable thereness" (*RP*, 15). This assertion casts poetry as an aleatory event that cannot be contained within the familiar circle of debt and repayment, a gift that neither offers nor requires any compensation other than its own singular presence. In a later redaction of this passage in "Frontiers of Writing," the essay that concludes *The Redress of Poetry*, Heaney describes this dimension of poetry in a manner that recalls the religious vocabulary of grace: "To redress poetry in this sense is to know it and celebrate it for its forcibleness as itself, as the affirming spiritual flame which W. H. Auden wanted to be shown forth. It is to know and celebrate it not only as a matter of proffered argument and edifying content, but as a matter of angelic potential, a motion of the soul" (*RP*, 192).

The religious antecedents of Heaney's competing notions of poetry as sacrifice and gift surface most fully in his Nobel lecture, "Crediting Poetry." The title of this lecture and its repeated use of the term "credit" reveal the lingering appeal for Heaney of a framework that invests poetry with a tangible commensurable value. It is only later, in the middle of the lecture, that Heaney links this fiduciary conception of poetry to the Catholic theology of self-sacrifice. Recalling a particularly desolating incident of sectarian violence in Northern Ireland and how that as well as other contemporary instances of the barbarism of history caused him to question his poetic vocation, Heaney figures his initial response to this dilemma through the image of a monk engaged in a stultifying penitential ritual:

> for years I was bowed to the desk like some monk bowed over his prie-dieu, some dutiful contemplative pivoting his understanding in an attempt to bear his portion of the weight of the world, knowing himself incapable of heroic virtue or redemptive effect, but constrained by his obedience to his rule to repeat the effort and the posture. Blowing up sparks for meager heat. Forgetting faith, straining towards good works.[22]

Poetry is envisioned here as an attempted act of atonement. Like the monk in his cell, the poet adopts a sacrificial posture, offering up his work in the hope that it might alleviate a burden of collective guilt. Such vicarious suffering is ostensibly what Christ exemplified on the cross and what devout Catholics are called upon to emulate. Heaney, although habitually disposed to this belief, presents it here as both futile and theologically distorted. In describing his eventual escape from this position, he implicitly identifies it with the warped servility—the ressentiment—fostered by his culture: "Then finally and happily, and not in obedience to the dolorous circumstances of my native place, but in spite of them, I straightened up" (*OG*, 423).

To elucidate this shift in his orientation towards poetry, Heaney provides an account of another monk who adopted a quite different devotional posture. This story, drawn from one of the most famous incidents in Irish hagiography, relates how St. Kevin was "kneeling with his arms stretched out in the form of a cross" when a blackbird mistook his outstretched arm for a tree branch and laid its eggs in the saint's open hand. The saint, dedicated "to love the life in all creatures," remained immobile until the eggs hatched and the nestlings finally flew off (*OG*, 424). In contrast to the image of the dutiful monk bent over the prie-dieu, St. Kevin's actions cannot be cast as a sacrificial exchange. Rather than the quid pro quo repayment of a debt that the crucifixion is reduced to in the theology of atonement, the saint's adoption of a cruciform posture is gratuitous in every sense of the word. His openhandedness transcends calculation and resists reciprocity. What the saint receives in return for his devotion is unanticipated and seemingly nugatory: fleeting contact with another, less encumbered dimension of being. For Heaney, St. Kevin's story manifests "that order of poetry which is true to all that is appetitive in the intelligence and prehensile in the affections" (*OG*, 424), which responds, in other words, not to the demands of reason but to the deeper, more inscrutable imperatives of desire. In summarizing the change in attitude epitomized by this second monastic image, Heaney refers to his willingness "to make space in . . . [his] reckoning and imagining for the marvelous as well as for the murderous" (*OG*, 423). The monastic image to which this statement is appended evokes the possibility of considering the appearance of the marvelous as an occasion of grace. And indeed, like grace, the marvelous arrives suddenly from out of nowhere to disrupt the expected order of things. Its manifestation does not just broaden but ruptures our horizons, opening consciousness to that which can be neither anticipated nor assimilated.

Heaney makes a similar point in another passage that employs a religious analogy to illuminate the essential nature of poetry. At the end of the title essay of *The Government of the Tongue*, he equates poetry with the writing in the sand that, according to the Gospel of John, Jesus produces when the Pharisees confront him with an adulterous woman and the prospect of her punishment by stoning:

> Poetry, like the writing, is arbitrary and marks time in every possible sense of that phrase. It does not say to the accusing crowed or the helpless accused, "Now a solution will take place," it does not propose to be instrumental or effective. Instead, in the rift between what is going to happen and whatever we would wish to happen, poetry holds attention for a space, functions not as distraction but as pure concentration, a focus where our power to concentrate is concentrated back on ourselves. (*GT*, 108)

Poetry operates, this passage suggests, on the margins of consciousness, in a liminal space and time, where it serves as a "threshold . . . at which reader and writer undergo in their different ways the experience of being at the same time summoned and released" (*GT*, 108). It is, in other words, both product and agent of inspiration, conductor of an ineffable spiritual energy.

In this tentative linkage of poetic inspiration and grace, Heaney follows a precedent established by his first poetic master, the Jesuit Gerard Manley Hopkins. As J. Hillis Miller notes, the images that Hopkins used to describe poetic inspiration—"flowing water, flame, impregnation"—were strikingly similar to the ones that he employed to "define the descent of God's grace."[23] In an early essay on the priest-poet, Heaney stresses this equivalence between the "central event in Hopkin's religious life and . . . the experience of the poetic act itself," ascribing both to "a bolt from the blue."[24] There is, of course, a profound difference between Heaney and his predecessor that qualifies any parallels in this area. While Hopkins underwent a startling conversion to Catholicism, Heaney has confessed to experiencing a gradual lapse in his faith. It is not surprising then that the distinctively Catholic notion of "actual grace"—that is, grace accrued through penitential acts of self-sacrifice and participation in the sacraments—is embraced by Hopkins but rejected by Heaney. As we have seen, it is precisely the economic framework undergirding the Catholic theology of sacrifice and suffering from which Heaney struggles to extricate himself. However, the deeper notion of "uncreated grace" articulated by Hopkins still has currency for Heaney. This force, which Hopkins associated with the Holy Spirit, is nothing less than the "energy of being" that sustains and shapes all things.[25] A similar notion, albeit shorn of any Trinitarian associations, is at play in Heaney's attribution of the origin of his poems to "the notion of grace" and "a certain unforeseen energy."[26] And it is present as well in his assertion that the sonic force field generated through the interplay of rhyme and rhythm in Yeats's "The Cold Heaven" may be seen as radiating from "a much greater, circumambient energy and order within which we have our being" (*RP*, 149). Here as elsewhere in his critical commentaries and interviews, Heaney associates the deepest and most authentic dimensions of poetry with something approximating the idea of grace that he also inherited from his Catholic background. For Heaney, the nature of this phenomenon remains irrevocably indeterminate: less than divine gift but more than purely secular serendipity.

Regardless of that ambivalent status, its effect, as Heaney's poetry attests, is salutary if not salvific.[27]

2

In his Nobel lecture, as we have seen, Heaney used the figure of a penitent monk at the prie-dieu to mark that period in his career when he was fixated on the murderous to the exclusion of the marvelous. This phase culminated in *North* and its notorious bog-body poems. These poems arose, as Heaney himself indicated, from "a search for images and symbols adequate to . . . [the] predicament" posed by the rapidly escalating sectarian violence of Northern Ireland.[28] He found those symbols in P. V. Glob's *The Bog People* with its startling photographs of the victims of ancient sacrificial rites preserved in the peat bogs of northern Europe. In establishing a parallel between these archaic blood sacrifices to an indigenous nature goddess and the political violence committed by the devotees of Mother Ireland, Heaney was, as he put it in the Nobel lecture, "pivoting his understanding in an attempt to bear his portion of the weight of the world" (*OG*, 458). He sought to alleviate that burden first by surfacing the sacrificial mythos that underlies the more extreme forms of Irish nationalism and then by defusing it through an intensive focus on the victims of these rites. As Daniel Tobin and Helen Vendler have shown, the figures in Heaney's most well-known bog poems—the Tollund man, the Grabualle man, the Windeby girl—are invested with an incommensurable identity that calls into question the ritualized violence that reduced them to ciphers in a sacrificial exchange.[29] But despite its ameliorating ethical implications, Heaney's fascination with the mutilated bodies of these victims is also disturbing. The "rapturous horror" manifested by these poems cedes to the nightmarish aspects of history a Medusa-like power of entrancement.[30]

In "Kinship," the poem that serves as summa to the bog poems, the bog itself radiates an almost paralyzing magnetic power. As the title indicates, the hold that this womb-like maw exerts over the poet's consciousness is as strong as the bonds of consanguinity. The quatrain that concludes the poem's fourth section highlights the contradictory effect—at once generative and stunting—that this "floe of history" (*P*, 196) has had on his development:

> I grew out of all this
> like a weeping willow
> inclined to
> the appetites of gravity. (*P*, 198)

With its evocation of the poet stooped in sorrow by the gravity of his homeland's troubles, this image rhymes closely with the monastic figure that Heaney used in the Nobel lecture to emblematize his earlier inauthentic sense of his vocation. The connection suggests that Heaney recognized even in the midst of his effort to fashion an art "adequate" to the murderousness of history that this endeavor was potentially warping, that tethering his verse to these dark terrestrial powers hampered his imagination. This note of self-questioning becomes even more pronounced in the poem's final section where the introduction of the ancient Roman historian Tacitus provides a more detached perspective. When the speaker appeals to Tacitus to "come back to this / 'island of the ocean' / where nothing will suffice" (*P*, 200), he is referring not just to the futility of the various political efforts, violent and otherwise, to resolve the sectarian conflict in Northern Ireland. The allusion here to Wallace Stevens's famous dictum, written at the outset of World War II, that modern poetry "has to think about war / And it has to find what will suffice" indicts Heaney's own attempt to redress the violence afflicting his community through art.[31] This disheartening admission that "nothing will suffice" in the face of the Troubles belies his claim that the bog-body poems offered "images and symbols adequate to our predicament." It betrays a sense of guilty inadequacy that deepens in this volume's final poem, "Exposure."

The dampening of spirit effected by this chronic sense of culpability permeates "Exposure," tellingly, the only one of his own poems that Heaney quotes in the Nobel lecture. It is also the first of Heaney's works to be set in the small Wicklow estate to which he moved his family in 1972, eager to escape not so much the violence as the constraints that life in Northern Ireland imposed upon his poetry. But despite its pastoral seclusion, Wicklow in this poem manifests the same downward gravitational pull as the bog. This depressive atmosphere is crystallized in the poem's images of sodden trees, fallen leaves, and the pattering rain telegraphing its complaint of failed responsibilities and retreat. These elements of the external landscape serve as an objective correlative for the poet's psyche, burdened by anxiety over the purpose of his art: "I sit weighing and weighing / My responsible *tristia.* / For what? For the ear? For the people?" (*P*, 228). In a manner that anticipates the Nobel lecture, "Exposure" reveals the cost exacted by the belief that art should be an instrument of atonement. Obsessively dwelling on his unfulfilled obligation, longing to be a David-like hero whose seemingly insignificant gift would save his community, the speaker misses out on the marvelous—"the once-in-a-lifetime portent / the comet's pulsing rose" (*P*, 227–28). Here, as well as elsewhere in Heaney's poetry, natural wonder comes cloaked in a supernatural aura. Not only is the comet associated with the celestial rose that appears at the end of Dante's *Paradiso,* but its mass is rendered ethereal through the poem's constellation of liquid consonants and high-frequency vowels: "Those million tons of light / Like a glimmer of haws and rose-hips" (*P*, 227). Even though the speaker misses out on this epiphany, some compensation for this loss is offered in the form of the "diamond absolutes" evoked by the glittering of the rain drops (*P*, 228). In its immediate context, this phrase hints toward the freedom implicit in the poet's anomalous and marginalized social position: "neither internee nor informer; / An inner émigré" (*P*, 228). But it takes on a heightened significance when it is read in light of its later appropriation in the Nobel lecture. There it is used along with other citations from "Exposure" to elaborate the inadequacy of Heaney's earlier sacrificial approach to poetry when he was aping a monk bent over the prie-dieu, "attending insufficiently to the diamond absolutes, among which must be counted the sufficiency of that which is absolutely imagined" (*OG*, 423).

Such an assertion of the self-validating, self-absolving nature of poetic utterance seems far removed from the doubts about the political responsibilities of the poet that pervade "Exposure." But this more exculpatory attitude is not entirely absent in the poem. It lingers in the allusions scattered throughout "Exposure" to the Russian poet Osip

Mandelstam whose second book was titled *Tristia* and who underwent a period of internal exile before eventually dying in Stalin's gulags. The privileged status that Mandelstam occupies in Heaney's poetics springs from his apparent resolution of the dilemma facing the poet in a time of political crisis. Should the poet write "for the ear," cultivating the intrinsic potency of the language itself, or should he write "for the people," deploying his art against their oppressors? Mandelstam's appeal derives from the fact that he eludes this double bind. In a totalitarian state such as the Soviet Union, the linguistic playfulness of Mandelstam's poetry was in itself an assertion of individual freedom and, as such, a blow against the hegemony of the state. Thus, in serving the principle of artistic autonomy, Mandelstam offered up his art as well as his life for the greater good of his community. But whatever corroboration this exemplar provides for Heaney is, to say the least, problematic since the gratuity of the poet's art is ultimately sanctioned by his martyrdom. However laudable, Heaney's admiration for Mandelstam reveals just how deeply interlaced the notions of gift and sacrifice were in both his thinking about his poetry and his practice of it.

The untangling of this conceptual knot began in earnest in Heaney's next volume, *Field Work* (1979). "Oysters," the poem that inaugurates the book, serves as the catalyst for this process of extrication. It is this poem, according to Heaney, that revivified his writing in the aftermath of *North* by allowing him to get "to the bottom of something inside myself, something inchoate but troubled."[32] While the source of this confusion emerges gradually in the poem, from its outset there is evidence of a new poetic perspective. For perhaps the first time, the palpable sensuosity that had been a hallmark of Heaney's early verse conveys an experience of unalloyed pleasure. Instead of the "warm thick slobber / of frogspawn" (*P*, 5), the "rat-grey fungus" of rotting blackberries (*P*, 10), the tar-like deliquescence of a thousand-year-old corpse, here we are given the heavenly "tang" of oysters. Not surprisingly, this delightful moment stirs up the troublesome residue of colonial displacement and exploitation. The discarded oyster shells call to mind the native Irish, who were similarly torn from their habitat, while recollected tales of Roman soldiers transporting oysters over the Alps serve as reminder of the colonizer's "glut of privilege."[33] But in this case, these feelings of guilt and resentment are quickly exorcized when the speaker upbraids himself for allowing them to undermine his faith in the adequacy of what is given to him every day.

> And was angry that my trust could not repose
> In the clear light, like poetry or freedom
> Leaning in from the sea. I ate the day
> Deliberately, that its tang
> Might quicken me all into verb, pure verb. (*FW*, 11)

In these last lines, this primal trust in existence is recovered through a Nietzschean commitment to the "innocence of becoming," a sacramental savoring of the passing day that brings consciousness into communion with the flux.

The dangerous consequences of refusing to embrace life in the present indicative become apparent in "Badgers," another of this volume's animal-based allegories. An element of mystification surrounds the poem's central trope. But its second stanza grounds the metaphorical framework in familiar political terrain, tentatively identifying the nocturnal predator with the specter of an IRA bomber. This reading garners support in the speaker's subsequent refusal to accede to those who credit the badger with "honour," insisting to the contrary that his true nature bears the mark of the "pig family." The coarseness of this insult is cancelled out by the subtlety of the passage that follows and concludes the poem:

> How perilous is it to choose
> not to love the life we're shown?
> His sturdy dirty body
> and interloping grovel.
> The intelligence in his bone.
> The unquestionable houseboy's shoulders
> that could have been my own. (*FW*, 26)

This final anthropomorphizing of the badger fuses the image of the young IRA man scurrying for cover with that of the servant boy of the eponymously titled poem from *Wintering Out*. What binds them together is a shared demeanor of sullen disaffection. Here, more explicitly than anywhere else in his poetry, Heaney identifies ressentiment as a root cause of Catholic political violence in Northern Ireland. The candor of the critique is accentuated by the fact that he includes himself within it. But it is the initial question, highlighted by the perfect rhyme it triggers, that sharpens Heaney's diagnosis. Ressentiment and the acts of vengeance that are its poison fruit arise when we refuse to receive life as it is given rather than as we desire it to be. Far from counseling complacency, Heaney is once again echoing harsh truths gleaned from Nietzsche. To be precise, he is evoking one of the central paradoxes of Nietzsche's philosophy: the recognition that "it is only when I can affirm existence just as it is that I become free to transform it"; otherwise, "any attempt to transform it falls back into the negatively oriented spirit of revenge that can do nothing."[34]

"At the Water's Edge," the third section of "Triptych," complements "Badgers" by spotlighting more precisely the religious posture that inhibits Irish Catholics from engaging in this kind of transformative political action. Like so many other poems in the first part of *Field Work*, "Triptych" is set against the rising tide of sectarian violence in 1970s Ireland. In this case, the incident that elicited the poem was the IRA's assassination in 1976 of Christopher Ewart-Biggs, the British ambassador to Ireland.[35] The poem's first section, "After a Killing," traces the pedigree of this act back to the violent birth of the Irish Free State, "as if the unquiet founders walked again" (*FW*, 12). Against that long history of violence, the poem holds out the beauty and fecundity of the Irish countryside. But any solace generated by the pastoral is quickly abrogated by the atavism prophesied in the poem's second part, "Sybil." Both the setting and the analysis become more personal in the poem's third panel. The shoreline alluded to in the title of this section is that of Lough Erne in County Fermanagh, located a short distance from Lough Derg, the site of Station Island. The poem surveys several of the islands in the lough, cuing in on the ruins found there: crumbling monastic statuary on Devenish, a hollowed-out stone icon of a Celtic god on Boa, the hearthstone of a derelict cottage on Horse Island. With their vestiges of a more honorable and spiritually vibrant past, these sites elicit a familiar response from a poet instinctively drawn towards elegizing:

Everything in me
Wanted to bow down, to offer up,
To go barefoot, foetal and penitential,

And pray at the water's edge. (*FW*, 14)

Heaney discerns in this inclination to genuflect before a lost past the self-abasing devotional posture cultivated by Irish Catholicism. Such veneration, he realizes, presupposes a need to make amends for what has been lost—to atone for its disappearance and solicit its salvaging through sacrificial acts of penitence.[36] That this obeisance is figured as infantile exposes its regressive nature. For more enlightened acts of political resistance to occur—such as the one alluded to at the poem's conclusion, a peaceful protest march that took place in Newry a week after Bloody Sunday—this habitual bias toward grievance and contrition must first be overcome.

Fittingly, it is the dead artistic masters elegized in *Field Work* who exemplify, as Seamus Deane notes, the "choosing [of] the bold course" as opposed to the skulking of ressentiment.[37] The sharpest counterpoint comes from the composer Sean O'Riada who re-energized traditional Irish music before his premature death in 1971. In his creative process, he forswore any punitive regimen of labor and dared, instead, to open himself to the play of unknown forces. Rather than a penitential bowing and scraping at the water's edge, he ventured into the sea, "trusting the gift, / risking the gift's undertow" (*FW*, 29). As a result, he was never weighed down by the backward-looking political agenda that others attached to his art but was lifted through his "grace notes" to transcendence (*FW*, 30). The trajectory traced by "Triptych" and "In Memoriam Sean O'Riada" reaches from the shoreline of an insular lough to the open expanse of the ocean, from familiar rituals of self-sacrifice to faith in an uncertain and unfathomable grace. The journey adumbrated here is mapped much more precisely in the title sequence of Heaney's next book, *Station Island*. There it is cast as a redaction of one of the most famous devotional practices of Irish Catholicism, the penitential pilgrimage to Lough Derg in County Donegal, the alleged site of miraculous deeds by St. Patrick and the putative entryway to purgatory. Many Irish writers, including, as we have seen, Denis Devlin and Patrick Kavanagh, produced works focused on this pilgrimage. But none committed themselves as deeply as Heaney to the transformation of the "self-afflicting compulsions" of Irish Catholicism that it traditionally exemplified.

3

In its movement from the archaic blood sacrifices of the bog-body poems to the penitential exercises of "Station Island," Heaney's career recapitulates the "introversion of sacrifice" that, according to Horkheimer and Adorno, characterizes the development of Western civilization and reaches its apotheosis, as Nietzsche reminds us, in Christian asceticism.[38] The self-sacrifice demanded by the Lough Derg pilgrimage was rigorous, incorporating fasts, sleepless vigils, and repeated circuits of walking (usually barefoot) and kneeling in prayer around the island's stony rings or "beds."[39] In both its three-day time frame and its tribulations, the pilgrimage was designed to evoke the Paschal sacrifice of Christ. Through their suffering, the pilgrims participated vicariously in Christ's expiation of humankind, becoming agents of atonement who sacrificed themselves (at least temporarily) to alleviate the debt incurred through their own and other's sinfulness. As a young man, Heaney undertook the pilgrimage to Lough Derg three times.[40] Given that personal connection and the ritual's centrality in Irish Catholicism, it is not surprising that Heaney returned to this experience as he struggled to extricate himself and his poetry from a sense of guilty indebtedness. But there were historical factors as well that directed Heaney's poetry in the early 1980s towards Station Island. As he himself recently indicated, the 1981 hunger strikes at Long Kesh Prison that resulted in the death of ten IRA prisoners were very much on his mind during the time in which "Station Island" was being written.[41] The Lough Derg pilgrimage shared some superficial similarities with the hunger strikes at Long Kesh, including not only the fasting but the designation of the site of the pilgrim's initial vigil—at first the Church of St. Patrick, later rebuilt as a Basilica—as the "prison."[42] But as Michael Parker astutely notes, Heaney's affiliation of the two events arose from a deeper ideological connection: their common emphasis on a "path of renunciation and sacrifice" deeply embedded in Irish Catholicism and sanctioned by the theological principle of atonement.[43] The hunger strike is directly referenced only once in "Station Island," in canto 9, which addresses the death of Heaney's one-time neighbor Francis Hughes, the second of the strikers to die. Still, its importance to this twelve-part poetic sequence cannot be underestimated. The deaths occasioned by the hunger strike and the violence that followed publicly validated Heaney's suspicion of the impetus toward self-abnegation and sacrifice fostered by Irish Catholicism.

Both the 1981 hunger strikes and the "blanket" and "dirty" protests that preceded them were political strategies fashioned by a group that had few other weapons. Subjected to internment without trial as well as physical and mental torture, IRA prisoners finally rebelled when in 1976 their special status was revoked and they were classified as ordinary criminals. Rejecting the regular prison uniforms, they first draped themselves in their blankets and then eventually refused to leave their cells, which soon became excrement-lined hell holes. When this protest lagged, the IRA prison leadership doubled down and intensified their struggle against the British military and political authorities in charge of Long Kesh prison. The ostensible strategic purpose of the hunger strike was to elicit British acceptance of five demands, which centered upon the reinstatement of special status for the prisoners. But at a deeper level, its goal was a total reinvigoration of Irish Catholic support, in both the North and the South, for the republican cause. In that regard, the hunger strike's appropriation of the sacrificial mythos long associated with Irish nationalism was crucial. Richard Kearney, the preeminent elucidator of this connection, traces its revival during the Troubles to the provisional IRA's "deep identification with the heroes of Easter Week," especially Patrick Pearse.[44] The leader of the Easter Rising provided these latter-day militants with a politically potent variant of the Christian ideal of sacrificial atonement. Among the places where Pearse articulated this idea was a poem written shortly before his execution, "A Mother Speaks," in which "he identifies himself with the sacrificed Christ 'who had gone forth to die for men.'"[45] As further evidence of the currency of Pearse's trope in the Northern Ireland struggle, Kearney cites the Catholic journalist and civil rights advocate Eamonn MacCann's remark that "one learned quite literally at one's mother's knee, that Christ died for the human race, and Patrick Pearse for the Irish section of it."[46]

Such associations were readily evoked both by the hunger strikers themselves and their supporters in the outside community. Bobby Sands, the preeminent hunger striker, followed Pearse in writing poetry that implicitly linked his own mortifications to Christ's: "Blessed is the man who stands / Before his God in pain, / And on his back a cross of woe."[47] When challenged by Fr. Denis Faul, a priest who sought to end the hunger strike, Sands reportedly defended his actions by reciting Christ's words from the Gospel of John: "What greater love hath a man than to lay down his life for the life of his friends."[48] Other prisoners "made handkerchiefs for their relatives that juxtaposed images of Christ and a hunger striker in imitation of Veronica's veil."[49] Those who marched in support of the strikers often carried posters that portrayed the strikers as the crucified Christ, adorned with prison barbed wire shaped as a crown of thorns. In these marches, some of their family members "wore blankets and wire crowns to symbolically express their conviction that the hunger-strikers . . . were sharing in Christ's martyrdom."[50]

Even if this Christological dimension was, as some have insisted, simply a propagandistic overlay, the military strategy that it cloaked still hinged upon the mythic power of sacrifice. Allen Feldman, whose exhaustive anthropological analysis of the 1981 hunger strikes was based on interviews with IRA prisoners who witnessed firsthand the planning and implementation of the prison protests, argues convincingly that the strike's primary purpose was to inaugurate a new and more comprehensive phase of "mass insurrectionary violence."[51] The idea of sacrificial atonement was central to that project. Serving as "surrogates" for their fellow IRA prisoners, the hunger strikers sought through their self-sacrifice to cleanse themselves and the republican movement as a whole from the taint of criminality. Purified by their tragic ordeal, their dead bodies would expose the inherent evil of British rule and trigger a "cathartic uprising" against it.[52] Heaney recognized this "realpolitik" dimension of this "sacred drama" enacted by hunger strikers as well as the brutal intransigence of the British government.[53] But as Danny Morrison, Sinn Féin's director of publicity in 1981, brusquely points out, the poet found "nothing life-affirming in . . . [their] sacrifice."[54] While Morrison's charge concerning Heaney's attitude toward the hunger strikers is valid, what he intends as criticism testifies instead to the acuity of Heaney's insight into the fatalism inherent in this deadly politics of sacrifice. Heaney realized (as we have seen and will see even more clearly in "Station Island") that the calculus of sacrificial exchange, with its recursive cycle of debt and repayment, leaves no room for the startling breakthrough of the unexpected. The implications of that closure are not just poetic but political. For as Hannah Arendt has argued, transformative political action always bears the shock of new beginnings, always depends upon the performance of what is "infinitely improbable."[55] Heaney echoes this in *The Cure at Troy* (1991), his adaptation of Sophocles' *Philoctetes*, where after citing the shared suffering of the hunger strikers' and murdered policemen's families, the chorus proclaims that this fractured community must "hope for a great sea-change / On the far side of revenge," must "believe in miracles."[56]

When Francis Hughes appears in the climactic canto 9 of "Station Island," Heaney's portrayal of the hunger striker's death is unsparing. Unlike the other ghosts in the sequence, Hughes reveals himself through soliloquy rather than conversation with the poet-pilgrim. Such solitary discourse seems fitting for a prisoner whose slow deterioration during his fast ultimately left him speechless, immured within his own dying body. But this self-enclosure as well as the depletion of Hughes's starving body also reflect the moral vacuity of a gunman responsible for an estimated twenty-five to thirty deaths, including reputedly those of boyhood acquaintances and possibly an infant who was "collateral" damage in a bombing.[57] Indeed, hollowness is the keynote of his concluding description of himself as "a hit-man on the brink, emptied and deadly."[58] In the account of the burial that follows, Heaney envisions an alternative ceremony, one devoid of the religious and military tributes that accompanied the actual event. By positing a more appropriate grave site at the locus of the gunman's first attack, the poem casts the trajectory of his career as a vicious circle. It presents his self-sacrifice not as ennobling or generative but rather as a fruitless reversion back to the murderous actions that marked his entry into manhood. Heaney's intention here is not to mock

Francis Hughes, whose death he greeted with sorrow and anger (*RP*, 186–87). Instead, by revealing the futility of the IRA hunger strike, he hopes to break the hold of the sacrificial imperative which it perpetuates. His use of the weasel to capture the atavism of Hughes's actions echoes Yeats's application of a similar image ("the weasel's twist, the weasel's tooth") in "Nineteen Hundred Nineteen" to evoke the bestiality of both World War I and the Anglo-Irish conflict.[59] It is not just Yeats's imagery that Heaney imitates here but the disjunctive nature of the poetic sequence in which it appears. The five loosely rhymed sonnets that comprise canto 9 shift suddenly after the initial two describing Hughes's death and burial to a phantasmagoric exploration of the poet's own interior struggle. As in Yeats's sequence, there is a logic that links these apparently discontinuous parts. But to elucidate that connection, we need first to examine how "Station Island" as a whole collates Heaney's conflicted sense of his poetic vocation with the ritualized self-sacrifice of the Lough Derg pilgrimage.

Heaney's long-standing struggle to see his poetry in terms of freedom rather than guilt-laden obligation is mirrored in the two literary figures that stand behind "Station Island"—Dante Alighieri and Sweeney, the pagan Celtic king who is the hero of the medieval Irish poem *Buile Suibhne*. With its recounting of a poet-pilgrim's journey into a psychic underworld populated with ghostly interlocutors drawn from a personal and communal past, Heaney's "Station Island" is clearly modeled after Dante's *Inferno*. Given that fact, it is not surprising that in 1985 shortly after the appearance of *Station Island*, Heaney published a long essay on Dante and modern poetry. In that essay, he seeks to rescue Dante from T. S. Eliot's ossifying praise. For a counter to Eliot's casting of Dante as a model of the poet who tethered his imagination to religious doctrine and duty, Heaney turns, as he has done previously when in quest of a more liberating vision of poetry, to Osip Mandelstam. According to Heaney, Mandelstam's Dante is not a promulgator of Catholic or scholastic orthodoxies but "an exemplar of the purely creative, intimate, and experimental act of writing itself."[60] This freedom is so deeply embedded in Dante's poetry that Mandelstam describes it primarily as "a free, natural, biological process, as a hive of bees, a process of crystallization, a hurry of pigeon flights."[61]

Sweeney is similarly associated with the instinctive wildness of nature. After his assault upon St. Ronan, the cleric put a curse upon Sweeney that transformed him into a bird and exiled him to the wilderness from whence he flew across Ireland from bog to mountain, lamenting his fate and praising the natural beauty of the landscape. Perhaps even more than Dante, Sweeney is the tutelary figure who presides over "Station Island." He is the focal point of the poem, "King of the Ditchbacks" that precedes "Station Island" and of the sequence "Sweeney Redivivus" that follows it. Moreover, it is his surrogate, an Irish traveler named Simon Sweeney, whose specter Heaney encounters upon first arriving at Lough Derg. Reprising his role as an "old Sabbath-breaker" and childhood bogeyman, this Sweeney counsels the poet as he is about to embark on his penitential ritual to "stay clear of all processions!" (*SI*, 61, 63). The advice gestures toward the conflict that lies at the heart of "Station Island." It is a conflict that, according to Heaney, the original Sweeney epitomizes. In the preface of *Sweeney Astray*, the translation of the *Buile Suibhne* that Heaney published in 1983, he identifies Sweeney "as a figure of the artist, displaced, guilty, assuaging himself by his own utterance," caught up in "the quarrel between free creative imagination and the constraints of religious, political, and domestic obligation."[62]

It is not until the latter half of "Station Island" when the poet is confronted by victims of sectarian violence that these anxieties about his artistic vocation become overt. Prior to that, the poem extirpates the religious attitude that lies at the basis of his conflict and previews its transcendence. Thus, canto 4 confronts us with a familiar exemplar of the Catholic theology of sacrifice—the missionary priest. In this case, the priest is Heaney's childhood neighbor, Terry Keenan, whose short tenure as a missionary in the tropics ended with his death by malaria.[63] The priest renounced the world and its pleasures in order to "save" those mired in ignorance and sin. But like Francis Hughes, whose hunger strike was motivated by a similar, albeit secularized, notion of redemptive suffering, the priest's self-sacrifice ultimately proves to be bankrupt. The talents and energy that he offered up to a religious obligation are simply dissipated: "Bare-breasted / women and rat-ribbed men. Everything wasted. / I rotted like a pear. I sweated masses." (*SI*, 69). To the extent that his sacrifice accomplished anything, it simply shored up his own community's religious beliefs against the threat posed by a secularized modernity: through the mere fact of his presence "something in them would be ratified" (*SI*, 70). The priest himself frames his vocation not as a choice but a concession to these communal expectations. During his school days at St. Columb's, Heaney experienced similar pressures to pursue the priesthood.[64] But unlike Keenan, he turned his back on this call for him to forfeit his freedom and do "the decent thing" (*SI*, 70). It is all the more ironic then that in his chosen role of poet he found himself saddled with a similar sense of tribal duty. Whether priest or poet, whoever comes under the sway of Irish Catholicism is deeply imprinted with its imperative of self-sacrifice. That vexing legacy of his childhood faith leads Heaney towards an act of apostasy that is, paradoxically, completed for him by Keenan's ghost. However, this renunciation, which merely inverts the renunciation of the world demanded of the priest and, to a lesser degree, the Lough Derg pilgrim, suffers from the same unilateralism that it ostensibly rejects.

A more subtle parsing of Catholicism's influence upon the poet's consciousness occurs in canto 6, which recounts his halting entry into sexuality. Both the intensity of his early intimations of sexual desire and their repression are marked linguistically. For his first object of affection, his partner during a childhood game of "secrets," he appropriates kennings—"pod of the broom, / Caitkin-pixie, little fern-swish"—that invest her memory with the attractive power of his natal landscape (*SI*, 75). But his fellow pilgrims' singing of hymns to the Virgin Mary, the icon of purity, induces a flashback of an adolescent sexual repression so severe that it led him to scavenge dictionaries for words that might quench his desire. When he recalls his eventual access to the realm of sensual delight via a later sweetheart, this opening is arched by counterpoised images—"the breathed-on grille of a confessional" and the "wide keyhole of her keyhole dress" (*SI*, 76). This antithesis insinuates that the gift of fully incarnate love comes only to those who have passed beyond the penitential regime of Catholicism. The allusion that follows infuses this gift with an element of transcendence. There, Heaney describes his long-awaited sexual awakening by citing the passage from canto 2 of the *Inferno* in which Dante is revivified by his discovery that Beatrice had intervened to rescue him. The fact that this intervention is initiated and delivered via a heavenly relay—from the Blessed Mother to St. Lucia to Beatrice—makes it a prototype of supernal grace. That Dantean ray of celestial radiance hovers in the background of Heaney's account of how he was "translated, given" through the requiting of sexual desire (*SI*, 76), bringing a higher pitch to what might otherwise have seemed a purely natural transformation. A pattern is sketched here at this medial point in "Station Island" that emerges more clearly in the sequence's last several cantos. When the self-abnegating, sacrificial mind-set fostered by Catholicism is cast aside, the doors of consciousness are opened to the possibility of the gift. What had previously been forgotten or forfeited suddenly appears to have been miraculously given.

This tension between the freedom of the gift and the obligations of sacrifice drives the central conflict that Heaney faced in his vocation as a poet. That quarrel intensifies in cantos 7 and 8 of "Station Island." In the aftermath of an old acquaintance William Strathearn's recounting of his murder by a Protestant death squad, Heaney's guilt over his unfulfilled responsibilities toward such victims bursts forth in a plea for forgiveness. His angst deepens when he recalls how he left the deathbed of a mortally ill friend, Tom Delaney, "feeling I had said nothing / and that, as usual, I had somehow broken / covenants and failed an obligation" (*SI*, 81). If the problem with William Strathearn and Tom Delaney was not saying enough, in the case of Heaney's second cousin, Colum McCartney, it was a matter of saying too much. At the end of canto 8, McCartney's ghost attacks Heaney for an earlier poem, "The Strand at Lough Beg," that aestheticized the young man's death at the hands of Protestant paramilitaries. He calls for the poet to do penance for that sin at the stations of Lough Derg. Advanced by this innocent victim of sectarian violence, the demand for sacrificial atonement that lies at the heart of the Station Island pilgrimage is rendered all the more compelling.

That is perhaps why the figure of the dead hunger striker, who in his own way answered that demand, elicits such an intense reaction. In the third of canto 9's sonnets, after the ghost of Francis Hughes has been given his say and laid to rest, the poet's guilt becomes horribly palpable:

"Strange polyp floated like a huge corrupt / Magnolia bloom, surreal as a shed breast, / My softly awash and blanching self-disgust" (*SI*, 85). This Bosch-like vision defamiliarizes Heaney's habitual self-reproach. The distance it brings lays bare the root cause of this malignant condition and facilitates a definitive judgment of it. The lines that follow denounce the ressentiment that links the poet to the dead paramilitary in a voice freighted with scriptural authority: "And I cried among night waters, 'I repent / My unweaned life that kept me competent / To sleepwalk with connivance and mistrust'" (*SI*, 85). As with Dante, this moment of despair initiates a transformation, but one that in this case repudiates rather than embraces a penitential posture. When ressentiment goes, so too does the sense of abjection that fuels the need for atonement. The slough of self-disgust is transmuted into a luminous wellspring. And in a manner presaged by canto 6, the abandonment of ressentiment opens access to the gift. In the next sonnet, an old brass trumpet that the poet had as a child thought too good for him is now envisioned as rising out of the lough and offering itself to him once more. His delighted acceptance of this music-making gift hints towards a shift away from his previously guilt-ridden approach to his own art. These two sonnets cast the change from self-abnegating sacrifice to the liberating embrace of life's gratuity as an epiphany. This lightening flash captures the essential character of this transformation by reducing it to a single decisive moment. What it leaves out is the seemingly insurmountable difficulty of overcoming a deeply embedded disposition.

The canto's final sonnet provides the necessary corrective. A series of anaphoric lines mock the assumption that conversions such as this can be accomplished through the self's own agency. Openness to the presence of the gift cannot be willed, but is itself given. To put it in religious terms, grace is not at our disposal; we can only put ourselves at its disposal. Like "the tribe whose dances never fail / For they keep dancing till they sight the deer" (*SI*, 86), we must bide our time, vigilantly awaiting the advent of an unforeseeable benison.

Even when the gift arrives, it remains vulnerable to false expectations and susceptible to being perverted to ends for which it is not suited. This is the gist of the parabolic anecdote of the muddied kaleidoscope that

Heaney evokes at the outset of canto 11: "As if the prisms of the kaleidoscope / I plunged once in a butt of muddied water / surfaced like a marvellous lightship" (*SI*, 89). The motive for this careless act of destruction comes in the version of the episode recounted in a lecture that Heaney delivered during the composition of *Station Island*. There he describes how the kaleidoscope was a Christmas gift, but when he compared it with a Protestant neighbor's present—a magnificent toy battleship—he was consumed with jealousy. His attempted conversion of the kaleidoscope into a military vessel resulted in its sinking in a mud puddle. Afterwards, he discovered that "its insides had been robbed of their brilliant inner space, its marvellous and unpredictable visions were gone."[65] The message of the parable is clear: poetry's inadequacy when measured against the instrumental power wielded by the colonial ruling class leads to the depreciation and sullying of this visionary gift. The canto, however, focuses less on the loss than on the process of salvaging.

Not surprisingly, the recovery of the gift is linked once more to the nullifying of Catholic penitential practices. The guide for this process is a Carmelite priest, whose advice to the poet is delivered in the confessional. But his message abrogates the ritual over which he presides, making the poet "feel there was nothing to confess" (*SI*, 89). To recover the gift that had been "mistakenly abased," the monk tells Heaney to "read poems as prayers" and to translate a poem of the great Carmelite mystic Juan de la Cruz as his "penance" (*SI*, 89). Rather than implying that poetry should be subordinated to familiar Catholic principles of guilt and atonement, the priest's advice suggests that the poetic act itself is inherently redeeming. We get a crucial clue as to how that might be from the translated poem that constitutes the rest of the canto. It is important to note that both the injunction to translate and the object of that translation were additions that Heaney made to the remembered episode underlying this canto.[66] Heaney's choice of this particular poem from the Spanish master of the *via negative* is especially telling, as these opening stanzas of his translation make clear:

That eternal fountain, hidden away,
I know its haven and its secrecy
    although it is the night.

But not its source because it does not have one,
which is all source's source and origin
  although it is the night. (*SI*, 89–90)

Poetry constitutes an act of prayer in Juan de la Cruz's poem through its acknowledgment of existence as something given, as the overflow of a divine wellspring. The fact that this eternal fountain is unfathomable, that the source of this gift is unknowable, releases this revelation from the economic framework of sacrifice. It means that, as Jean-Luc Marion, the Catholic phenomenologist, puts it, "The gift is perfectly reduced to givenness—that nothing which tears everything away from nothingness."[67] When there is no thing that gives, there can be no demand that the gift be reciprocated with propitiatory sacrifices. And likewise no expectation that the grateful recognition of the gift will be rewarded by a divine Giver. The gift comes with no strings attached; it is delivered and accepted gratuitously.

The mystical paradoxes expressed in Heaney's translation of Juan de la Cruz's poem augment a crucial passage from earlier in "Station Island." At the end of canto 3, recalling the childhood death of a paternal aunt, Heaney displaces the "circuits" of the pilgrimage, that is, the prayerful walking around the island's sacred stations, with a more problematic image of circling:

I thought of walking round
and round a space utterly empty,
utterly a source, like the idea of sound;

like an absence stationed in the swamp-fed air
above a ring of walked-down grass and rushes
where we once found the bad carcass and scrags of hair
of our dog that had disappeared weeks before. (*SI*, 68)

The emptiness, the miasma of decay, the positioning of death at the heart of things—all of these point toward a nullity that renders the pilgrim's "circuits" futile. But in the passage's conjoining of emptiness and source, there is a counter-note. As Daniel Tobin notes, this evocation of "an ultimate source or space that cannot be fully revealed and is therefore transcendent" resonates with Juan de la Cruz's mystic insights into the *deus absconditus*.[68] Around this hidden center, there can be no processions, only halting steps in the surrounding darkness.

Such "probes" into the unknown are precisely what the specter of James Joyce calls for at the end of "Station Island." In lieu of the closed circle of debt and repayment conjured from a conventional theology of atonement, Joyce charts a path to artistic redemption that is idiosyncratic and centrifugal: "You lose more of yourself than you redeem / doing the decent thing. Keep at a tangent. / When they make the circle wide, it's time to swim // out on your own." (*SI*, 93–94). It seems inevitable that Heaney's quest to extricate himself from what he referred to as "the penitential sub-culture of Irish Catholicism" would culminate in an encounter with Joyce's ghost.[69] In his escape from the nets of family, nation, and religion woven so tightly in Ireland, Joyce epitomizes the ideal of artistic freedom. The fact that he gives voice to this freedom in this sequence's most fully realized version of Dante's terza rima identifies that earlier master as a kindred spirit and confirms Heaney's choice of Mandelstam's Dante over Eliot's. Joyce, having purged himself of the spirit of ressentiment that he identified as a source of his countrymen's paralysis, calls upon his successor to do the same: "This subject people's stuff is a cod's game, / infantile, like your peasant pilgrimage" (*SI*, 93).[70] He counsels Heaney to forgo the rituals of his inherited faith and to devote himself instead to his art. In an earlier version of this section of "Station Island," Joyce's reversal of Catholic orthodoxy is rendered even more explicitly: "When I refused to take the sacrament / I made my life an instrument of grace."[71] The passage paraphrases Stephen Dedalus's culminating epiphany in *A Portrait of the Artist* that he will become "a priest of eternal imagination, transforming the daily bread of experience into the radiant body of everliving life."[72] Given the argument that has been advanced above, the omission of these lines from the final version of "Station Island" might seem surprising. But the deletion reflects Heaney's reluctance to embrace Joyce's view of omnipotence of the artist, his unwillingness to deify the artistic imagination by placing grace under its purview. The Joyce that ultimately enters Heaney's poem is not the godlike creator of the work of total plenitude but rather the advocate of a more tentative and fragmentary form of poetic discourse—"echo soundings, searches, probes, allurements, // elver-gleams in the dark of the whole sea" (*SI*, 94). In this revised Joycean portrait, the artist does not sanctify his life by the sheer force of his creative will. Instead he surrenders his work to the gratuitous play of existence, unmooring it from the foundational beliefs of his culture in quest of an unforeseeable transcendence.

4

That Heaney's subsequent forays into this fathomless domain trigger a significant shift in his poetics has been noted by many critics. Helen Vendler, for instance, characterizes his next book, *The Haw Lantern* (1987), as forsaking "the tactile and the palpable" world that he inhabited in his early poetry for a realm of the "virtual," in which things "are almost invisible, or soon to be."[73] Vendler casts this transformation, which culminates in *Seeing Things* (1991), as primarily aesthetic in nature: a shift away from a "mimetic" or "memorial" style that invests language with the density of the material world and the actuality of the past towards a symbolist one in which the poetic imagination preserves an evanescent reality by elevating it to "an abstract and symbolic plane."[74] For Henry Hart, on the other hand, *Seeing Things* is primarily an exercise in a visionary poetics, a heightened version of the Kantian sublime whereby a "boringly mundane reality" gives way to "scenes made sublime by altered perspective or poetic tropes."[75] Both critics attenuate the significance of the transformation that occurs in these volumes by positing it as essentially subjective in nature. They reduce the poet's newfound perspective to something akin to the kaleidoscope that appears at the outset of canto 11 of "Station Island"—a form of artifice that renders a familiar reality wondrous. In doing so, they overlook the deeper message of that canto and others in "Station Island": the gift of vision debased by ressentiment is recovered not through the agency of the subjective imagination but through a revelation of reality as something given. To recognize the real as something that "appears as giving itself," as an event of disclosure, as Martin Heidegger and more recently Jean-Luc Marion have taught us to do, is to see phenomena as imbued with a dynamic potency that resists our efforts to apprehend and orchestrate them.[76] It entails a posture of what Wordsworth referred to as wise passivity, an acceptance that we cannot conjure or manipulate the marvelous into appearing but only hold ourselves open to its arrival. In both *The Haw Lantern* and *Seeing Things*, Heaney registers that truth by highlighting the erratic nature of such manifestations of the marvelous—by casting them in the form of anomalous weather ("Hailstones"), accidents ("The Milk Factory"), play ("Markings"), tricks of light ("Squarings xlvii & xlviii"), folkloric miracles ("Fosterling," "Squarings viii"). The ontological status of what is revealed in these poems always remains in doubt. For Heaney, like the philosopher John Caputo, recognizes that between the "gratuity" of the phenomenal world and a divinely imparted "grace," there is at best an "undecidable link."[77]

The trajectory of this transformation in Heaney's poetry is spotlighted in "The Milk Factory" from *The Haw Lantern* and "Fosterling," the medial poem of *Seeing Things*. In the former, a seemingly trivial event—a sudden eruption of milk from its containment vessels at a local dairy plant—garners a deeper significance when it is cast in terms of the sacrificial outpouring of blood and water from the pierced side of the crucified Christ:

> We halted on the other bank and watched
> A milky water run from the pierced side
> Of milk itself, the crock of its substance spilt
> Across white limbo floors where shift-workers
> Waded round the clock.[78]

The deft pleonastic description of the "milky water" emanating from "milk itself" recalls the shared essence of the blood shed by Christ and the wine consecrated in the eucharistic sacrifice of the Catholic mass. But no debt can be repaid, no atonement effected through the accidental discharge of this milk. It is no longer a commodity capable of being exchanged. Yet despite this loss of its calculable value, this spilt milk is nothing to cry about. Released from the "crock of its substance," the milk becomes something other than a familiar fungible entity. Incommensurable, exceeding the limits of objecthood, this overflowing substance is a source of astonishment for those who do not seek to contain and grasp it. Thus, while the workers in the factory remain trapped in a "white limbo," the young speaker and his companions, not yet immersed in the human routine of conceptual apprehension, are transported into something akin to a heavenly radiance, "astonished and assumed into fluorescence."[79]

"Fosterling" begins with Heaney ruefully noting how a schoolroom painting of a typical low-country scene crystallized his early attraction to the similarly waterlogged landscape in which he grew up. But his fascination is directed less to the natural environment of these northern places than to the human constructs that crisscross the painting. There is a tight correspondence between these artifacts, evoked through the compacted partial rhymes—"windmills," "millhouses," "still," "outlines," "canals"—of these opening lines.[80] These water-driven mechanisms capitalize upon the "immanent hydraulics" of the land, participating in a reciprocal exchange of forces that renders this excess liquidity productive. In that capacity, Henry Hart sees them functioning as a "metaphor for the dynamics of the visionary imagination" as it strives to counterbalance "the heaviness or sinfulness of existence."[81] Such a view aptly characterizes Heaney's poetry when its primary domain was the mud-clotted fields of rural Derry—evoked here as in the earlier poetry through the use of Hiberno-English dialect—and its highest aim the fashioning of an imaginative construct adequate to the historical predicament of the poet's tribe. But it is a mistake to circumscribe the more buoyant poetry that Heaney generated in the aftermath of *Station Island* within this reciprocal framework. This sharp transition in Heaney's poetics is marked here by the break, highlighted through added spacing, between this sonnet's octave and sestet. In that final section, it is only when poetry forsakes, rather than redresses, "the doldrums of what happen" that the marvelous appears, in the form of a dazzling "tree-clock of tin cans / The tinkers made" (*ST*, 52). Conjured into being by travelers, this epiphany is fugitive and seemingly frivolous. But its flashing was sufficient, according to the folktale that was the image's source, to fool the devil intent on collecting souls as recompense for a benefit he had bestowed.[82] The marvelous, no matter how seemingly insubstantial, thwarts the devilish economics of sacrificial exchange.

Whether it is the coruscations of the imagined tin tree clock or the glow of effluent milk, the issue of what status we should grant these emanations is profoundly vexing. Are they too little or too much? Tending toward vacuity or repletion? Insufficiently or extravagantly charged with the energy of being?[83] The question remains all the more open when we locate these poems and others in which the marvelous is manifested in context. Both "The Milk Factory" and "Fosterling" appear next to poems (the eighth section of "Clearances" and first of "Squarings") that ostensibly describe the postmortem disappearance of the soul into the void. For Helen Vendler, these adjacent poems account for the presence of the numinous in the others: such apparitions arise, she suggests, when "the phenomenal world" is "contemplated through eyes made intensely perceptive by unignorable annihilation."[84] This assertion becomes more tenuous when the culminating poems of *Seeing Things* are considered. "Squarings xlvii & xlviii" come at the end of a long sequence of twelve-line poems in which the impromptu play of the marble shooter—colloquially referred to as squarings—becomes a heuristic strategy. It is here that Heaney fully embraces the exploratory, provisional poetics of "searches, probes, allurements" that Joyce's ghost called for at the end of "Station Island." If the form itself is aleatory, so too was its discovery since Heaney claims it to be something "given, strange and unexpected" rather than consciously chosen.[85]

The final two poems of "Squarings" focus, as do so many others in this sequence, upon phenomena that hover on the horizon of perception. They address the spatial and temporal aspects of this liminal perceptual experience. In "Squarings xlvii," Heaney ponders the phenomenon of the "offing," that is, the distant, barely visible part of the sea glimpsed from shore. Far from inducing vacuity, the vacancy of the offing is cast, in Daniel Tobin's felicitous phrase, as a "generative emptiness."[86] It evokes the numinous while allowing it to remain intangible:

> Then, when you'd look again, the offing felt
> Untrespassed still, and yet somehow vacated
>
> As if a lambent troop that exercised
> On the borders of your vision had withdrawn
> Behind the skyline to manoeuvre and regroup. (*ST*, 101)

In the last poem of the sequence, the offing is restored to its more familiar sense of the near future—what lingers on the edge of foresight rather than eyesight. The offing becomes here, as in the previous poem, the locus of an intimated spiritual illumination. Or as Heaney playfully puts it, "Seventh heaven may be / The whole truth of a sixth sense come to pass" (*ST*, 102). The poem's second half extrapolates this elusive epiphany and envisions its realization during a sunstruck drive along the river Bann. For Vendler, this vision confirms rather than cancels the pervasive sense of annihilation that governs this volume. The frisson it induces is "ecstatic but wintry," like the chill of the void that accompanies Wallace Stevens's "mind of winter."[87] Such a reading refuses to acknowledge the poem's final promissory note, the anticipated reintegration of an overlooked or lost radiance. What such an experience might entail is best gleaned from Heaney's gloss on a later poem, "Known World," from *Electric Light* (2001) in which he describes a moment strikingly analogous to the one envisioned in "Squarings xlviii."

> Often when I'm on my own in the car, driving down from Dublin to Wicklow . . . I get this sudden joy from the sheer fact of the mountains to my right and the sea to my left, the flow of the farmland, the sweep of the road, the lift of the sky. There's a double sensation of here-and-nowness in the familiar place and far-and-awayness in something immense. When I experience things like that, I'm inclined to credit the prelapsarian in me. It seems, at any rate, a greater mistake to deny him than to admit him.[88]

The encounter with the marvelous, this passage suggests, revives a belief in the potency of a radical innocence that lies latent in the adult psyche. For Heaney, such credence is necessarily tentative, an act of trust tinged with uncertainty. Repeatedly throughout *Seeing Things*, and especially in "Squarings," he invests the phenomena registered in these poems with an evocative indeterminacy. Nowhere is that more evident than in "Squarings x," where as so often throughout this sequence it is a trick of light—specifically, the reflected sunlight rising off a quarry pool—that is observed. The witnessing of that "cargoed brightness" poses a challenge to the observer that is encapsulated in the poem's last lines: "Were you equal to or were you opposite / To build-ups so promiscuous and weightless? / Shield your eyes, look up and face the music" (*ST*, 64). The dilemma epitomized here, as we have seen, pervades Heaney's career: how does one regard the gratuitous nature of art and, indeed, of existence itself? That culminating injunction demands that we address this question, but offers no clear resolution. Tracing that "cargoed brightness" back to its source could lead to a vision of harmonious transcendence or to an acknowledgment of the harsh truth of absolute nothingness.

Not definitive revelations nor even "hints and guesses" such as proffered by T. S. Eliot in *The Four Quarters,* what Heaney gives us instead is exposure to a mystery that can never be resolved but only plumbed ever more deeply.[89] Yet despite the fact that Heaney's poetic "probes" remain provisional, that they eventuate in nothing more substantial than "elvergleams," their effect on those disposed to receive them is liberating. Their superfluous shimmering dissolves ressentiment and disrupts the narrow notions of equity that foster sacrifice. Or at least that is what Heaney insinuates in "Squarings xxvi," the only poem in this long sequence to evoke the historical predicament afflicting Heaney's community of origin. At its outset, the poem reminds us of the persistence of the oppression imposed upon the members of this community, who perennially find themselves following British army trucks filled with gun-laden soldiers. In the face of this imminent threat of violence, the poem advises not only circumspection but a deeper kind of awareness: "steer and concentrate / On the space that flees between like a speeded-up / Meltdown of souls from the straw-flecked ice of hell" (*ST,* 80). That evanescent gap between the fragile shell of the poet's Volkswagen and the potentially lethal army truck is the space between now and then, here and there, being and nothingness. It is the interval that makes the givenness of existence available for contemplation. This opening at the heart of the space-time continuum resembles what Martin Heidegger referred to as *die Lichtung,* the clearing where entities arise and recede in the ineffable and interminable process of being's giving of itself. There is a saving grace in even a glimpse of this aperture, as yet another allusion to Dante's *Inferno* reveals. As we noted with Montague's similar evocation of the icy nether regions of the *Inferno,* this domain of fratricidal violence and treachery resonates strongly with a country entrapped in sectarian conflict. And indeed, Heaney has long regarded the most famous scene of this section of the *Inferno*—Ugolino's endless gnashing of his betrayer Ruggerio's head—as the ultimate emblem of the futility of a politics driven by ressentiment and the sacrificial imperative that it fuels. Appended to *Field Work,* Heaney's translation of this episode was first occasioned by the "'dirty protests' in the Maze prison."[90] The rendition of Ugolino's final actions—*"And his teeth, like a dog's teeth clamping round a bone, / Bit into the skull and again took hold"*—that he later added to "The Flight Path" in *The Spirit Level* (1996) directly evokes the hunger strikes of 1981 that followed in the aftermath of the "dirty protests."[91] The hope that Heaney proffers at the end of "Squarings xxvi" is that in acknowledging the gratuity of our lives, we will be released from the narrow calculus that demands compensation for the losses of history through the sacrifice of oneself or others. That grace, however tenuous and uncertain in its provenance, is foremost among the gifts bequeathed by Heaney's poetry.

5

Relics and Nuns in Eiléan Ní Chuilleanáin's Poetry

Sifting the Remains of Irish Catholicism

By the turn of the millennium, the once imposing edifice of Irish Catholicism appeared increasingly derelict. Over the previous decade and a half, the authority of the Catholic Church had been badly damaged by legislative defeats on contraception and divorce as well as a series of scandalous revelations about sexual impropriety and abuse, beginning with the shocking disclosure in 1992 of the popular Bishop of Galway Eamonn Casey's secret affair with a young American woman who had borne his child. Then in the summer of 2001, the relics of St. Thérèse of Lisieux came to Ireland and during their eleven-week tour of the country were venerated, according to the estimates of the event's organizers, by 3 million people, three-quarters of the island's population. The *Sunday Business Post* went so far as to designate the crowds that greeted the relics as "the greatest mass movement of the Irish people in the history of the country."[1] This extraordinary outburst of traditional Catholic devotion seemingly indicated that Catholicism in Ireland, despite the persistent rumors of its demise, was still a vital presence in Irish society. It was as if an act of cultural homeopathy had been performed. The enthusiastic reception of these sacred relics apparently inoculated the Catholic Church against the charge that it had itself been reduced to a relic.

If so, the revival was timely. During this period when Ireland's incredible economic boom was reaching its apex, Catholicism seemed to be one of the few viable counter-forces to the rampant consumerism spawned by the Celtic Tiger. That assumption was belied by the fact that the tour of St. Thérèse's relics was marketed like the rollout of some cutting-edge consumer good or the appearance of a celebrity pop star, with posters announcing that she "would draw bigger crowds than rock legends U2" and that she "was more popular than pop star Madonna."[2] Moreover, the response to the relics that Bishop Brendan Comiskey of Ferns, the chief organizer of the event, promulgated—a "child-like" exercise of imagination that supersedes critical intelligence and submits to a mysterious presence—was less a counter to than an extension of a consumerist ethos.[3] In this regard, we might recall that Marx fashioned his notion of "commodity fetishism" from the analogous relationship between the enthrallment of the consumer with the commodity in capitalism and the worship of objects like relics in religions such as Catholicism. In each case, the originating context of the object is obscured and the object itself is seen as imbued with a quasi-magical aura. When considered from this demystified perspective, the extraordinary popularity of St. Thérèse's relics would appear to derive from their reification of an ostensibly purer Catholic faith while their well-publicized introduction into twenty-first-century Ireland looks suspiciously like an attempt to rebrand (à la Classic Coke) a superannuated and compromised product.[4] In Eiléan Ní Chuilleanáin's poetry, we find a similar conjunction of relics and religious women, designed in this case not to shore up the existing structure of the Catholic Church so much as to radically destabilize it. Instead of fostering traditional pieties, Ní Chuilleanáin effects through this poetic motif a winnowing of Irish Catholicism that brings forth both the seeds of future liberation and the chaff of past oppression. As such, her poetry epitomizes the twofold process of critique and creative refashioning that characterizes the Catholic element in the strand of Irish poetry that we have been examining.

For Ní Chuilleanáin, no aspect of Irish Catholicism is more culturally resonant nor more in need of a thoroughgoing recuperation than the role of religious women. She identifies this "preoccupation with nuns, and the reasons for their existence" as foundational to her effort to understand her cultural heritage, insisting that it "explains or rather provides always the first syllable of an explanation of the world I grew up in and the many worlds I inherit."[5] The definitive role that nuns play in Ní Chuilleanáin's poetry has been acknowledged by critics as well. In the article that first introduced Ní Chuilleanáin's work to an international critical audience, Peter Sirr designated her art as "cloistered," not only because so many of her poems referred to "nuns and convents," but because the form of the poetry itself—"in its deliberate choice of marginal location, in its quiet rhetoric, in its discrete presentation of material"—had a "cloistered" quality.[6] According to Ní Chuilleanáin, nuns entered her poetry not so much as invited guests but rather as unbidden emissaries from the recesses of her imagination. In the essay from which I quoted above, "Nuns: A Subject for a Woman Writer," she describes how as a young writer in her late twenties she sought a "vantage point" for her poetry that was based in experience, a theme "really there, not made up, but intractably in the world I and others have lived in, hard and resistant to explanation." But as her imagination groped for this experiential perspective, Ní Chuilleanáin was surprised to discover that her poetry was repeatedly invaded by "the figure of a nun [who] would be standing quietly in the middle of a poem, as in a room in my house, before I had asked her in."[7] While this fascination with nuns has a biographical basis—Ní Chuilleanáin was educated at convent schools and has three paternal aunts who were nuns—her interest in these religious women is ultimately driven by a deep-seated recognition of their cultural significance in Ireland. Existing on "a border, both inside and outside Irish society," nuns occupied a crucially liminal position in relation to the dominant patriarchal social structure of late nineteenth- and twentieth-century Ireland.[8] As such, they provide a kind of threshold experience that ostensibly upholds but more often interrogates the cultural codes in Ireland that have regulated the emplacement of women in society and in their own bodies.

Despite the primacy that Ní Chuilleanáin assigns to nuns in her imagination, they, like so many other entities in her poems, have a spectral rather than a substantive presence. They are never fully realized but manifest themselves instead in brief glimpses and oblique gestures and allusions. Neither these nuns nor the poetic texts in which they appear can be reduced to commodities that are easily apprehended and readily consumed. Instead of being rendered as "atomized, self-encapsulated things . . . [whose] meanings and properties appear to lie within themselves alone"—the ontological perspective that according to Michael Taussig defines commodity fetishism—Ní Chuilleanáin's nuns are always presented in terms of a "relational gestalt,"[9] always located in the context of her culture's formative assumptions about women's roles. One such assumption casts the social marginality of nuns as a form of diminution. It regards the lives of these women as attenuated because of their subjection to strict disciplinary regimes and their exclusion from the socially normative patriarchal family. Such an attitude is exemplified by the comment that one of Ní Chuilleanáin's uncles made in reference to the nuns who populate her poetry: "When I see a nun I always think, 'none.'"[10] This "depersonalization" of nuns was widespread in Irish culture where, according to the historian J. J. Lee, "nuns were de-humanized in public images to a far greater extent than priests."[11] Against this prevailing view of the unattached female as defined by lack, Ní Chuilleanáin, paradoxically, emphasizes how the international nature of Catholic religious orders bestowed an expansiveness upon these cloistered women that was generally unavailable within the narrow provincialism of twentieth-century Irish middle-class life. Similarly, the nuns in Ní Chuilleanáin's poetry, despite their spectral nature, are never seen as having been reduced to a kind of dismal ethereality by their ascetic practices. Instead, Ní Chuilleanáin evokes in her poetry what she emphasizes in her prose: the intensely corporeal nature of their religious practice, "the way their lives, their attention were disciplined and directed to the physical world at all times." Nowhere is this more evident than in their attire. The conventional assumption is that the long robes, wimples, and veils that nuns traditionally wore inhibited their bodies. But from Ní Chuilleanáin's more nuanced perspective, the nun's habit served as a kind of habitat, an extension of the body that while containing it offered it room to move as freely and "intently as a fish in water."[12]

This willingness to invest the body with a heightened spiritual significance has long been a hallmark of Catholic women religious. Tellingly, one of its primary manifestations was in the prevalent role that they often gave to relics. In her analysis of relics in their late medieval apogee, Caroline Bynum points out how they were predominantly associated with religious women and reflected an awareness and appreciation of the spiritual potency of female somatic experience.[13] This association of nuns with relics did not end with the Middle Ages, but continued well into the modern era. Thus, in the rich flowering of convent life that occurred in nineteenth-century Ireland, relics were a primary mark of distinction: "the more influential friends a community had, the greater was their supply of relics."[14] A deeper understanding of these feminized talismans emerges throughout Eiléan Ní Chuilleanáin's poetry—a conception of the relic that resists its reduction, as in the case of St. Thérèse's fragmented bones, into a determinate perdurable entity. In fact, Ní Chuilleanáin subverts precisely this conventional fetishizing of the relic in the ironically titled poem "The Real Thing," from her volume *The Brazen Serpent* (1995). There, the relic is envisioned as something more akin to the philosopher Emmanuel Levinas's enigmatic notion of the "trace." For Levinas, the trace is a vestige that brings the past into proximity without rendering it tangible; it is the wake inadvertently left by something as it passes, a ripple in the fabric of things that lingers after that which produces it disappears. "An absence radically withdrawn from disclosure . . . [but] not reducible to concealment," the trace hovers in the hinterland between past and present, absence and presence, nonbeing and being. It is a remainder that resists representation and is manifested only as "a disturbance imprinting itself . . . with an irrecusable gravity."[15] In Ní Chuilleanáin's "The Real Thing," Sister Custos, whose name is Latin for "guardian," adopts a posture similar to that of the conservators of the Thérèsian relics. She regards "her major relic, the longest / Known fragment of the Brazen Serpent"—the Mosaic staff that was a type of the true cross—as "the real thing."[16] That is to say, she treats it as the hypostatization of the essence of the faith, a treasure to be worshipped, sequestered, and safeguarded. Against this popular understanding of the relic, the poem posits an alternative vision in which the heirloom of the faith is identified with "true stories / [that] wind and hang like this / Shuddering loop wreathed on a lapis lazuli / Frame" (*BS*, 16). At the poem's conclusion, these stories are associated with the vestiges of Sr. Custos's own cloistered life. For Ní Chuilleanáin, this is the true relic: a remnant of a corporeal existence that is not memorialized but that reveals itself instead in its disruption of the officially sanctioned and sanitized versions of the past:[17]

The torn end of the serpent
Tilts the lace edge of the veil.
The real thing, the one free foot kicking
Under the white sheet of history. (*BS*, 16)

"The Real Thing" reveals that relics that Irish Catholics should cherish are not piecemeal fragments detached from the lifeless bodies but the restive traces engendered by the lives of women religious.

The touchstone for Ní Chuilleanáin's assessment of the impressions left by these often forgotten women is the poem "J'ai mal à nos Dents." First published in *The Magdalene Sermon* (1989), this poem reappears as an epigram to Ní Chuilleanáin's essay on nuns and then again, along with a brief commentary, as her contribution to a book of essays entitled *Religious Women and Their History: Breaking the Silence*.[18] Dedicated to the memory of Anna Cullinane or Sr. Mary Anthony, who was one of Ní Chuilleanáin's paternal aunts, "J'ai mal à nos Dents" does not represent this woman's attributes but instead contextualizes the linguistic traces of several disparate episodes of her religious life, most of which was spent as a Franciscan of Calais. The fact that these verbal remnants are in French and that the first of them is the strange solecism that constitutes the poem's title highlights the anomalous nature of the nun's life as epitomized by Sr. Mary Anthony. Through the poem's opening and closing lines, Ní Chuilleanáin echoes the more conventional view of nuns by casting these women as vitiated—passive servants of a patriarchal Church that has stripped them of their freedom and alienated them from their own bodies.

The Holy Father gave her leave
To return to her father's house
At seventy-eight years of age
. . . .
They handed her back her body,
Its voices and its death.[19]

The poem's framework directly acknowledges the harsh fact of the convent's containment within a disempowering patriarchal structure. But in doing so, it challenges readers to move beyond this familiar yet limited truth and to discern the richer and more complex reality that it obscures. Some will show themselves incapable of surmounting this initial impression of the nun's life, as for instance the critic who categorizes the poem as "coldly angry," brimming with resentment at "a patriarchal church [that] has exploited this woman's strength until there was none of it left."[20] This myopic characterization of Sr. Mary Anthony's life as one of mere victimhood is exposed and critiqued within the poem itself. For her brother back in Ireland listening to the war news on Radio Éireann, Sr. Mary Anthony remains nothing more than a distant and occluded object of concern, a "name [that] lay under the surface" (*MS*, 29) of the reports of the German army advancing on Calais. Blinkered by his own assumptions about his sister's cloistered life, he cannot envision her active participation in the historical events to which he is merely a bystander:

> he could not see her
> Working all day with the sisters,
> Stripping the hospital, loading the sick on lorries,
> While the Reverend Mother walked the wards and nourished them
> With jugs of wine to hold their strength.
> *J'étais à moitié saoûle.* It was done.
> They lifted the old sisters onto the pig-cart.
> And the young walked out on the road to Desvres,
> The wine still buzzing and the planes over their heads. (*MS*, 29)

In lieu of the sterile asceticism stereotypically associated with religious women, these nuns, as the interposed French phrase indicates, participate in a kind of bacchanal. Their drunken ecstasy contrasts, though, with that of the ancient Maenads in that it is conjoined with acts of succor rather than violent sacrifice. The physical engagement evoked in this passage—the communal sharing of the pleasures and burdens of the body—confirms the significance of the French phrase that appears as the poem's title and that is reiterated in the stanza prior to the one above. This bizarre locution (I have a pain in our teeth) that the young Sr. Mary Anthony utters during a visit to the dentist casts her body not as a reified and isolated substance owned by the self, the "possessive individualism" that characterizes modern self-identity,[21] but as an amorphous and shared corporeality that emanates, as the poem puts it, "out of her first mother" (*MS*, 29). As the last of the poem's French phrases *"(Une malade à soigner une malade)"* (A sick woman to care for another sick woman) neatly illustrates, this blurring of the boundaries of self and other that characterizes Sr. Mary Anthony's experience as a religious woman continues when she returns to the family home, ill herself, to tend to her sick sister. Through its revelation of the hidden plentitude of this nun's life, "J'ai mal à nos Dents" exposes the limits of the commonplace attitude that would equate the cloister with confinement, enclosure with erasure.

The dynamism that Ní Chuilleanáin attributes to Sr. Mary Anthony and, by implication, women religious in general, runs counter to what the Irish historian and Dominican nun Margaret Mac Curtain identifies as the stereotypical image of "the nun in mid-century Ireland," that is, "a docile and submissive figure clad in a black or white or blue sweep of garment with a medieval headdress who rarely raised her voice or eyes."[22] In her dismantling of this stereotype, Ní Chuilleanáin anticipates the work of several historians, including Mac Curtain herself. Mary Peckham Magray's comprehensive historical analysis of nuns in nineteenth-century Ireland establishes their foundational role in the process of reform that revitalized and consolidated Irish Catholicism. Even more significantly, her study provides substantial evidence that convent life "was far richer than . . . constitutions and rule books would suggest . . . [and] offered a style of living found highly desirable by many Irish women."[23] Mac Curtain identifies as a key component in this vocation's desirability the enhanced opportunities for education available to nuns in early and mid-twentieth-century Ireland. In the case of the Medical Missionaries of Mary founded in 1936, she points out how this education included professional training in medicine, a field from which Irish women at this time were generally excluded.[24] Yvonne McKenna's extensive interviews of women who were nuns in mid-twentieth-century Ireland offers firsthand testimony in support of these claims. If these women lament the constrictive rules imposed upon them, they also highlight the compensatory outlets that made their lives more sustaining in some regards than those of their secular counterparts, a point that McKenna stresses in her summary of this phase of her research: "Although remarkably structured and regulated, religious life did present women with opportunities not always available to them outside. It gave them the opportunity to pursue a respectable alternative path to marriage and motherhood, to be educated, receive training, work and travel."[25] In poems published before this ground-breaking research, Ní Chuilleanáin similarly counterpoises the life of the nun against the role of motherhood culturally and legally enshrined as the preferential option for Irish women throughout much of the twentieth century.

"Chrissie," a poem from later in *The Magdalene Sermon*, employs this contrapuntal theme to particularly powerful effect. Suffused with the elusive mythic atmosphere that makes so much of Ní Chuilleanáin's poetry seem as though it emerges from the recesses of the cultural imaginary, this poem focuses on a young woman marooned in a wrecked ship near a bleak shore. The precise nature of the traumatic loss that she has suffered remains unknown, but the imagery associates it with sexual penetration and parturition. Using one of her favorite tropes whereby the female body is recapitulated in an external structure, Ní Chuilleanáin casts the skeletal shipwreck as a uterine form:

> Escaped beyond hope, she climbs now
> Back over the ribs of the wrecked ship,
> Kneels on the crushed afterdeck, between gross
> Maternal coils: the scaffolding
> Surviving after pillage.
> . . . .
> Four notches down the sky, the sun gores the planks;
> Light fills the growing cavity
> That swells her, that ripens to her ending. (*MS*, 35)

The allusion to the placenta and umbilical cord in the reference to "crushed afterdeck" and "gross / maternal coils," the reference to the "growing cavity," coalesce to present maternity as a kind of shipwreck whereby women are either stranded in a socially sanctioned but desolate domesticity or else driven into hiding, as may be the case here, to avoid the scandal of an illegitimate pregnancy. The littoral setting as well as the implication of a secretive childbirth call to mind the contemporaneous Kerry babies case. The scandal centered upon a twenty-five-year-old unmarried mother, Joanne Hayes, who, having just given birth to a stillborn child, was subsequently charged with the infanticide of a newborn baby washed up on the strand near Cahirciveen, County Kerry. The aggressive nature of the prosecution of Hayes, which continued despite the absence of any substantial evidence, and the attacks upon her in the press revealed the deep stigma still attached to unmarried mothers in late twentieth-century Ireland.[26] "Chrissie" does not directly address this issue but rather the underlying cultural code that coercively identifies femininity with maternity and marriage. The critique surfaces with characteristic obliquity in the poem's conclusion.

> And she goes on fingering
> In the shallow split in the wood
> The grandmother's charm, a stone once shaped like a walnut
> . . . .
> She clings, as once to a horned altar beside the well. (*MS*, 35)

In these lines, the young woman at the heart of the poem is associated with artifacts and sites—the walnut-shaped stone, the well, the horned altar recalling the Celtic fertility god Cernunnos[27]—that bind her over to something akin to an ancient fertility cult. Against this, the poem sets the image of another kind of mother, a mother superior, whose willingness to expose herself to the unfamiliar imbues her with the sublimity of an epic hero—"(Her tanned forehead more dreadful now / Than when helmeted and veiled)"—and who leads her charges, "shoulder to the stern," in "pushing out boats" (35) into the open sea. As Ní Chuilleanáin does in her prose, the poem positions the mother superior and her followers on the margins of society. But in its final action, "Chrissie" links the threshold experience of these religious women to the traditional Irish *imram*, casting it as a courageous voyage away from the well-known terrain of domestic life and into an unfathomable realm suggestive of the infinite depths of both the feminine psyche and the divine.

In "La Corona," from Ní Chuilleanáin's next book, *The Brazen Serpent*, the juxtaposition of nun and mother occurs in a mundane rather than mythic context. Here the poem's obliquity arises not so much from the setting as from the elliptical and disjunctive nature of the poem's narrative.

The poem's central figure is a bedridden woman identified only as "the mother" (*BS*, 17). The status of this woman is ambiguous since she possesses the kind of religious accoutrements—relics, a leather-bound prayer manual—of a mother superior, yet is positioned via references to her wedding day and "a daughter" as a more secular mother (17). This blurring of identities insinuates that the sterility conventionally associated with the nun's life is equally applicable to the traditional domestic role of wife and mother. The key to the riddle of this woman's identity lies in the poem's allusion to St. Rita (1381–1457), upon whose feast day the poem is set and who provides one of the relics just referred to—"A flower from the Holy Thorn" (17) that pierced the saint's forehead as she meditated upon the crucifixion. St. Rita, as the story goes, wanted to be a nun but was coerced by her family into a loveless and abusive marriage from which she was released only by her husband's death.[28] The character at the heart of this poem would seem to be in an analogous situation. She aspires to the religious life of a nun but has been immured within a domestic sphere that, as in Joyce's *Dubliners*, is characterized by a kind of moribundity. The fact that she has taken to her bed, perhaps in grief, and that black-bordered funeral cards appear at the poem's conclusion suggests that, like St. Rita as well, she may have been widowed.

The Joycean character of this poem extends to the way in which the paralysis of the poem's opening scene culminates in an epiphany, occasioned here by a solar eclipse that rends the quotidian routine of the mother's life just as it severs the poem itself:

> Through the high window light forces its wedge
> To blot the calendar; the mountainside
> Flooding, the water fanned in veins, backs
> Against a dark cloud with a bright snake at its edge. (*BS*, 17)

Both the imagery here ("light forces its wedge") and the homonymic link between the aureole of light surrounding the eclipsed sun and the crown of thorns connect this epiphanic event back to the holy thorn that is St. Rita's relic. The implication is that the rupture in consciousness signaled by the eclipse should be equated with the hopeful aura that ultimately emanates from this saint's tenebrous life. The possibility of redemptive transformation is highlighted by the figure that Ní Chuilleanáin uses to describe the corona since the image of the snake eating its tail, the *ouroboros,* is an archaic emblem of rebirth and resurrection. For the mother in this poem, then, the eclipse portends a change that would release her, like St. Rita, from a desiccated domesticity into a new and richer life as a nun. This hoped-for liberation is evoked once more at the poem's conclusion where the mother is described as dealing "herself a new hand" (17). Against the "black borders" of the cards that she shuffles, emblems of her own death-in-life, are set the "grey hatchet faces" (17) of her cousins, an image that calls to mind the sharp-edged profile of a nun wearing a wimple, a profile that Ní Chuilleanáin in another context describes as "firm-faced" and "formidable."[29]

Ní Chuilleanáin's recognition of the nun's borderline status in Irish culture leads her not only to counterpoint this figure with the socially sanctioned roles of wife and mother, but also to align nuns and other religious women with women who were ostracized for violating the sexual norms of a rigidly patriarchal culture. This point is amplified in Ní Chuilleanáin's essay on nuns, where she suggests in reference to Kate O'Brien's convent novels that in twentieth-century Ireland, the choice of the vocation of the nun involved "a liberation from social constraints as wild as that of any girl who caused a scandal in her parish."[30] In positing this affiliation, Ní Chuilleanáin sets herself squarely athwart the mainstream of Irish public opinion. The revelations in the 1990s concerning the abusive conditions that pervaded the Magdalen asylums and mother and baby homes run by orders of religious women in Ireland have justifiably provoked outrage and demands that the orders who ran these institutions be held accountable for their actions. But these horrifying disclosures have also resulted, less legitimately, in another rigid stereotyping of nuns, one that this time presents them not as victims but rather as agents of patriarchal oppression. Nowhere is this more apparent than in Peter Mullan's harrowing film *The Magdalene Sisters* (2002). Based on Steve Humphries' documentary *Sex in a Cold Climate* (1998), Mullan's film details the physical and psychological abuse inflicted upon three young Irish women consigned to a Magdalen laundry in 1964. Blame for this abuse is primarily directed at the nuns overseeing the laundry, who are cast in the film as the frontline defenders of a puritanical and patriarchal church.[31] I will postpone until later the consideration of how Ní Chuilleanáin addresses the collusion of religious sisters with the oppressive disciplinary regimes of the Irish state. For now, though, I want to focus on the way in which her poetry exhumes a hidden congruence between these divergent but similarly marginalized feminine figures and thereby elucidates a more radical transgressive strand in the traces left by religious women in Ireland.

One of the most significant ways in which Ní Chuilleanáin affiliates women identified as spiritually superior and those labeled as sexually debased or deviant is by focusing upon a traditional figure—Mary Magdalene or St. Margaret of Cortona—in whom these roles are conflated. In the poem treating the latter figure, the eponymous "Saint Margaret of Cortona" from *The Brazen Serpent*, the relics of this medieval saint are presented as exerting an unsettling influence on the sexual politics of modern Ireland. Often referred to as the second Magdalene, St. Margaret of Cortona (1247–1297) was the mistress of a nobleman with whom she had a son. After his murder, she was disowned by her father and entered a Franciscan community where she spent years redressing her earlier sins through harsh penitential practices until she eventually established her own community of religious women to serve the poor and sick.[32] The poem focuses, however, less on St. Margaret herself than on the appropriation of her legacy by institutional authorities, a point highlighted by the epitaph that follows the poem's title and identifies Margaret as "Patroness of the Lock Hospital, Townsend Street, Dublin." Established in England and Ireland in the latter half of the nineteenth century, Lock hospitals were originally designated as places where prostitutes, ostensibly contaminated with venereal diseases, could be quarantined and rehabilitated.[33] This context is indirectly evoked at the poem's outset where a priest uses the occasion of her feast day to employ the saint as a homiletic tool. In the course of emphasizing the illicit status of her early life—"*She had become,* the preacher hollows his voice, / A name not to be spoken" (*BS*, 24)—the priest inadvertently reveals the extent to which St. Margaret's life, and by implication the lives of women like her, resist the labels that society imposes upon them.

It is, however, her relics that most fully manifest St. Margaret's refractory nature:

> Behind the silver commas of the shrine,
> In the mine of the altar her teeth listen and smile.
>
> She is still here, she refuses
> To be consumed. The weight of her bones
> Burns down through the mountain. (*BS*, 24)

The location of the relics parallels the syntactical placement of the epithets that would categorize and encapsulate this anomalous woman's life story. But what remains of St. Margaret is an uncontainable trace, fragments of a body that, like the Cheshire cat's smile, mock those who would seek to reduce it to an apprehensible presence. The incendiary power of these relics links them to the fallen women in the Lock hospital, whose bodies burn alternatively with desire and disease. Reversing the trajectory of the traditional spiritual ascent through purgatorial flames that consume the vestiges of corporeality, the residue of St. Margaret's bodily existence continues to exert a terrestrial influence. In Ní Chuilleanáin's rendering, St. Margaret's relics are no longer tethered to the orthodox religious agenda of penitential reformation but instead serve a more radical deconstructive purpose, proffering the possibility of a release from the social codes that would confine and regulate female sexuality.

All of this is recapitulated in the poem's typically evocative but enigmatic conclusion:

> Her death did not make her like this:
>
> Her eyes were hollowed
> By the bloody scene: the wounds
> In the body of her child's father
> Tumbled in a ditch. The door was locked,
> The names flew and multiplied; she turned
> Her back but the names clustered and hung
> Out of her shoulderbones
> Like children swinging from a father's arm
> Their tucked-up feet skimming over the ground. (*BS*, 24)

What consecrates St. Margaret, the poem suggests, is not her transcendence of the body through a process of mortification culminating in death. It is rather her illicit love and the suffering that she endures because of the loss of that love. The constrictive labels thrust upon her are transmuted here into markers of the fleeting movement of a life suspended between heaven and earth. Her position contrasts starkly with the cruciform figure of the Son whose Father wills—at least in the conventional theology of atonement—that he hang in agony, a testament to the irreconcilable opposition of worldly and celestial powers. The legacy of Ní Chuilleanáin's St. Margaret is the vision of a different kind of patriarch, one who enables a playful straddling between the contravening demands of body and spirit.

A similar re-envisioning of the transcendental ideal underpinning patriarchy occurs in another poem from *The Brazen Serpent*, "The Architectural Metaphor." In this poem, however, the figures of the religious woman and the sexually transgressive woman are differentiated rather than conflated and the sociocultural context in which the conjunction of these women actually occurred is foregrounded. The title of this poem reminds us that in Ní Chuilleanáin's poetry, as Eamon Grennan has noted, "one of the first things to strike a reader is the presence in it of some architecturally rendered space."[34] Grennan casts Ní Chuilleanáin's use of architecture in exclusively spiritual terms, seeing it as "sacramental, a solid outward sign of some inward truth: a monument, often literally, to an act of faith."[35] But this poem registers her close attention to the way in which such spaces also manifest the agency of more secular powers, such as the nation-state. This realization, in turn, precipitates a reconfiguration of a faith tainted by its complicity with state power. At its outset, "The Architectural Metaphor" stresses how a shift in the border has moved the convent from its sheltered position on the periphery of society into the midst of the public sphere. The exact nature of the change brought about in this architectural space is hinted at in the poem's juxtaposed references to the cloister and the laundry, a linkage that calls to mind the Magdalen asylums in which such spaces were conjoined. Ní Chuilleanáin acknowledges here the convent's incorporation in what James Smith refers to as Ireland's "architecture of containment," the constellation of mother and baby homes, Magdalen asylums, and reformatories that shored up the tenuous social structure of the Irish Free State.[36] As Smith's painstaking research establishes, this "architecture of containment" was primarily fashioned in the 1930s in response to the concerns about juvenile prostitution and the high level of illegitimacy, both of which threatened the newly independent Ireland's identity as a distinctively Catholic nation. Ostensibly designed as an alternative to traditional state-controlled forms of incarceration, the mother and baby homes and Magdalen asylums—expanded now to include not just prostitutes but unmarried mothers and other "troublesome" women—were placed under the direction of women religious. Despite that fact, these Catholic institutions continued to exercise a "punitive rather than rehabilitative function."[37] Smith lays the blame for this not only on "a male patriarchal hegemonic social order," but on the women religious who collaborated with it.[38] While Ní Chuilleanáin acknowledges the key role of nuns in implementing this malign disciplinary regime, she contends that they are to some degree convenient scapegoats for the primary perpetrators, "the real authority figures: priests, doctors, and policemen . . . politicians and bureaucrats who decide how little would be paid, and when nothing would be paid, for the up-keep of the powerless."[39]

"The Architectural Metaphor" adopts a similarly nuanced stance but strives even more forcefully to rehabilitate the legacy of nuns in Ireland from the stain of their entanglement with the patriarchal state. It does so by juxtaposing the dead foundress of the convent and a young girl on the verge of being assaulted by a man, precisely the type of girl who in the aftermath of such an assault could have found herself confined to a Magdalen laundry.

Now light scatters, a door opens, laughter breaks in,
A young girl barefoot, a man pushing her
Backwards against a hatch—

It flies up suddenly—
There lies the foundress, pale
In her funeral sheets, her face turned west

Searching for the rose-window. (*BS*, 14)

This poem's power lies in the way in which the contiguous events of this scene evoke something more than recrimination. This quasi-encounter between the young woman and the foundress elicits the possibility of a reciprocal act of rescue. Just as the girl is delivered from the male aggressor by the sudden appearance of the dead nun's effigy, so too does the girl's arrival reanimate the long deceased foundress. This exchange reminds us of the convent's original sheltering mission. Because of pronominal ambiguity, the vision that concludes the poem cannot be consigned to either the foundress or the young girl, but must be seen as generated by the interfusion of their divergent yet coincident experiences. What most distinguishes this vision is its supplanting of the rose window, a possible referent for the "architectural metaphor" of the poem's title. This symbol embedded at the heart of countless Catholic churches epitomizes a conception of the divine as centripetal, harmoniously unified, and hierarchal—in short, as phallocentric. In lieu of this transcendent rose (the prototype of the flower associated with the relics of St. Thérèse of Lisieux), the poem offers a glimpse of a weed-choked graveyard with a foraging hen:

> It shows her
> what she never saw from any angle but this:
> Weeds nested in the churchyard, catching the late sun,
>
> Herself at fourteen stumbling downhill
> And landing, and crouching to watch
> The sly limbering of the bantam hen
>
> Foraging between gravestones—
> Help is at hand
> Though out of reach:
> The world not dead after all. (*BS*, 14–15)

In this vision, the heterodoxy of which is marked by the concluding offset lines, the pain and suffering of human existence are acknowledged as they are not in the artificial perfection of the rose window. Hope is placed not in a distant panoptic deity but in a cunningly resistant and proximate femininity that offers the possibility of salvaging new life from out of the detritus of patriarchy.

As the poem's penultimate sentence—"Help is at hand / Though out of reach"—suggests, a utopian aura hovers over this effort to recuperate the feminist potency of convent life. Ultimately, the poem aspires to a goal that remains unrealized: a redemptive synthesis that elides the tensions between the convent's dual roles as a protective enclosure that fostered a vibrant female-centered community and a place of near penal confinement that sequestered the most vulnerable of those women that patriarchy deemed recalcitrant. In Ní Chuilleanáin's recent book, *The Girl Who Married the Reindeer* (2002), she abandons this dream of reconciliation and infers that the legacy of nuns and convent life in Ireland must ultimately remain an unresolved dialectic. This is most clearly revealed in the poems from this volume that evoke the motif of relics, "Cloister of Bones" and "Translation."

"Cloister of Bones" culminates a set of loosely linked poems that can be seen as synopsizing the provocative role that convents have played in Ní Chuilleanáin's imaginative life. The first of these poems, "The Anchoress," acknowledges the recession of the figure of the nun from the contemporary social scene in Ireland and elsewhere. In the past, as the poem reveals in its final lines, there was a rich and enlivening exchange between cloistered religious women, such as the anchoress, and the surrounding community, an open sharing of their intimate and wondrous spiritual feats with those on the outside. But as these lines with their reiterated initial "when" so insistently remind us, this condition belongs to an anterior time. In the poem's present, the engagement between the anchoress and the external world has become increasingly rare and attenuated, reduced to "a few words, a command" and a promise of prayers exchanged at the "mossgrown window beside the church porch."[40] The subsequent companion poems "Sunday" and "Chestnut Choir" expand upon this point by presenting us with a convent whose spatiotemporal location—the misty reaches of a mountain at winter's solstice—situates it not so much in the realm of actuality as in a mythic landscape. It functions there more as a way station than a destination, the locus of a spiritual impetus that the persona of these poems cannot fully embrace but that pulls her away from the familiar pleasures of ordinary life. Having journeyed to this site, she decides against remaining there to keep vigil for the divine and opts instead for the freedom and danger of the darkness outside.

If these preceding poems can be read as acknowledging the declining viability of the convent as an external religious institution, "Cloister of Bones" is Ní Chuilleanáin's most overt extrapolation of its lingering emancipative potential. The cloister in this poem is no longer the repository of relics but has become one itself. This evocation of the convent as ruin all too accurately reflects the precipitous decline in late twentieth-century Ireland of women choosing the vocation of nun and the accompanying widespread closure of convents. As Margaret Mac Curtain's bleak demographic analysis reveals, during the 1980s over thirty convents closed and by the outset of the '90s, 57 percent of nuns were over sixty years old while only 2 percent were under twenty-nine.[41] In the face of this loss, the poem's speaker imaginatively reconfigures the cloister from its ruins. But instead of recreating this remembered space as a spectacle, as her initial detached perspective might suggest she will do, she finds herself subsumed within this retrospective scene. This process of interanimation reaches its climax when in fulfillment of the promise of the poem's title, the cloister is transmogrified into the female body: "arched and bouncing / Naves, a corseted apse" (*GWMR*, 9). By casting the female body as a sheltered space invested with sacral power, this poem brings to fruition what the experience of cloistered religious women had long heralded—that is, a new conception of the relationship of women and the divine or what the poem in its last line refers to as "the women's Christmas" (*GWMR*, 9). In this gynocentric theophany, the female body is no longer merely a receptacle for a patriarchal deity but becomes a sacred site in itself. And the eruptions of its somatic and psychic energy—the "tremble / Of women's laughter . . . [and] mile-high panics" (*GWMR*, 9)—are no longer regarded as manifestations of disease, what patriarchy refers to as hysteria, but rather as a form of jouissance that the poem presents as a correlative to the act of worship.[42]

This eulogizing of the cloister for its engendering of a distinctively feminine spirituality must, however, be juxtaposed with the lamentation for the victims of the Magdalen laundries in "Translation." The specific occasion for this poem, as its subtitle informs us, was the transfer in 1993 of the cremated remains of inmates from an unmarked mass grave at the Sisters of Our Lady of Charity's convent in High Park, the site of Ireland's largest Magdalen asylum, to Glasnevin cemetery, where a memorial stone with the names of those whose remains could be identified was subsequently erected. If the preservation and veneration of relics such as St. Thérèse of Lisieux's represents an act of commemoration that fetishizes an idealized past, the heedless dumping of the corpses of the Magdalen inmates in a mass grave fosters a collective amnesia that would erase the past sins of church and state. There is a retributive logic at play in the translation of the Magdalen remains that, as Ní Chuilleanáin ironically puts it, "evens the score" (*GWMR*, 18). While alive, these women were regarded as impure or dirty and as punishment were charged with the task of expunging the dirt of others. Now in death, the shifting of the dust that they have become exposes the dirty laundry, the humiliating trappings of a repressive past, that the nation has tried in vain to hide.

The amorphous ashes of the Magdalen inmates contrast quite obviously with the carefully preserved and elegantly enshrined bodily fragments that constitute the traditional religious relic. As this poem develops, they increasingly resemble the uncontainable and disruptive trace that characterizes the notion of the relic articulated by Ní Chuilleanáin in "The Real Thing" and repeatedly evoked throughout her poetry. This becomes especially apparent when we contrast "Translation" with another work of art occasioned by the exhumation and reburial of the High Park Magdalens—the author and performance artist Gerard Mannix Flynn's "extallation" "'Call Me by My Name': Requiem for Remains Unknown" erected in 2003. Prominently situated at the corner of Leeson Street and Stephen's Green, the very heart of Dublin and site of its first Magdalen laundry, this "extallation" consisted of a large mortuary wall with plaques, some of which contained the names and dates of deceased women buried in the mass grave at High Park, others of which simply indicated "remains unknown."[43] As Geraldine Meaney points out, Flynn's monument to these forgotten victims of the state directly challenged the "official" heroic narrative of Irish history embodied in the myriad plaques and statues honoring Ireland's literary and political champions as well as its victims of colonial oppression.[44] Moreover, this work's naming of these previously anonymous women was in itself a powerful and profoundly moving act of reclamation.

Ní Chuilleanáin's poem, on the other hand, resists any such traditional memorializing of the Magdalens. It insists that what remains after their death is unnamable, beyond words, that the residue of their painful lives is ultimately untranslatable. Yet at the same time, it acknowledges their unappeasable claim upon the present. Like the victims of the Holocaust, the Magdalens make themselves heard even in their silence. From the persecuted dead there emanates what the French philosopher Maurice Blanchot refers to as "the voiceless cry, which breaks with all utterances . . . the cry [that] tends to exceed all language . . . [to] remain outside of sense—a meaning infinitely suspended, decried, decipherable-indecipherable."[45] Ní Chuilleanáin suggests something similar in a passage that brilliantly conjures this cry from out of the very forces, both natural and institutional, that would stifle it:

> Assist them now, ridges under the veil, shifting,
> Searching for their parents, their names,
> The edges of words grinding against nature,
>
> As if, when water sank between the rotten teeth
> Of soap, and every grasp seemed melted, one voice
> Had begun, rising above the shuffle and hum
>
> Until every pocket in her skull blared with the note—
> Allow us now to hear it, sharp as an infant's cry
> While the grass takes root, while the steam rises. (*GWMR*, 18)

In its conclusion, the poem intimates what effect this cry would have. It does so by adopting a persona that, in a manner characteristic of Ní Chuilleanáin, blends the identities of the deceased Magdalen penitents and the nuns who were their overseers.[46] Such a blurring of the distinction between inmate and professed sister was central to the illusion that sanctioned the Magdalen asylums. The implication, conveyed by both government officials as well as the religious women in charge of these institutions, was that the young women who came to these places and remained there, in some cases for the rest of their lives, did so voluntarily, out of a commitment to a religious life of penance analogous to that of a nun.[47] Indeed, there was much about the lives of the Magdalen penitents that mimicked that of the sisters who served as their guardians. They too abandoned their former names and were assigned overtly religious ones, engaged in a daily regime that included large periods of prayer and silent meditation, and could advance to a stage in which they were decreed to be "consecrated" and allowed to wear something akin to a habit.[48] But the lack of educational opportunities, the constant routine of tedious labor, the frequent persecution—all of these shattered the pretense of a shared vocation and left the Magdalens "irredeemably marked . . . as socially and intellectual inferior."[49] Ní Chuilleanáin's merging of the Magdalen and the nun reflects the recent change in the status of both groups whereby they have been "washed clean of idiom," purged of the customary distinctions that had once separated them from each other. The stigma previously attached to the Magdalens has been transferred to the nuns who were ostensibly their guardians.

> Washed clean of idiom: the baked crust
> Of words that made my temporary name:
> A parasite that grew in me: that spell
> Lifted: I lie in earth sifted to dust:
> Let the bunched keys I bore slacken and fall:
> I rise and forget: a cloud over my time. (*GWMR*, 18)

If the public acknowledgment of the inexpressible suffering that the Magdalens endured during life somehow releases them in death from the burden of that past, these revelations have cast a pall over the memory of women religious in Ireland as well as the nation-state whose disciplinary aims they served. Detached from its particular context in this poem, the poem's last line with its concurrence of liberating transcendence and miasma might serve as Ní Chuilleanáin's synecdoche for the legacy of nuns in Ireland. Her poetic sifting of the remains of these religious women has disclosed that the hope for emancipation from patriarchal religious and social structures that their experience fosters must be tempered by a realization of their own role in enforcing those oppressive structures. As such, Ní Chuilleanáin's poetry powerfully demonstrates that the appropriate response to the tradition of Irish Catholicism is not a reification of the more venerable vestiges of its past but rather an anatomizing of the conflicting traces that it bequeaths to the future.

6

Paul Durcan's Priests

Refashioning Irish Masculinity

If nuns remained largely occluded figures in Irish culture until the notorious revelations of abuse at mother and baby homes and Magdalen asylums brought them unwillingly into the national spotlight, that was distinctly not the case with priests. The preeminent status of the priest in Ireland was such that as late as 1969, the Irish historian John A. Murphy asserted that "anti-clericalism of the negative secular type has of yet put down no roots in Ireland" because it could not "contend with a massive weight of historical tradition." He proceeded to note that "for the old and middle-aged, no matter what the degree of sophistication or religious commitment, respect for the cloth is inbred and virtually automatic" and that "even the questioning young have shown no real change in this regard."[1] In Paul Durcan's poetry, priests continue to occupy a position of centrality; however, it is not one that is granted the sort of unreflective reverence that Murphy describes.

Indeed, a quick glance through Durcan's poetic corpus reveals a number of poems with sensationalistic titles mocking the hierarchy of the Irish Catholic Church: "The Archbishop Dreams of the Harlot of Rathkeale," "Irish Hierarchy Bans Colour Photography," "Bishop of Cork Murders His Wife," "Archbishop of Dublin to Film *Romeo and Juliet*," "Archbishop of Kerry to Have Abortion," "Cardinal Dies of Heart Attack in Dublin Brothel." The topicality and offhand humor emblematized by these titles as well as Durcan's eschewing of prevailing formal expectations account for the critical establishment's general neglect of his poetry. His reliance upon fantastic and grotesque imagery for shock effect, his colloquial style, and his prolixity seemingly mark Durcan more as a popular versifier than a poet worthy of serious consideration. Certainly his poetry readings are legendary for their crowds and their entertainment value.[2] Yet that popularity has not prevented esteemed poetic contemporaries, such as Seamus Heaney and Derek Mahon, or preeminent cultural commentators such as Fintan O'Toole from asserting the significance of Durcan's poetry.

In each case, these commentators accentuate the deeper purposes driving his seemingly slapdash, manic outbursts of poetry. O'Toole puts it best when he notes that the strange disjunctions and absurd vignettes so characteristic of Durcan's poems are not the work of a surrealist but of "a great realist . . . a brilliant describer of a reality so dislocated, so imbued with political, religious, and psychic myths that it will not yield to prosaic language or to literal minds."[3] These lingering cultural myths, O'Toole suggests, are most fully "embodied for Durcan in the figure of his father."[4] The poet's struggles with his father, John Durcan, a native of Mayo who eventually moved to Dublin and became a circuit court judge, defined his adolescence and generated his most critically acclaimed book of poetry, *Daddy, Daddy* (1990). This conflict reached its apex when Durcan's father had him involuntarily committed to a psychiatric institution in his late teens. At the heart of the matter was the fact that the younger Durcan did not conform to the prevailing standard of masculinity in early 1960s Ireland. That normative notion of Irish masculinity was grounded, as we shall see, in the figure of the celibate Catholic cleric, whose self-control and juridical authority established him as a manly exemplar. Throughout his poetry, Durcan travesties this masculine ideal and cultivates an androgynous alternative that is, ironically, epitomized by Jesus as well as the more sensitive form of priest that emerged after the Second Vatican Council.

While Durcan's poetry has often alluded to the trauma of his institutionalization, it is only recently that he has publicly described the circumstances that led to it. In 1964, when he was nineteen and a student at University College, Dublin, Durcan was kidnapped by relatives and consigned to a psychiatric clinic, where he was subjected to extensive electric shock therapy and threatened by the prospect of a lobotomy.[5] This extreme response to his late adolescent eccentricities was triggered, according to Durcan, by his anomalous masculinity: "From a fairly early age I was aware that certain kinds of people disapproved of me—particularly certain kinds of male. These men had the idea that boys had to be soldiers, chaste soldiers, and had to fit into a mould and if they didn't there was something not quite right. My father would say: 'Paul is a sissy. Come on, be a man.'"[6] The standard of masculinity that Durcan describes himself being measured against—the chaste soldier—was a distinctively Irish variant of the prevailing notion of manliness established in Western modernity. The cornerstone of that normative masculine construct was the principle of self-control.[7] In Victorian Britain, as Joseph Valente summarizes, a "muscular ideal of manhood" arose that "consisted precisely in the *simultaneous* necessity for and exercise of this capacity for rational self-control—in strong passions strongly checked—from which the virtues of conventional 'masculinity' (fortitude, tenacity, industry, candor) were assumed to derive."[8] For colonized Irish males, such a standard of masculinity created an intractable dilemma. Valente elaborates upon the nature of this "double-bind." On the one hand, if Irish men under British rule exhibited the requisite manly restraint, they were seen as obeisant to colonial domination and thus as weak or feminine. Yet on the other hand, if they actively opposed colonial authority, they were considered to have forfeited this self-control and regressed into a kind of unmanly barbarism.[9] The search for an exemplar that overcame this dilemma intensified after the fall of Charles Stewart Parnell, whose aristocratic hauteur and steadfast advocacy of Irish independence had seemingly resolved the conflicting pressures imposed upon Irish masculinity.[10] Since Parnell's downfall had been precipitated by a sexual scandal, it is not surprising that the new ideal of Irish masculinity cultivated in his aftermath linked manly assertiveness to chastity. It manifested itself, as Joseph Nugent has carefully elucidated, in a late nineteenth-century cult of Irish saints, centered upon Colmcill who by "mastering his nature yet remaining boldly masculine . . . displayed precisely that gentlemanly equilibrium of which his latter-day compatriots were patently devoid."[11] But this new exemplar only became truly effective in shaping Irish masculinity when it was concretized in the contemporary real-life figure of the Irish priest. As a modern-day surrogate for the Irish saint, the priest constituted "the authorized positive stereotype" for "the Irish Catholic male subject."[12]

The efficacy of this priestly exemplar in twentieth-century Ireland is well supported by a variety of sources. In his well-reviewed *L'Irlande Contemporaine* (1907), the French writer Paul Dubois described the preeminence of the priest in early twentieth-century rural Ireland by stressing his heightened masculine presence and paternal aura: "As one meets him in the small towns of the West with his high hat and somber garb, his great strong frame and ruddy face leave a striking image in the mind . . . He is in truth the father of his people . . . and, no doubt, an authoritative enough father."[13] Over half a century later, priests still retained the status of revered patriarch among Irish Catholics. In an extensive cross-cultural survey of native Irish Catholics and their Irish-American counterparts conducted in 1964, the Jesuit sociologist Bruce Biever found that among his sample of over nine hundred Irish, there was unanimous agreement with the statement "I think priests should be given a great deal of respect both by individuals and society," with 92 percent agreeing strongly and 8 percent indicating a more tempered agreement. In contrast, the Irish-American sample revealed only 53 percent agreement.[14] Even more strikingly, two-thirds of Irish Catholics, more than five times their American counterparts, endorsed the statement that "Priests have the right and the obligation to tell me how to run my life; if I follow their advice, I can't go wrong."[15] Not surprisingly, a recent sociological analysis of masculinity in late-modern Ireland confirms that up until the last decades of the twentieth century, "the celibate priest was the role model for Irish masculinity."[16]

In "Polycarp" from Durcan's second complete book of poems, *Teresa's Bar* (1976), he acknowledges the persistence of this priestly standard of masculinity even while celebrating its usurpation. The poem's use of a traditional ballad measure and rhyme scheme, in contrast to Durcan's usual open form, signals its interrogation of a deeply rooted cultural attitude.

Polycarp has quit the priesthood
And he is living back at home;
He wears a smile upon his lips
That blooms from the marrow bone.

It's a smile that flowers and withers
Like fruit upon a tree;
In winter he stands at corners
In the streets all nakedly.

They are waxing pretty angry—
Are Respectability's crew;
It's a crime against all decency
To be one of the very few

Who has had the courage like Polycarp
To be his own sweet self;
Not to mind the small town sneers
When they call him a "fucking elf"

Or the do-it-yourself-men boors
Who despise men with feminine souls.[17]

Durcan connects Polycarp's departure from the priesthood and his fierce condemnation by social authorities to his free-spirited androgynous nature. In doing so, the poem evokes the anti-type of the priestly ideal of masculinity—that is, the cleric corrupted by his failure to cultivate an appropriately masculine asceticism, seduced into worldliness by an overly feminine sensibility. The positive exemplar of the manly priest has always been haunted by this spectral counterpart. Therefore, as Joseph Nugent notes, in Canon Sheehan's early twentieth-century autobiographical novel *Luke Delmege*, the popular priest-novelist reinforced his typically honorific representations of Irish priests with a scathing portrayal of their opposite—"the limp unmuscular, artificial cleric, who . . . is perpetually aping the manners and customs of the world, and in dress and manner and conversation is forever changing and shifting, like a mime on stage."[18] In contrast, Durcan exonerates this despised motley figure. Not only does his Polycarp avoid the martyrdom suffered by his early Christian namesake, but his flitting presence undermines the self-restraint advocated by priests and the rest of "Respectability's Crew": "Desire under the steeples and spires, / Polycarp's back in town" (*LD*, 33). This concluding refrain, with its allusion to Eugene O'Neill tragic drama of father/son rivalry, *Desire Under the Elms*, highlights the challenge that Polycarp's rebellious and anomalous sexuality poses to such paternal authority.

That threat explains why real-life Polycarps, such as Durcan himself, were so thoroughly disciplined to adapt themselves to the normative standard of masculinity. This inculcation in the masculine principle of self-control began early, as Durcan indicates in one of the most disturbing poems of the "Daddy, Daddy" sequence. In "Study of a Figure in a Landscape, 1952," toilet training occasions an absurd simulacrum of a judicial inquest as the judge-father interrogates his young son about his bowel movements: "—Did your bowels move today? / —Yes, Daddy. / —At what time did your bowels move? / —At eight o'clock, Daddy" (*LD*, 231). This prolonged series of questions—they go on for more than a page—exposes the father's obsessive commitment to enforcing this masculine ideal as does the physical aggression that he resorts to at the poem's end. Such policing extended beyond the body to include the emotions. Any trace of affectionate feeling towards other males was regarded as evidence of homosexuality and, as such, actively suppressed. And so the speaker in "I Was a Twelve-Year-Old Homosexual" from *The Berlin Wall Café* (1985) is "flogged" by his father and sternly rebuked by his priest until he "agreed and . . . gave up homosexuality."[19] The poem's title, with its echoes of 1950s pulp fiction and horror films ("I Was a Teenage Werewolf"), mocks the hysterical response of these arbiters of masculinity who regard any deviation from the norm as monstrous.

In Ireland as elsewhere, sport served as a mechanism for converting such tenderhearted boyish affection into a more manly fraternization. As the sociologist Harry Ferguson notes, the Gaelic Athletic Association, founded in the late nineteenth century, supplemented the Catholic Church by also playing "a key role in the production of the disciplined, Catholic, self-reliant male body."[20] The poems in the long sequence "Daddy, Daddy" that recount the poet's participation in the GAA-sanctioned sports of hurling and Gaelic football are especially poignant, for they expose the desperation of the father's effort to establish his son's "masculinity." On the surface, "The One-Armed Crucifixion" appears to be a rare wistful portrait of filial harmony occasioned through hurling practice. But the references to the interminable and repetitious nature of the activity cast it less as play than as a kind of torture:

> How many thousands of hours on the shore at Galway,
> In the drizzle off the back of the sea,
> On the sodden sands,
> Did we spend hurling together, father and son?
> Pucking the *sliothar*, one to the other,
> Hour in, hour out, year in, year out. (*LD*, 231)

Such suspicions are confirmed by the allusion encoded in the poem's title and its epigraph. Here, as in a number of other poems in "Daddy, Daddy," Durcan foregrounds his citation of a visual artist—in this case, the Italian sculptor Giacomo Manzù, who was both a Catholic and a committed antifascist. Manzù's bas-relief sculpture *Christ and the General* (1947) replaces the traditional crucifixion scene with an image of Jesus as a member of the resistance hanging by a single arm from a telephone pole and being taunted by a piggish German general.[21] The posture of the hanging Christ in Manzù's sculpture mirrors that of the young boy in the poem reaching to "pluck the ball one-handed out of the climbing air" (*LD*, 231). The implications of this iconographic parallel are clear. The boy, required to leap repeatedly after the hurling ball or *sliothar*, is paying the price for resisting the imposed masculine ideal. The fact that this standard is identified as fascistic, tacitly here and then more overtly throughout the sequence, will be considered more fully when we examine Durcan's linkage of this masculine ideal to nationalism. Even more heart-wrenching is "Sport," which recounts a Gaelic football match between the inmates of two psychiatric hospitals. The young poet's successful goalkeeping for the Grangegoran Mental hospital elicits a rare expression of praise from his father. The absurd incongruity of the father's pride in the son's athletic feats and the boy's debilitated condition infuses this poem, like so many of Durcan's, with a tragic-comic aura.

Durcan exorcises the trauma of being judged negatively by his father and other upholders of the Irish masculine ideal by repeatedly exposing their hypocrisy, their inability to be true to the very standard that they enforce. Hyperbole and paradox are his favored instruments for this cultural anatomizing. In "Two Little Boys at the Back of the Bus," a poem positioned near the middle of "Daddy, Daddy," Durcan foregrounds the infantilism and displaced homosexual desire that anchor the manly cult of sport. Having described how his mother fulfilled a similar role for father and son—"as well as being my mother / She was your mother also"—the poet portrays this masculine dyad as they

> Enact in the muck and lawn
> Of the playing fields of Ballsbridge
> A parody of homosexual aggression:
> Scrum, hook, tackle, maul. (*LD*, 252)

The poem ends with the kind of bizarre mash-up of absurdist theater and magical realism that marks Durcan's poetry with an indelible distinctiveness. The mother enters the scene piloting a Fokker 50, a not-too-subtle symbol of her usurpation of phallic authority, and pacifies her male charges by sedating them with sodium amytal. The fact that this drug is more popularly known as "truth serum" emphasizes the poem's revelation of the hidden truth that belies the Irish masculine ideal.

The origin of that ideal is signaled in the poem's references to the Jesuit educational background that father and son have in common. "Chips," another poem from this sequence, is even more overt in identifying the prototype underlying the standard of manliness epitomized by the poet's father. After detailing the contradictory nature of his attitude toward his father—"at once saint and murderer"—Durcan provides a litany of epithets that, among other things, casts the older man as "Priest of Priests, / Melchisedech of the Ox" (*LD*, 270). That phrase links the elder Durcan to the hierarchy of the Catholic Church, the bishops and cardinals, who occupied pride of place among their clerical brethren and exerted control over them. And indeed, just as Durcan's father attempted to wield authority in the family, so too did the Irish hierarchy in the public sphere. Their success in that regard in the first decades of Irish independence is widely recognized and evinced by their legislative victories in banning divorce and instituting strict censorship laws. Even in the late 1950s and early '60s, they retained extraordinary authority in public affairs. Extrapolating from his sociological analysis of Irish Catholicism during this time period, Jean Blanchard asserted that the Catholic hierarchy in Ireland had "more power in practice than those of any other country in the world" and that, typically, a congregant "listens much more readily to his Bishop" than to his elected political representatives.[22] By a decade later, that stance had undergone a sea change. The results of a comprehensive survey of the attitudes and practices of Irish Catholics conducted in 1973–74 revealed that "two-thirds of the respondents agreed that the leaders of the Catholic Church were out of touch with the real needs of its members."[23]

That did not prevent the bishops from continuing to assert their juridical authority over the Irish polity, oftentimes with considerable success. In a 1971 pastoral letter read at Sunday masses throughout the diocese of Dublin, Archbishop John Charles McQuaid, the doyen of the Irish hierarchy, addressed the hot-button issue of contraception in his typically authoritarian manner:

> Any contraceptive act is always wrong in itself. To speak, then, of a right to contraception, on the part of an individual, be he Christian or non-Christian or atheist, or on the part of a minority or of a majority, is to speak of a right that cannot even exist . . . Any change in legislation that would allow the sale of contraceptives would be an insult to the faith, gravely damaging to public and private morality, and would remain a curse upon our country.[24]

A statement on contraceptive legislation released seven years later by the Irish bishops' conference was considerably more nuanced in tone, but no less confident about the Catholic hierarchy's prerogative to direct both private judgments and public policy: "In the area of contraception, laws can affect the way people think about marriage, about the family, about fidelity . . . conscience itself can become confused and weakened by society's attitudes. A change in the law can deceive people into thinking that morality has changed also."[25] While a bill legalizing the use of nonmedical contraceptives was narrowly passed in 1985, the Catholic bishops were effective in delaying its passage and ensuring that it preserved the ban on male and female sterilization.[26]

On the issue of divorce, the Irish Catholic hierarchy was equally determined to assert its authority and even more successful in doing so. With a referendum on the legalization of divorce on the horizon, the Irish bishops in February 1985 issued a lengthy pastoral letter, "Love Is for Life." At first glance, this document seemed to exhibit a more tempered sense of the bishop's role in public life. It acknowledged "that morality and civil law do not necessarily coincide" and stressed that it did "not ask that Catholic doctrine as such be enshrined in law."[27] But that more humble posture was belied by the pastoral's firm indictment of the catastrophic social consequences of the proposed legislation:

> The very notion of commitment is weakened . . . It is not just broken marriages which are affected. All existing marriages are in principle implicated. The "multiplier effect" of divorce as a factor making for instability in marriage is unavoidable and it is irreversible. The mounting statistics of divorce which have been experienced worldwide follow inevitably from this logic. (Sec. 191)

As the voting day for the referendum approached, the bishops resorted to increasingly aggressive rhetoric in advocating their position. Kevin McNamara, archbishop of Dublin, outdid his precursor McQuaid by proclaiming in a magazine interview that the impact of legalized divorce would be similar to that of the nuclear disaster at Chernobyl. Just as the latter event showed "how negative radiation can filter across and permeate society," so too had "divorce legislation . . . had a somewhat similar effect in the way it has permeated western societies and undermined the stability of marriage."[28] As a result of such statements being reiterated in the media and at pulpits, the divorce referendum, which had previously polled favorably, was resoundingly defeated. It was only ten years later, after the bishops' power had been irrevocably undermined by a string of scandals, that a similar referendum narrowly passed.

During this period when the Catholic hierarchy fought to forestall secularization and preserve its control over the Irish body politic, Durcan wrote a series of poems attacking the basis of their patriarchal pretensions. The first of these, "The Archbishop Dreams of the Harlot of Rathkeale" from *Teresa's Bar* (1976), undermines the premise of self-control that sanctions masculine authority. Unwittingly, the archbishop identifies his erotic dream of a naked women, the "harlot" of the title, as the source of the manly vigor displayed in his homilies: "And I wake up in the morning feeling like an old bull / Plumb to charge through my brethren in my sermon" (*LD*, 41). In the background of this and similar Durcan poems are W. B. Yeats's earlier ripostes against Catholic episcopal oppression in the 1920s and '30s. In the most notable of these poems, "Crazy Jane Talks with the Bishop," Yeats adopts the mask of a mad peasant woman and mocks the Manichean dualism underlying the bishop's strict regulation of sexual desire. Crucial to this broadside against episcopal power, as Elizabeth Cullingford has noted, is Yeats's appropriation of "the carnival folk grotesque," a literary mode epitomized by Rabelais and elucidated by the Russian literary theorist Mikhail Bakhtin.[29] Among other things, Bakhtin identifies the literary carnivalesque with a process of "*profanation*" that undercuts all forms of hierarchal authority through "carnivalistic debasings and bringings down to earth, carnivalistic obscenities linked with the reproductive power of the earth and the body, carnivalistic parodies of sacred texts and sayings."[30] Durcan follows Yeats in wielding this weapon against the representatives of Catholic hierarchy while leveling it more directly at the internal contradictions of their idealized masculinity.

In "Bishop of Cork Murders His Wife" from *Sam's Cross* (1978), for instance, Durcan brings the eminent cleric of the title down to earth by casting him as a stereotypical working-class husband, an Irish equivalent of Archie Bunker. Angered by his wife's desire for intimacy and her effort to prevent him from watching an English football match on TV, he kills her. This "carnivalistic debasing" strips the luster from the exalted masculine standard exemplified by the Irish prelate. It exposes how this supposed guardian of women is in actuality a crude misogynist. The public impact of the Catholic hierarchy's misogyny is the subject of "Archbishop of Kerry to Have Abortion," a poem from *The Berlin Wall Café* (1985), occasioned by the 1983 referendum on a strict anti-abortion amendment to the Constitution. The topsy-turvy role reversal so characteristic of the carnivalesque drives this poem's satire. The archbishop, whose real-life counterparts forcibly called for the amendment's passage, finds himself occupying the position of the voiceless object of that legislation—an unmarried pregnant woman. Having been impregnated by an "oversensitive member of the Nuns of the Big Flower," the archbishop fearfully faces the prospect of an abortion (*BWC*, 26). That he is being compelled to have the procedure by the Vatican constitutes something more than just a cheap shot at papal corruption. It presciently exposes the hypocrisy of an institution that promulgates a code of sexual restraint yet conceals its own deviations from that code, even when doing so imperils the innocent.

There is a further irony at play here. In both these poems as well as others in this vein, Durcan adopts yet another strategy of the literary carnivalesque—the playful exploitation of nonliterary forms of discourse. Specifically in these cases, Durcan mimics the sensationalized news reports of the mass media. In doing so, he calls attention to the shift in discursive power occasioned by the arrival of television to Ireland in the early 1960s. Not only is the Catholic hierarchy no longer able to monopolize public discussion of moral issues, but its authority, as these poems imply, is being supplanted by this new and more clamorous voice. Elsewhere in these two books, Durcan elaborates upon this point by showing how the hierarchy's attempts to suppress or co-opt elements of the mass media backfire. "Irish Hierarchy Bans Colour Photography" from *Sam's Cross* unfolds the obvious allegorical implications of the action described in its title: the hierarchy's moral absolutism fosters a world view that is drab and rigidly dualistic. The poem's conclusion emphasizes the bishops' impotency by indicating that in the wake of this ban "Ireland is expected to become / The EEC's largest moneyspender in colour photography" (*LD*, 72). More intriguing is "Archbishop of Dublin to Film *Romeo and Juliet*" from *Berlin Wall Café*, which mocks the Irish bishops' long-standing censoriousness towards any representations of sexuality. Not only is their stance mendacious—they want to "spread the gospel of love" yet "stamp out sexuality" (*BWC*, 24)—but it is anachronistic since this purified rendition of Shakespeare apes the expurgations of the late eighteenth-century editor of Shakespeare, Thomas Bowdler. Far from eradicating carnality, such acts of suppression elicit new and seemingly more perverse means of sexual satisfaction. Thus, in the archbishop's bowdlerized *Romeo and Juliet*, the star-crossed lovers are isolated in "separate refrigerators" located tellingly in Rome and Armagh, the center of papal authority and site of the titular head of the Irish Catholic Church. When the lovers consummate their relationship via "television link / Courtesy of Eurovision," critics herald this act of virtual intercourse as an advancement in pornographic cinematography rivaling Bertolucci's *Last Tango in Paris* (*BWC*, 24–25).

Other poems continue the critique of the Catholic hierarchy while also intimating Durcan's prescription for its reformation. "Cardinal Dies of Heart Attack in Dublin Brothel" from *Going Home to Russia* (1987) once again spotlights the canker of hypocrisy eroding the institutional authority of the Irish Catholic Church. But what makes this cardinal's death while in flagrante delicto with his favorite prostitute "edifying," as the poem reiterates in its opening line, is not the revelation of his apparent moral duplicity (*LD*, 154). It is rather this ostensibly celibate man's acknowledgment that the incarnation can only be fully realized, body and soul be united, when masculinity and femininity are interfused. The cardinal serves as an exemplar here not because of his exertion of manly self-restraint but because of his surrender of control, his "submission / to that lovely, ephemeral woman" whose "compassion . . . / was as tender as it was fiery" (*LD*, 154). In contrast to its precursors, this poem concludes on a note of praise rather than mockery. The speaker's wife converts the site of the cardinal's death, the locus of his shame, into something laudatory when she colloquially extols him as an outstanding cleric: "our belovèd cardinal who has died in a brothel / Was, in the very last analysis, 'a broth of a cardinal'" (*LD*, 154).

The last of Durcan's poems directed at the Irish Catholic hierarchy, "Letter to the Archbishop of Cashel and Emly" from *Greetings to Our Friends in Brazil* (1999), stresses even more forcefully the necessity of jettisoning an unflinching masculinity in favor of a more balanced gender formation. The cleric in question here, Archbishop Dermot Clifford, wrote a strident pastoral letter in March 1994 against the second referendum on legalizing divorce, which narrowly passed in 1995, warning that divorce would "undermine stable family life."[31] In a later sermon, Clifford presented evidence of how divorce would negatively affect society in the form of a series of sensational statistics that claimed that "divorcees smoke and drink more than married people, are more prone to psychological problems, and their stepchildren are more prone to sexual abuse," and even "were three times as likely to cause road accidents" as married couples.[32] Such charges were particularly stinging to Durcan whose marriage to Nessa O'Neil, the subject of many of his poems, had broken up in 1984. As punishment for promulgating "sordid / statistics" about separated spouses, Durcan proposes that the archbishop exchange places with the Irish swimmer Michelle Smith who won multiple gold medals at the European Championships of 1995 and the Olympics in 1996.

Let's ask her to preach to us in Holy Cross
The stroke of compassion.
Let's enter you—truth-addicted Archbishop Dermot—
In next Sunday's women's 200-metre butterfly,
Tog you out in black bikini becoming to your statistics
With purple skullcap and goldrimmed googles
And watch you pound the pool—
Pure spirit, pure bubbles, not a squeak of flesh.[33]

This carnivalesque transformation ridicules the archbishop's abstraction from the shared corporeality that undergirds all acts of compassion. The public exposure of his own fleshly vulnerability provides payback for his pontificating over the carnal lapses of others. But the retribution envisioned here also contains the seeds of a possible rehabilitation. It comes in the form of a muscular female athlete who shows that the race goes not to the physically and psychologically monolithic but to the androgynous.[34]

The malign effects of the Irish masculine ideal manifested themselves not only in the intransigency of the Catholic hierarchy but in the equally rigid posturing of Irish nationalists. This was particularly important to Durcan, whose maternal heritage linked him to some of the most famous paragons of Irish nationalism. (His great-uncle was John MacBride, one of the executed leaders of the Easter Rising, who had married Maud Gonne, the republican virago and object of W. B. Yeats's unrequited love.) Not just in Ireland but throughout modern Europe, as the historian George Mosse has shown, "the manly ideal was co-opted by modern nationalism, giving it an additional powerful basis."[35] As we previously noted, Joseph Valente has shown how such an alignment was complicated in colonial Ireland where assertions of nationalist identity always bore the risk of evoking violence and thus violating the masculine code of self-restraint. However, in the aftermath of Irish independence, such tempering of the patriotic spirit was no longer necessary. The "chaste soldier," as Durcan labeled the standard bearer of Irish masculinity, could openly express his militancy. Here as elsewhere, the darker undercurrents of this exemplar come to light in the poet's father. Throughout the "Daddy, Daddy" sequence, the elder Durcan is exposed as a proto-fascist, a secret sympathizer with the Germans in the World War II and an admirer of Mussolini. "Poem Not Beginning with a Line from Pindar" traces the roots of his totalitarian proclivities to his involvement in the political party Fine Gael, an outgrowth of General Eoin O'Duffy's fascistic Blueshirt movement. Durcan's description of Fine Gael corroborates Mosse's assertion that "fascism represented the fullest expression of modern masculinity."[36]

> The party of the Fine Gael is the party
> Of respectability, conformity, legitimacy, pedigree,
> Faith, chivalry, property, virility,
> The party of Collins, O'Higgins, O'Duffy, Cosgrave,
> Great men queuing up at the bride's door.
> Walk tall to the altar rail in pinstripe suit and silk tie.
> Talk the language of men—*bullshit, boob, cunt, bastard*—
> And—*teach the Protestants a lesson.*
> The law is the law and the law must take its course. (*LD*, 255)

Those last two lines are the father's response upon hearing news of the Kingsmill massacre of January 1976. Described in the poem's opening section, this incident in which ten Protestant workers were stopped at a roadblock and murdered by the IRA constituted one of the worst atrocities of the Troubles. But it elicits no empathy from Durcan's father, only a declaration of sectarian hatred that reflects the dogmatic rectitude characteristic of the Irish masculine ideal. Having exposed how such evil is interlaced with the most intimate threads of our identity, Durcan's poem remains unremittingly dark. It refuses, as the allusion in its title emphasizes, even the slight compensation that the American poet Robert Duncan allows himself in "A Poem Beginning with a Line from Pindar" when he opens his diatribe against American jingoism on a hopeful note borrowed from his classic precursor—"*The light foot hears you and the brightness begins.*"[37]

An earlier Durcan poem from *Sam's Cross* on another famous incident of the Troubles, the killings of three members of a northern Irish band by Protestant paramilitaries, lays bare the binarism that governs both sectarianism and normative conceptions of masculinity. The partisan "versifier" who is the poet's interlocutor in "In Memory: The Miami Showband—Massacred 31 July 1975" insists that "You must take one side / Or the other, or you're but a fucking romantic." The poem traces this rigid dualism back to the warrior cult that still drives modern manliness:

> It is in war—not poetry or music—
> That men find their niche, their glory hole;
> Like most of his fellows
> He will abide no contradiction in the mind (*LD*, 75).

Set against this deadly either/or mind-set is the cross-cultural eclecticism of the showband's music, whose redemptive potential Durcan signals with a scriptural allusion.

As with the doctrinal obduracy of the bishops, the corrective that Durcan envisions for hard-line nationalism requires a shift from hegemonic masculinity toward gender hybridity. He found a real-life model for such androgyny in Mary Robinson, the first female president of the Republic of Ireland. During her tenure as president (1990–1997), Robinson redefined an office that had been largely ceremonial. She used the stature of her position to fashion a more expansive notion of Irish national identity, one that welcomed marginalized groups such as emigrants, homosexuals, and Anglo-Irish Protestants. She recognized in her own mixed marriage—her husband was a Protestant—the possibility for a more constructive relationship between Ireland and Britain and worked to foster that by breaking with tradition and inviting members of the British royal family to the official presidential residence. Occupying a position of masculine authority, Robinson brought a woman's perspective and experience to her official duties. As Durcan notes in one of several poems from *Greetings to Our Friends from Brazil* (1999) occasioned by her presidency, Robinson herself called attention to "the way women *organize* / Things in a fundamentally different fashion" (*GB*, 235). Feminist theorists such as Julia Kristeva and Hélène Cixous have claimed that the porousness of the female body, its incorporation of otherness, engenders a different structuring of reality than does the more monolithic male body; Durcan's Robinson, however, believes that such heterogeneity is not biologically limited but available to both genders. Therefore, upon taking office in 1990, she "issued her first and only commandment: / First and last you must learn to love your different self" (*GB*, 236). The fact that the poem's title, "The First and Last Commandment of the Commander-in-Chief," evokes both the religious and martial authority typically reserved for men highlights Robinson's revision of normative masculinity's insistence upon a single, stable identity. The extent to which Durcan identifies Robinson with a traversal of gender boundaries becomes even more apparent in the "The Mary Robinson Years," the culmination of this series. The poem exhibits the loose conversational structure that becomes increasingly prevalent in Durcan's poetry. What might seem to be formal laxity could be considered a virtue from a Bakhtinian perspective. According to the Russian theorist, poetry as a genre tends towards a narrow monologisim that privileges the author's voice to the exclusion of the word of others.[38] That is not the case in this poem constructed around snippets of dialogue that occur at a party in Rio de Janeiro marking the end of Robinson's presidency. In the second section, the poet encounters a hyperbolic character outside the Copacabana Hotel who comically encapsulates Robinson's openness to alterity—a mulatto transvestite émigré from County Tipperary who works for an international aid organization. The transgendered relief worker succinctly explains her reason for being in Brazil: "Faith and good works and all that. / The Gospel according to St. Matthew" (*GB*, 256). The liberation that Durcan associates with Mary Robinson's demolition of the Irish masculine ideal is given a theological basis here, a point emphasized by an exchange earlier in the poem with the Franciscan friar Leonardo Boff, a founder of liberation theology.

Durcan's positing of androgyny as a counter to a constrictive masculine ideal is far from being unprecedented. In particular, the Beat writers, whose improvisational style Durcan imitates, executed a similar maneuver in 1950s America. As James Penner notes, the "nonnormative masculinity" cultivated by this group hinged upon "their ability to role-play and oscillate between the masculine and the feminine positions."[39] Yet Durcan's poetic gender-bending differs from that of his precursors in crucial ways. As the poems on Mary Robinson as well as many others demonstrate, Durcan refused to follow the Beats in restricting androgyny to males; instead, he repeatedly highlights its empowering effects on the women who actualize this principle.[40] Even more strikingly, he found sanction for his advocacy of androgyny not in avant-garde psychology or exotic religious traditions as the Beats did but rather in the Christian faith that was the bedrock of Western culture. In conjuring the image of Jesus Christ as androgynous, Durcan turns the tables on the Victorian cult of "muscular Christianity" that was a central pillar of the Irish standard of masculinity. It is an altogether more pliant Christ figure that Durcan evokes, abstractly in the recent "The Origin of Species," which pays homage to "Christ, all-fathering mother!"[41] and more concretely in the earlier "The Haulier's Wife Meets Jesus on the Road Near Moone." The latter poem from *The Berlin Wall Café* focuses upon the travails of a woman trapped in a loveless, and virtually sexless, marriage to a prototypical Irish businessman: "A popular and wealthy man, / An alcoholic and a county councilor" (*LD*, 117). Granted a brief reprieve from her marriage, she dresses up like a "femme fatale" and heads off to Dublin for a night out at the Abbey Theatre. Having gotten lost, she is rescued by Jesus, who describes himself as a "travelling actor." Her description of her "savior" identifies him as being as capacious as her husband is constricted:

> Jesus turned out to be a lovely man,
> All that a woman could ever possibly dream of:
> Gentle, wild, soft-spoken, courteous, sad;
> Angular, awkward, candid, methodical;
> Humorous, passionate, angry, kind;
> Entirely sensitive to a woman's world. (*LD*, 120)

Durcan's androgynous Jesus harkens back to the early period of Christianity when a new life in Christ was associated with an overcoming of gender divisions, as Paul's letter to the Galatians makes clear in its baptismal formula: "there is not male or female, for you are all one in Christ Jesus." But the Christ-like androgyny sanctioned by scripture operates, according to Daniel Boyarin, at a purely spiritual level. In this Pauline formation, being "male-and-female means [being] neither male nor female."[42] Such disembodied androgyny is not what Durcan's Jesus exemplifies. When the neglected wife invites him to spend the night with her,

> he waved me aside with one wave of his hand,
> Not contemptuously, but compassionately.
> "Our night will come," he smiled,
> . . . .
> At closing time he kissed me on both cheeks
> And we bade one another goodbye and then—
> Just as I had all but given up hope—
> He kissed me full on the mouth. (*LD*, 120)

The familiar romantic notion that androgyny is consummated through heterosexual love relationships certainly attracted Durcan. In "The Man Whose Name Was Tom-and-Anne" from *Jesus, Break His Fall* (1980), a poem written when his own marriage was falling apart, he posits an ideal matrimonial arrangement where the partners jettison their own single-sex identities in lieu of a more holistic blending of genders. But Durcan, ever self-critical, was wary of the tendency of men to exploit this principle in their relationships with women. That danger is exacerbated when the figure upholding the standard of androgyny is so culturally potent. In the poignantly funny "The Pietà's Over" from *The Berlin Wall Café*, Durcan reveals how easily masculine sensitivity morphs into wounded pathos. The speaker's wife ridicules her husband's piteousness by revealing it as childish self-aggrandizement: "The Pietà's over . . . / It is time for you to get down off my knees / And learn to walk on your own two feet." Through his "messiahing about in his wife's lap / suffering fluently in her arms," the husband seeks to exonerate himself from responsibility for his misdeeds and to reduce his wife to the marmoreal posture of the *mater dolorosa* (*LD*, 140). In *Greetings to Our Friends in Brazil*, "Man Circling His Woman's Sundial" reiterates this critique. The male speaker's deference to his absent lover lapses first into drunken self-pity and then, more dramatically, into a death wish. He insists that only when his ashes have been buried under the sundial, only after he has been subsumed within the feminine domain of nature, will he garner his lover's appreciation. Here again, masculine submissiveness in romantic love is exposed as a form of narcissistic self-abasement. But this poem, unlike its precursor, also offers a positive example of a Christ-like androgyny. It takes the form of the local parish priest whom the speaker phones in his despair and whose tender response reveals him to be "sympathetic, solicitous, soulful—sisterly even" (*LD*, 394).

While bishops and cardinals, as we have seen, are repeatedly ridiculed throughout Durcan's poetry, priests fare considerably better. In stark contrast to the Catholic hierarchy, Durcan generally portrays these ordinary men of the cloth as emotionally open, eager to reconcile the sacred and quotidian, and sympathetically attuned to the complex corporeal nature of their Christian faith. Their common touch reveals and partially salves the wounds occasioned by an otherwise aloof and severe patriarchal institution. This image of the priest as a beloved figure who shares in the suffering of his flock recuperates the earlier pre-famine attitude of the native Irish towards the Catholic clergy, famously epitomized in the early nineteenth-century Irish novelist John Banim's poem, "Soggarth Aroon." The "dear priest" of this poem's title is represented by its speaker as "a friend / . . . who never did flout me yet / . . . [who] gave while his eye did brim."[43] But as Joseph Nugent indicates, the traditional image of the "loving, caring, gentle Irish priest" ended with the Devotional Revolution. That formalization of Irish Catholicism refashioned the priest into "a more austere, more authoritative, more controlled, more formidable figure . . . [who was] in his bearing, a more manly man."[44]

It was only in the 1960s that this standard lost its hold and a less rigidly masculine type of priest reemerged in Irish culture. The Irish journalist Mary Kenny has noted the distinctive presence of these "Sixties priests" who were "progressive and involved with social reform," less concerned with policing sexual morality than with nurturing the poor and disadvantaged both at home and abroad.[45] These priests, like their counterparts in the United States and Europe, reflected the democratizing reforms occasioned by the Second Vatican Council, most notably, the shift from "a cultic model of priesthood . . . to more of a 'servant-leader' model."[46] In abandoning the perch of exalted patriarch, these new-style clerics openly acknowledged their own human fallibility. The challenge facing them was succinctly described in a 1972 lecture delivered by Fr. Michael Buckley to a group of seminarians at the Jesuit School of Theology in Berkeley, California. Buckley asserted that the crucial question in determining the viability of a priestly vocation was whether "this man [is] weak enough to be a priest?" Or, as he elaborates it, "is this man deficient enough so that he can't ward off significant suffering from his life, so that he lives with a certain amount of failure, so that he feels what it is to be an average man?"[47] The prevalence of this softening of the priestly role is marked by the counter-reaction that it triggered. In a pamphlet published in 1972 by the conservative *Irish Messenger of the Sacred Heart*, Robert Nash S.J. argued against this removal of the priest from his pedestal. He quotes approvingly the comments of James Dunne, former president of the Irish Congress of Trade Unions:

> The overwhelming majority [of laity] expect the priest and brother to be a man of religion. We don't want him to be a jack of all trades, putting himself so stupidly at their feet as to become a clown, an object of contempt . . . Time was the enemies of the Church wanted to keep the priest in the sacristy. Now, believe me, it is his friends who want to keep him there, for his place is in the church, at the altar and in the pulpit, and the farther he strays from there, the more chance that he will get lost.[48]

More recently, this backlash against the priesthood's shift away from an exclusionary patriarchalism has intensified. Catholic traditionalists in Ireland and America now blame the emasculation of priests for virtually everything plaguing the church from declining mass attendance to a loss of vocations to the abuse scandals.[49]

Durcan's positive representations of sensitive, down-to-earth priests deviates sharply from the norm in contemporary Irish culture. In the wake of the abuse crisis, as Harry Ferguson notes, a new stereotype of the "paedophile priest" has emerged. The trauma caused in Ireland by the clerical abuse of children cannot be overestimated. But restrictively linking pedophilia to priests not only stigmatizes an entire group for the crimes of a relatively small minority, but it obscures the more extensive abuse perpetuated by men outside the priesthood.[50] Nonetheless, priests have become a convenient vehicle through which the Irish public can convey its contempt for the Catholic hierarchy's myriad failures. In recent Irish films, as Martin McLoone has noted, the priest functions as a surrogate for a corrupt institutional church and invariably finds himself ridiculed and debased. A particularly striking example is the seemingly benign Fr. Fitzroy from Peter Mullan's *The Magdalene Sisters* (2002) who is observed abusing a mentally handicapped inmate. Revenge occurs when his clothes are rubbed with a noxious plant and the priest, driven mad with itching, publicly disrobes and runs naked into the woods while being denounced by his victim.[51] In contrast to such cinematic portraits, the priests most fully evoked in Durcan's poetry are characters, not caricatures, more richly variegated in texture than their attenuated screen counterparts.

Fr. Peter O'Brien, CC, the central figure of the title poem of *Greetings to Our Friends in Brazil*, possesses all density of the real-life priest upon whom he is based. At the heart of this rambling recounting of a day in the poet's life is the long afternoon that he spends with this "compatible man" (*LD*, 367). Most of it centers around the masculine activity of watching a Gaelic football match between Mayo and Kerry, but prior to that, Durcan attends the Sunday Mass presided over by his priest-friend. The priest performs the Mass with a heightened emotional tenor that is spiritually affecting yet sincere:

> Every inflection, every gesture
> Effected a rescue of innocence:
> Not so much as an iota of unctuousness
> Or melodrama or power-tripping or patronage. (*LD*, 369)

His homily offers an even more direct assault upon clerical hypocrisy in its account of how Archbishop McQuaid once censored an editorial in a Catholic newspaper that quoted the Epistle of St. James verbatim. The salutary effect of this day is evinced by the poet's corporal act of mercy when he picks up a middle-aged woman hitchhiker on his drive back to his Achill Island cottage. The tables are turned when the woman recognizes his depression and consoles him by describing her own perseverance in the face of many hardships. The link between this woman and the priest becomes apparent at the conclusion when Durcan, overwhelmed by thoughts of genocide in Rwanda and ethnic cleansing in Bosnia, recalls his friend's evocation of a divine mercy that surpasses human understanding. Such hope is essential for the promise of global interconnectedness heralded in the poem's title to be realized. That promise is realized in the next poem through the ministry of an Irish missionary priest, Fr. Frank Murphy, who founded a school in Recife, Brazil, for the children of prostitutes. As the caretaker of this "crèche," as he refers to it, Fr. Murphy is imbued by poet with the qualities of both Mary, Mother of God, and the prototypical masculine revolutionary hero, Che Guevara (*LD*, 375–76).

The pattern manifested in "Greetings" occurs several other times in Durcan's poetry. In each case, a priest enacts his most important duty—the saying of Mass—in a manner that marks his deviation from the patriarchal ideal that he ostensibly epitomizes. "The 12 O'Clock Mass, Roundstone, County Galway, 28 July 2002" from *The Art of Life* (2004) is a poem written under the rubric of a palpable actuality. With its incorporation of a Sunday Mass as well as references to an impending hurling match, it seems like a belated response to Daniel Corkery's call for a literature that authentically represents the ordinary Irish Catholic's experience. But it is doubtful that an orthodox Catholic would approve of this particular priest's rendition of the Mass. This is partly due to the alacrity with which he conducts the service, an action that Durcan favorably interprets as marking the immediacy of the Incarnation—"as if the Consecration was something / That occurs at every moment of the day and night." But the priest's heterodoxy is manifested more directly in his distinctively unmasculine revision of the Sign of Peace. Instead of the liturgically prescribed "Peace be with you," he calls for his congregation "to turn around and say to each other: 'You are beautiful'" (*LD*, 517).

The strangely titled "The Death of the Ayatollah Khomeini" from *Daddy, Daddy* recounts a Mass at Drogheda that occurs on the day of the Iranian leader's passing. The elderly pastor laments the hypocrisy of his generation, which sequestered its faith to Sunday Mass and "closed the doors of our emotions." Shockingly, he counsels his younger parishioners to remain "in bed on Sundays and dream / Of how life might be / When it is on earth as it is in heaven" (*LD*, 208). Such advice echoes the ayatollah's attacks upon the secularization of Iranian society and his call for a reintegration of Islam into everyday life. The analogy deepens with the concluding section's indictment of the patriarchal theocracy epitomized by the ayatollah and his counterparts in the Irish Catholic hierarchy. During the consecration, an infant girl waddles up the center aisle while the priest, who "looked like a young naked woman / looking down from a height," recites Christ's injunction "Do this in commemoration of me." Replying "I will," she walks out "like a young bride never to return" (*LD*, 209). The charm of this scene does not dull the edge of Durcan's satire, which deftly exposes the chauvinism of a Catholic Church that refuses to allow women to represent an institution that is traditionally referred to as the "bride of Christ." The fact that the infant girl is surreally identified as "the young mother-to-be / Of the Ayatollah Ruhollah Khomeini" warns against the disastrous consequences of this exclusion of women from positions of religious authority (*LD*, 209). But what is noteworthy for our purposes is the congruity between the feminine sensibility of the priest in the poem—his insistence upon emotional openness, his willingness to appear vulnerable—and this call for a truly androgynous priesthood.

The figure of the father, in both his spiritual and physical, clerical and secular formations, is the axis that governs Durcan's analysis of Irish masculinity. Its intricacies are most succinctly elaborated in the best of Durcan's "Mass" poems, "10:30 am Mass, 16 June 1985" from *The Berlin Wall Café*. Here the notation of the date constitutes more than just a nod toward verisimilitude, for the day highlighted in the title marks the coincidence of Father's Day and Bloomsday, the yearly celebration of the putative day of the events of James Joyce's *Ulysses*. Even more so than his counterparts, the priest here exudes a palpable charisma, the kind of indeterminate sex appeal that we typically associate with the male paragons of cinematic elegance:

> When the priest made his entrance on the altar on the stroke of 10:30,
> He looked like a film star at an international airport
>
> . . . .
>
> He was a small, stocky, handsome man in his forties
> With a big mop of curly grey hair
> And black, horn-rimmed, tinted spectacles.

I am sure that more than half the women in the church
Fell in love with him on the spot—
Not to mention the men.
Myself, I felt like a cuddle. (*BWC*, 32)

The rest of the poem unfolds simply. After liturgical readings that get a mixed reception from the poet, the priest delivers a homily in praise of his father and then asks all the fathers in the congregation to stand. But when considered in light of the larger cultural context, both actions resonate with deeper significance. The priest's anecdote about his father describes how he overcame a drinking problem by giving up alcohol when his son entered the seminary and how when he was dying of cancer a few years later he asked his soon-to-be ordained son to hear his confession. The father's acknowledgment of his own weakness is matched by his son, the priestly father's, forgoing of any sacerdotal prerogative as his father confesses "the story of his life" to him (*BWC*, 33). In both cases, priest as well as parent, the father is humanized, his larger-than-life status diminished. The Joycean connection hovers over the poem but comes into play more fully with its concluding action. Joyce's *Ulysses*, as has been often noted, dwells obsessively on the issue of fatherhood. Stephen Dedalus, like his creator and like Durcan himself, is cursed with a troublesome father. The imagined events of 16 June 1904 focus, in no small part, upon his efforts to fathom the mysteries of paternity and fashion an alternative to his dysfunctional relationship with his biological father. As such, he considers the possibility that the act of artistic creation will invest him, as it did Shakespeare, with paternal authority and allow him to become, as Buck Mulligan puts it, "Himself his own father."[52] In the background here is a notion of fatherhood as an essentially spiritual condition derived from Stephen's schooling in Catholic Trinitarian theology. His articulation of this concept identifies it explicitly as the basis of the Catholic Church's patriarchal structure: "Fatherhood, in the sense of conscious begetting, is unknown to man. It is a mystical estate, an apostolic succession, from only begetter to only begotten. On that mystery and not on the madonna which the cunning Italian intellect flung to the mob of Europe the church is founded."[53] Cloaked in that intangible aura, the patriarchal authority exerted by priests and the physical fathers who emulated them seems in every sense impregnable.

Durcan's priest defuses that when he calls upon the fathers in the church to stand for acknowledgment, to reveal themselves in "the profanity of their sanctity, / In the bodily nakedness of their fatherhood, / In the carnal deed of their fathering" (*BWC*, 33). That gesture recapitulates Stephen's eventual discovery of a more authentic father than his own biological parent or his self-engendering imagination. In casting Leopold Paula Bloom—a profoundly androgynous man—as a father figure, Joyce revises the prevailing Irish standard of masculinity. The difference for Durcan is that it is not an outsider but a figure from the heart of the culture—the priest—who facilitates this transformation of the ideal that he once exemplified.

7

Paula Meehan's Revised Marianism

The Apparitions of "Our Lady of the Facts of Life"

There is an immense gulf separating the cultural milieus in which Austin Clarke and Paula Meehan began writing poetry, especially evident in the dwindling authority of the Catholic Church and an increasing openness about sexuality, characteristics of late modern Irish society that Clarke himself anticipated. Yet even in the last decades of the twentieth century, as Paul Durcan's poetry testifies, the Catholic Church continued to fight a vigorous cultural war to preserve its regulatory power over sexuality in Ireland. Paula Meehan's main intervention in this conflict, "The Statue of the Virgin at Granard Speaks" from *The Man Who Was Marked by Winter* (1991), is perhaps the most notable public poem in recent Irish literary history. It is frequently cited by commentators examining the cultural crisis in 1980s Ireland occasioned by the fierce legislative battles on contraception, divorce, and abortion; the tragedies of Anne Lovett and Joanne Hayes; and the "moving statues" phenomenon.[1] But the poem's cultural significance reaches beyond its intrusion into these particular public controversies and its indictment of the lingering legislative and cultural oppression of Irish women. "The Statue of the Virgin at Granard Speaks" occupies a central position in Meehan's long-standing effort to cultivate a form of visionary experience that would redress the spiritual destitution of modernity without being co-opted by a patriarchal Catholicism opposed to the secularization of Irish society.

Certainly one of the strangest aspects of late twentieth-century Irish Catholicism was the outburst of Marian apparitions in 1985, an episode commonly referred as the "moving statues." It began in the tiny village of Asdee in County Kerry on February 14 when several young children claimed to have seen the statue of the Blessed Virgin in the back of the parish church move its hands and eyes.[2] What might have been quickly dismissed as a display of childish fantasy—triggered perhaps by a film shown at the parish hall about the modern-day Italian Franciscan mystic and ostensible miracle worker, Padre Pio—became something more interesting and disturbing when adults in Asdee validated these claims and when the apparitions there were followed by a rash of similar sightings throughout the rural countryside of Ireland.[3] These sightings culminated in late July in Ballinspittle in southwest Cork where a grotto erected like thousands of others throughout Ireland during the Marian year of 1954 temporarily became a site of national pilgrimage. After several local people claimed to have seen movement in the concrete statue of Our Lady of Lourdes, hundreds of thousands of their fellow countrymen and women flocked to Ballinspittle, where they prayed the Rosary aloud and in many cases experienced their own apparitions.[4]

As has often been the case throughout history, these Marian apparitions occurred during a period of cultural upheaval. The Irish economy was in its worst shape since the 1950s with unemployment and emigration rates once again soaring. But in contrast to that earlier period when the power of the Catholic Church was at its apex, by the late 1970s and early '80s there was a burgeoning drive to secularize a state that had been entangled with the Catholic Church since its inception. The result, as we noted in the prior chapter, was a series of acrimonious political debates on contraception, divorce, and abortion that reached a fever pitch with the constitutional referenda of 1983 and 1986. The first of these resulted in the easy passage of an amendment to the constitution guaranteeing the right to life of the fetus while the second led to the surprising defeat of a constitutional amendment legalizing divorce. The cultural angst occasioned by these issues greatly intensified in the aftermath of two shocking incidents in 1984 involving young unmarried mothers whose pregnancies eventuated in tragedies. The "Kerry Babies" case involved Joanne Hayes, an unmarried twenty-four-year-old woman from rural County Kerry. As was indicated previously, Hayes was accused of murdering a newly born infant whose mutilated body washed ashore on the south Kerry coastline. This accusation became untenable—although she continued to be subjected to aggressive legal scrutiny—after evidence revealed that Hayes could not possibly be the mother of this unidentified infant and that she had recently given birth to her own stillborn baby, whose body she had buried in a nearby field. It was the earlier incident, though, that highlighted the link between the cultural debate over female reproductive rights and Marian devotion. In January 1984, in the town of Granard in County Longford, Anne Lovett, a fifteen-year-old girl who had hidden her pregnancy from family and friends, went out by herself on a cold winter night to a grotto devoted to the Blessed Virgin where she died attempting to give birth.[5]

The Marian sightings that began scarcely a year after this tragedy differed from other well-known apparitions such as Lourdes and Fatima, for the Virgin never spoke to those who crowded the shrines and churches of the Irish countryside in 1985. Yet there was little doubt among those who witnessed the movements of her statues that the Blessed Virgin was sending a message to the Irish people. As the journalist Eamonn McCann reported of the crowd gathered at Ballinspittle, there was "almost unanimous agreement" that the miraculous movements of the statue "meant 'Our Lady' or 'God' was displeased by the trend of events in Ireland and was indicating that some reversion towards the way things were in the past would be in order."[6] Such an interpretation of the message of moving statues was hardly surprising given the affiliation of Marian apparitions throughout modern European history with reactionary political and social movements.[7] Indeed, as James Donnelly's detailed analysis reveals, Ireland was a particularly potent example of the deep-seated connection between Marianism and conservative resistance to modernity. The sociopolitical power of Irish Marianism peaked in the mid-twentieth century when groups such as the Legion of Mary, the Children of Mary, Our Lady's Sodality, and the Blue Army of Fatima played a vanguard role in opposing what they perceived as the concomitant threats of international communism and the secularization of the Irish polity.[8] Although these groups declined precipitously in both membership and influence in the aftermath of the Second Vatican Council, an intense strain of Marianism pervaded organizations such as the Society for the Protection of Unborn Children (SPUC), the National Pro-Life Rosary Movement, and Family Solidarity that came into being with the legislative battles of the 1980s. The SPUC, for example, employed the image of one of the most famous Marian apparitions, Our Lady of Guadalupe, in its campaign for the pro-life amendment and celebrated its passage with annual pilgrimages to a Marian shrine at Our Lady's Island in County Wexford, where the Blessed Virgin's assistance was likely enlisted in the ongoing struggle against contraception and divorce.[9]

Given this affiliation of Marianism with a hidebound conservatism, it is not surprising that the cultural elite in Ireland mostly dismissed the moving statutes phenomenon as a disturbing display of collective irrationality. But there were those who resisted the temptation of such pat explanations. The poet Eavan Boland, while refusing to credit the authenticity of the supposed apparitions or the legitimacy of the conservative agenda undergirding them, nonetheless saw them as evincing a residual desire for the kind of visionary experience that modernity has severely curtailed:

> If nothing else, that outbreak of an old mode of perception made me begin to look more inquiringly at those things we thought of as new. And one of the things I began to measure, without even being conscious of it, was a distance between ways of seeing. After all, those people in the farms and at the crossroads had spoken, for a brief moment that summer, of vision. Maybe a vision of impossible things. But vision all the same.[10]

Boland proceeded to indict modern poetry for its transmutation of this religious visionary impetus into a "religion of poetry."[11] By cultivating a hieratic notion of the imagination that rendered the poet into, as Wallace Stevens put it, "a metaphysician in the dark" and the poem into "an act of mind," the modern tradition of poetry sequestered visionary experience within the solitary imagination and divorced it from everyday communal existence.[12]

Throughout her poetic career, Paula Meehan has sought to remedy precisely this failure. In an interview with John Hobbs, she identified the integral link between poetry and dreams but stressed her desire "to write something that was both visionary and quotidian, because . . . that's where vision is, in the absolutely daily life as it is lived."[13] As an Irish woman and the product of a much-beleaguered urban working-class community, Meehan recognizes the oppressive force exerted by "common sense"—the prevailing "wisdom" of the dominant culture—which, in an eponymously titled poem from her most recent volume *Painting Rain* (2009), "dictates" that a group of inner-city children who thoughtlessly vandalize a tree are doomed to lives of misery.[14] Against the complacent fatalism of conventional rationality, Meehan holds out the hope that a shared visionary experience might serve as a resistant and potentially liberating counterforce. Through her poetry, she seeks to fashion a salutary alternative to the mass hysteria that conjured monitory gestures from statues of the Blessed Virgin throughout the Irish countryside. She begins with an act of re-envisioning that recuperates a pre-Christian mother goddess from a transcendental Marianism and reestablishes her roots in nature and the feminine psyche. But these apparitions of the mother goddess eventually give way to a more mundane form of visionary experience—exchanges between real women that remain charged with a numinous power. Meehan's desire not only to represent but also produce such exchanges is reflected in her long-standing emphasis on the public performance of her poetry, especially with those groups—inner-city school children, women prisoners, recovering addicts—left stranded in the wake of what passes for progress. In both her poetry itself as well as its presentation, Meehan aspires to a mode of vision that is postmodern yet non-esoteric, one capable of generating a collective moment of ecstasy that remains free and intractable, neither bolstered by nor tethered to any external agenda.

1

In "The Statue of the Virgin at Granard Speaks," contrary to the apparitions of 1985, the statue of the Virgin Mary remains fixed in place, a physical fact emblematic of the obduracy of Irish Mariolatry. Marian devotion came to Ireland, according to Margaret Mac Curtain's genealogy, at the heart of the Middle Ages, just prior to the invasion of the Normans, and rose to prominence during the seventeenth and eighteenth centuries as a mark of Catholic resistance to Anglo-Protestant oppression.[15] It reached its apogee during the post-famine Devotional Revolution, when this "cult of the Virgin Mary" manifested itself in "the rise of confraternity and abstinence movements which championed sexual purity."[16] Through Meehan's deft use of prosopopoeia, the statue of the Virgin at Granard repudiates this cultural appropriation of Mary. She voices her resentment at being immured within this constrictive theological framework and guiltily acknowledges how it prohibited her from protecting one deeply in need of her assistance:

> though she cried out to me in extremis
> I did not move,
> I didn't lift a finger to help her,
> I didn't intercede with heaven,
> nor whisper the charmed word in God's ear.[17]

A similar evocation of a captive and ineffectual Virgin Mary occurs in Margo Harkin's film *Hush-a-Bye Baby* (1990), another widely recognized work of art created in response to Anne Lovett's tragic death. The film focuses on Goretti, a Derry teenager struggling with a secret pregnancy. As Elizabeth Cullingford points out in her shrewd analysis of the film, the Virgin Mary appears throughout the film "not as a loving mother, but as a frightening bogey-woman."[18] At its conclusion, Goretti in the throes of childbirth experiences a recurrence of an earlier apparition in which an encased statue of the Blessed Virgin "with its swollen pregnant stomach [is] once more pressing against the glass," its distended hands an "image of imprisonment and disconnection."[19] Both film and poem employ this motif of the immured Virgin as an emblem of the lingering entrapment of Irish women within a rigid code of sexual purity sanctioned by Marian ideology.

If this figure also suggests the internment of a more life-affirming mythos within the conventional image of the Blessed Virgin, only the poem chooses to exhume that. It does so by juxtaposing passages in which Mary starkly disavows her traditional Catholic roles—consolatory Mother of Sorrows, Immaculate Virgin, merciful mediatrix—against ones in which she conveys her attunement to the natural world and her desire to be reintegrated within it.

> They call me Mary—Blessed, Holy, Virgin.
> They fit me to a myth of a man crucified:
> the scourging and the falling, and the falling again,
> the thorny crown, the hammer blow of iron
> into wrist and ankle, the sacred bleeding heart.
>
> They name me Mother of all this grief
> though mated to no mortal man.
> They kneel before me and their prayers
> fly up like sparks from a bonfire
> that blaze a moment, then wink out.
>
> It can be lovely here at times. Springtime,
> early summer. Girls in Communion frocks
> pale rivals to the riot in the hedgerows
> of cow parsley and haw blossom, the perfume
> from every rushy acre that's left for hay
> when the light swings longer with the sun's push north.
>
> Or the grace of a midsummer wedding
> when the earth herself calls out for coupling
> and I would break loose of my stone robes,
> pure blue, pure white, as if they had robbed
> a child's sky for their color. My being
> cries out to be incarnate, incarnate,
> maculate and tousled in a honeyed bed. (*MW*, 42–43)

Meehan's poem echoes an exhaustive body of scholarship that traces the Blessed Virgin worshipped in Catholicism back to early Mediterranean earth goddess cults. Indeed, it is from this primitive maternal deity that many of the most salient features of Marian iconography are derived, specifically "her dark blue cloak, turreted crown, link with the moon and the stars, with water and wind."[20] The statue of the Virgin at Granard ends her soliloquy with an impassioned supplication that she be restored to her animistic origins. The poem garners a bitter poignancy through this ironic reversal that places the Blessed Virgin in a position of entreaty similar to that of Anne Lovett when she died giving birth before this statue.

> On a night like this I number the days to the solstice
> and the turn back to the light.
>   O sun,
> center of our foolish dance,
> burning heart of stone,
> molten mother of us all,
> hear me and have pity. (*MW*, 44)

Through this redaction of the Marian apparitions of 1985, Meehan implies that if Irish women lived under the aegis of a nature goddess, in which the potency of feminine sexual energy was celebrated rather than denigrated, then the tragedies of Anne Lovett, Joanne Hayes, and countless others might have been averted.

The fashioning of this counter-vision of a pagan mother goddess was the major accomplishment of the first phase of Meehan's poetic career. The initial two poems of her first book *Return and No Blame* (1984) provide a helpful synecdoche of her efforts in this regard. In them, Meehan indicts the harsh disciplinary power of Marian ideology, exposes the disastrous consequences of idealized conceptions of feminine sexuality, and evokes the difficulty of finding a vantage point that that will allow her to address the depredations of urban life without being overwhelmed by them. Thus in the first section of "Echoes," the opening poem of this book, the persona, keeping vigil from a tenement window, watches a Corpus Christi procession "with gaudy bishops in tow / As the monstrance sways" and acerbically marks its domesticating intent: "The legion of Mary's virgins // Snare the small wild children / And arraign their innocence."[21] The grandeur of this Catholic ritual only accentuates the destitution of inner-city poverty: "Only the stench of urine lingers / Now, and only rats are revealed / In streams of gold through fanlights" (*RNB*, 8). The next poem, "Tempus Fugit," exposes both the inadequacy and the temptation of a more secular kind of idealization. Here a man's exalted vision of his lover in a pub gives way to her shocking discovery of a "discarded foetus on the floor" of the lavatory, a sight so horrible that she can assimilate it only by rendering it into a poetic image: "she will always swear she saw / A pale face staring, like a moon" (*RNB*, 15). Later in this volume, Meehan gives this aesthetizing of human suffering a typical poetic provenance, identifying it in "The Apprentice" with Yeats. Rejecting him as a master, she transmutes his images of ethereal feminine beauty into the bodily traces of a harsh urban environment:

> Your swanlike women are dead,
> Stone dead. My women must be
> Hollow of cheek with poverty
> And the whippings of history! (*RNB*, 27).

Rather than adopt the lofty perch of her visionary precursor—"his window is too high / For me to see out of"—she seeks in "Ariadne's Thread," a later poem from this volume, to locate herself in the midst of the city's welter without allowing her art to be consumed by its brutality. The sudden shift in this poem's second half to abrupt, discordant lines and the concluding reference to an "unraveling" skein intimate the young poet's doubts about her ability to establish such a stance (*RNB*, 41–42).

It is not surprising that Meehan's exposure of the horrors of inner-city poverty led her toward the pastoral. But Meehan ventures down this familiar literary path only to reveal it as a dead end and reverse its usual trajectory. While "Intruders" begins with the narrator's retreat to a remote Shetland island where she will learn the "ancient holy way," she soon discovers that her pastoral idyll is haunted by the specter of the city's human detritus, its beggar-women, delinquents, and drunkards (*RNB*, 36). This realization leads Meehan in her subsequent poetry to engage in an act of transposition whereby she renders nature into a spectral presence, a psychic force that can be activated in the heart of the city. Eventually, she will give this elemental power its own visionary sanction and identify it with the mother goddess. But long before that happens, it is manifested in the erotic energy that pulsates through Meehan's early verse. That energy receives its most explicit formulation in "The Dark Twin," first published in her second book, *Reading the Sky* (1985), where it is cast in Jungian terms as the anima hidden in the depths of the male psyche. But the poem complicates the archetypal opposition that identifies the masculine with history, the feminine with nature. The man, whose point of view the poem adopts, presents his sexual penetration of the woman as an act of enlightenment in which the knowledge of history is infused into his "dark twin," the feminized unconscious.[22] His presumption of mastery is undermined, however, by the woman's psychic attunement to the victims of history, an awareness that she inflicts upon him through the "little death" of sexual climax, which renders him speechless.

The resistant force of this feminized erotic energy is amplified when it is invested with its own mythos. Meehan provides this in "One Evening in May" from *Pillow Talk* (1994), where she transforms the Marian apparition into a revelation of a more archaic power. In appropriating the beginning of May as a time of devotion to the Blessed Virgin, the Catholic Church sought to subsume, as it did in so many other ways, the worship of a pagan mother goddess within its own Marian rituals. Here, though, Meehan completes the act of genealogy that she began in "The Statue of the Virgin at Granard Speaks," granting the Virgin's occluded precursor the splendor of her own visionary manifestation:

> The sultry lead and pewter sky
> opened on blue immensity
> which hung a moment,
> then sultry lead and pewter sky
>
> clanged back. I thought I was wise
> till I heard her voice; thought
> I had the art of mirror plumbing
> perfected. Then she showed me
>
> in a blue clearing of clouds
> how space can enrapture a mortal.
> . . . .
> Whatever happens now, I'll be bound
> to her rule for life. I pray I'll not rue
> the day she parted clouds,

revealed her starry body, her great
snakeshead, her myriad children,
feasting at her breasts. She spoke. She said,
"You're mine. Come. Do my bidding."[23]

In contrast to Marian apparitions, in which the Virgin serves as the messenger of an external authority, Meehan's counter-vision of the mother goddess blurs the distinction between what is outside and inside the self. The references to the "sultry lead and pewter sky" and the speaker's "mirror-plumbing" imbue this vision with a self-reflexive cast, but what is revealed is something more than just a subjective projection. The enjambments that proliferate throughout this poem associate this epiphanic experience with an act of cleaving. The breakthrough of "blue immensity" into the overcast sky signals a rift in inner space as well, exposing the presence of a long-buried power within the psyche. Not contained within nor controlled by the ego-self, this "shapechanging" force leaps the boundaries of the individual psyche, binding it to others, including, as in "The Dark Twin," those who are "sick and damaged" (*PT*, 16). More commonly, though, the connections sparked by this force are not just sympathetic but erotic in nature. Thus, the prayer derived in "Handmaid" from the revelation of this mother goddess is a declaration of desire rather than an abashed acquiescence. In this poem's profane rendition of the Annunciation, the Lord is a secular figure and Mary's familiar gesture of spiritual obedience—"Thy will be done"—is redacted as an erotic imperative: "O Lordy / do with me what you will" (*PT*, 13).

2

In invoking the myth of the mother goddess for its subversive power, Meehan is retrieving an abiding tradition in Western culture. As Joe Cleary points out, the appearance of Johann Jakob Bachofen's magisterial scholarly work *Das Mutterrecht* in 1861 engendered various discursive formations of the "Great Mother" mythos that militated against the instrumentalist rationality and hypermasculine capitalism that characterized European modernity.[24] What Cleary refers to as the "late twentieth-century Irish fascination with the figure of the Great Mother" emanates from a similar impetus—a recognition of "a lack or hollowness . . . posited at the heart of Irish modernity."[25] In his account of this myth's recrudescence in contemporary Irish culture, Cleary conflates the Marianism of the "moving statues" episode with contemporaneous secular visions of a "spirit-mother," most notably Jim Sheridan's popular film *Into the West* (1992).[26] Sheridan's film traces the journey of two young traveler boys as the spirit of their dead mother in the form of a white horse leads them from the destitution of contemporary inner-city Dublin into the enchanted domain of the Irish West. Both journey and film culminate in the younger brother's near-drowning in the maternal realm of the sea and his miraculous rescue by the apparition of this "spirit-mother." While acknowledging the possibility of more radical applications of this motif, Cleary concentrates upon the regressive nature of Sheridan's iteration of it. For Cleary, the resistant power of the mother goddess mythos is greatly diminished by the film's attenuated identification of this figure with only the benign aspects of a premodern pastoral domain and its emplacement in a Celtic Twilight never-never land divorced from the actual social sphere of contemporary Ireland. The upshot of Cleary's intriguing analysis is an alignment of both the religious and secular visions of the mother goddess in late modern Ireland with a "longing for some more maternal world [that] cannot get beyond a kind of gestural wistfulness."[27]

Meehan's appropriation of this mother goddess maintains its oppositional impetus towards post-Enlightenment modernity while at the same time avoiding the kind of nostalgic domestication that renders this mythic figure toothless. If Meehan recognizes the need for a visionary alternative to the hegemony of reason, she also acknowledges the importance of not reverting to naïve and unreflective forms of credence. The complexity of her attitude is encapsulated in the ambivalence of the phrase "age of reason," which appears in several crucial poems in the later part of Meehan's career. Its primary referent in these poems is to that chronological watershed when a child has ostensibly developed sufficient rational awareness of the world to distinguish it from fantasy. But lurking just beneath the surface is the familiar use of this phrase as the epochal label for the European Enlightenment. Thus, the aptly titled "The Age of Reason" from Meehan's most recent book, *Painting Rain* (2009), marks the moment when the speaker becomes aware of the acute disparity between the beautiful trappings of her family's Catholic faith and the harsh reality of their tenement life:

> My Grandmother Mary
> is picking lilac and roses to place on her May altar.
>
> I think grace looks like the mother-of-pearl cover
> on my eucharistic prayerbook.
>
> Later a broken window, raised voices, my uncle
> out of his head; all of us
>
> sleeping in my auntie's bed. (*PR*, 49)

If "The Age of Reason" registers the obsolescence of an inherited religious faith, "A Child's Map of Dublin" from *Pillow Talk* employs this signal phrase to expose the oppressive power of an alienated rationality that in the name of progress expunges the vibrant inner-city community of the poet's childhood:

> I walk the northside streets
> that whelped me; not a brick remains
> of the tenement I reached the age of reason in. Whole
> streets are remade, the cranes erect over Eurocrat schemes
> down the docks. (*PT*, 14)

The enjambment in the third line of this passage reminds us that this community, despite its many deprivations, possessed a semblance of organic unity and that its demolition left a gaping absence in the heart of the city. And the image of the cranes looming over the city identifies this bureaucratic remaking of the city as a display of phallocentric power. For Meehan, then, the phrase "age of reason" marks both the necessary supersession of naïve, credulous forms of religious vision as well as the pressing need for some imaginative counter to the post-Enlightenment regime of instrumental reason.

If *Into the West* offers a vision of the mother goddess as a ruthful maternal presence, Meehan identifies her instead as a ruthless Dionysian force. It was in part her firsthand experience of the vastness of the American Northwest during her stints as a graduate student and teacher in the MFA program at Eastern Washington University that enabled Meehan to locate the mother goddess in its aboriginal context, to discern in this well-worn cultural trope the lineaments of the untrammeled and awful wildness of nature from which it originates. The title poem of *The Man Who Was Marked by Winter* serves in many ways as a source text for this vision. In Meehan's poetic recounting of an event that she actually witnessed, a young man whose corpse is discovered on a mountain river bank in the spring thaw is seen as the victim of a nature goddess, who "clutched him to her breast . . . // made her mark / below his heart, a five-fingered gash—*Bondsman*" (MW 54–55). Glossing this figure, Meehan identifies her as "a female power like the force of nature, pitiless and blind to human concerns."[28] Throughout her first four books, Meehan repeatedly casts her personae as both avatar and victim of this mythic figure. As noted above, in Meehan's poetry the mother goddess manifests herself most powerfully in the bedroom. There, as the ironically named title poem of *Pillow Talk* indicates, she converts the smothering intimacy fostered by bourgeois notions of romantic love into a more primal and unruly form of ecstasy, a Maenad-like ritual of demoniac possession:

> What you don't hear is the other voice
> when she speaks through me
> beyond human pity or mercy. She wants you.
> . . . .
> I know she once tore a man apart,
> limb from limb with her bare hands
> in some rite in her bloody past. (*PT*, 32)

These visions of an elemental feminine presence serve, as Meehan indicates in "Not Your Muse" from the same volume, to counter the debilitating constructs that patriarchal tradition imposes upon the sexuality of women. But the power activated by the mother goddess extends beyond private relationships into the public sphere. In sharp contrast to Sheridan's regressive alignment of the "spirit-mother" with the premodern Irish west, Meehan's mother goddess does not retreat from modernity but operates within the heart of the urban metropolis. There she fosters a spatial practice that enables the female subject to evade the "official" cordoning of urban space into accepted and forbidden zones, thereby granting her the freedom of the city. Thus, in the sequence "City" from *Pillow Talk*, the erotic energy epitomized by the mother goddess leads the persona to flee the comfort and safety of the hearth for the danger of the city streets at night. This nighttime journey converts an urban space, purely functional in the daylight, into a sublime wilderness redolent of both beauty and terror. In the penultimate poem of the sequence, "City," Meehan associates this psychic wildness with the shamanistic role of the *"shapechanger"* (*PT*, 22).

This motif, which has roots both in Celtic and Native American folklore, recurs throughout *Pillow Talk*.[29] As Meehan notes in an interview, these references to shape-changing should not be relegated to a mere poetic device but instead describe a way of being in the modern as well as the premodern world, an everyday strategy for negotiating the threatening anonymity of urban existence:

> I think people shapeshift all the time. It's a natural thing. I know I do it walking through different areas. If I'm in a rough part of New York, I walk like those around me. We need protective coloring. The animal part of us . . . the more we trust that part of us, the more safe we are.[30]

In that regard, the persona's sojourn under the aegis of the mother goddess recalls the fearless posture that Walter Benjamin discerned in the poet laureate of the modern city, Charles Baudelaire, whose blending of the flaneur and the nomadic warrior Benjamin designated as "apachedom."[31] Meehan's final poem of this sequence, "On the Warpath," imports the "apachedom" infused from this cruising of deserted city streets back into the bedroom, where it completes the Dionysian transformation of the disciplined subject of capitalist society into "the human, suddenly, wild" (*PT*, 23).

As much as anything else, what distinguishes Meehan's poetic vision of the mother goddess from those that precede "the age of reason" (in both its individual and epochal sense) is her self-reflective interrogation of its efficacy. Her critique emerges sporadically and centers upon the way in which the erotic energy summoned through these visions replicates to some degree the corrosive effects of modernity that it seeks to counter. The self-destructive and isolating potential of eros is exposed through its conjunction with other forms of Dionysian excess, most notably the use of narcotic drugs. Meehan has frequently registered her concern with the heroin epidemic that spread like a plague through Dublin in the 1980s and devastated the inner-city community in which she grew up. In poems, such as "Letter to John B." from *Reading the Sky* and "Her Heroin Dream" from *The Man Who Was Marked by Winter*, the line distinguishing eros from narcosis is blurred. The first of these concludes with the persona confessing that the moon, a frequent talisman of the mother goddess throughout Meehan's poetry, "has me strung out on a man / again. A bad bad habit" (*RS*, 17). Even more significantly, the drug-induced vision recapitulated in "Her Heroin Dream" takes the form of an erotic fantasy in which motifs associated with the mother goddess are pervasive. The ecstasy detonated by the persona's imagined copulation with a moon-born dragon is volcanic—"the kundalini energy would shoot straight up her spine, / blow her head open like a flower" (*MW*, 35)—but utterly solipsistic. Like the opiate that conjured it, this vision evokes illusions of omnipotence and absolute freedom that eventuate not in action but in a numbed indifference to the devastation of the surrounding environment: "They'd slip from the cell hands twined, / glide over the prison wall into a new morning / to sport among the ruins" (*MW*, 35).

Meehan's brilliant coda to the mother goddess mythos, "Mother" from *Dharmakaya* (2002), foregrounds the paradoxical interfusion of creation and destruction inherent in the visions of this figure while warning against their atrophying into a fetishistic belief. "Mother" is the medial poem in a three-part sequence, "On Poetry," which counterpoints the phases of the poet's creative development against the conventional formations—virgin, mother, whore—that patriarchy imposes upon female sexuality. Like its more famous precursor Sylvia Plath's "Daddy," Meehan's "Mother" is an act of exorcism directed toward a composite figure that incorporates both the poet's actual parent as well as her mythic counterpart. In Meehan's case, however, the apostrophes that drive the poem exhibit an ambivalence not present in Plath's diatribe against the papa-patriarch. Thus, the declaration—"when you created time // mother you created plenty"—hovers between praise and complaint, registering not just admiration for the fecundity of this mother figure but resentment at the trouble she caused for her daughter.[32] Even the poem's more forthright denunciations are cunningly polysemous. The typically foreshortened line—"mammal self abuser" (*D*, 45)—accentuates the destructive power of the mother goddess mythos by linking it to the physical abuse that Meehan's mother directed towards her, described more fully in an earlier poem from this volume, "The View from Under the Table." But at the same time, this phrase evokes an autonomous erotic energy. In the penultimate stanza, the critique turns inward:

> mother fetishist
> heart breaker
> forsaker and fool
> in the pouring rain. (*D*, 46)

Here, Meehan suggests that when the mother goddess and the Dionysian ecstasy that she elicits are reified, liberation gives way to enervating isolation. As such, the act of mourning described in the poem's final stanza is occasioned not just by the memory of her long deceased mother but by the passing of the mythic vision that animated so much of her earlier poetry.

By inscribing this critique within a sequence titled after traditional masculine designations of women, Meehan highlights both the resistant power of the mother goddess mythos as well as its potential co-optation within the prevailing patriarchal social structure. This point is made even more directly in "On Being Taken for a Turkish Woman," the second section of the "Berlin Diary" sequence from *Pillow Talk*. In its focus on the persona's traversing of a threatening urban terrain, this prose poem recapitulates "City" from earlier in the volume. But in this case, female spatial autonomy is sanctioned not by a vision of the mother goddess but by a more prosaic gesture of cross-cultural female solidarity. This parabolic vignette reaches its climax with the reframing of another talisman of the mother goddess, a blue stone earring. As the persona navigates her way to a Turkish market through a newly unified Berlin, she discovers that her attire makes her look like a Turkish woman and thus establishes her as a potential target of ethnic as well as sexual violence. When she is lead astray by a man who mistakes her for Turkish and directs her towards a dangerous area along the canal, she recalls a lover who, the poem implies, also betrayed her after having given her the blue stone and designated it as *"the sign of one who's chosen the path of the warrior rather than the path of the lover"* (*PT*, 46). The lover embellishes this rubric with a disquisition on the significance of the stone's blue color: "a long rigmarole on Mariology, Earth goddesses, the power of the female, mid-Easter moon worship, blue as a healing colour, as Mary's colour" (*PT*, 47). What is cast here as "rigmarole" was previously the impetus for the visionary dimension of much of Meehan's early poetry. The lover's pedantic excursus on the mother goddess exposes how liable such a mythic vision is to being abstracted from the quotidian and invested with a coercive authority. Against this, the poem sets the Turkish market woman's simple yet auspicious avowal of a common bond: "A blue stone glitters at her throat, another on her baby's blanket. *Good luck,* she says, *and health to wear it"* (*PT*, 47). The shift in the talismanic blue stone's status from metaphor to metonym, a shift marked in the overall form of this prose poem, is indicative of a more extensive reorientation of Meehan's poetry in which mythic visions of the mother goddess give way to oracular exchanges, both real and imagined, between actual women.

3

It is not by accident that the movement that we have been tracing in the later part of Meehan's career—a shift away from mythic visions of the mother goddess to remembered gestures of solidarity among ordinary women—coincides with her deepening engagement with Buddhism. In its manifold forms and practices, Buddhism cultivates an awareness of the conditional nature of all perception, both phenomenal and visionary, in order to elicit "the free, clear transparency . . . the naked, pure intelligence" that is the goal of human existence.[33] For Meehan, who makes clear in her poems and interviews that she is not a practicing Buddhist, the appeal of this spiritual tradition lies in large part in its resistance to the authoritarianism characteristic of the Catholic faith in which she was raised. Meehan's entryway into Buddhism was through the Beat poets, most notably, her poetic mentor, Gary Snyder. What Charles Molesworth says about the impact of Zen Buddhism on Snyder's poetry could apply at some level to Meehan as well:

> The flexibility at the level of ritual, or more accurately at the level of ritualized awareness, is consonant with another important element in Buddhism that influenced Snyder's poetry and vision: the sense of a sacred tradition that extends in historical time but avoids strict adherence to a single master text. Buddhism as a whole, but Zen in a special way, transmits its values through personal instruction and discipleship.[34]

In Meehan's case, as we have seen in "On Being Mistaken for a Turkish Woman," this Buddhist emphasis on personal transmission as a source of vatic wisdom is grounded in face-to-face exchanges between women.

But perhaps even more significant is the way in which these exchanges revise the Marianism that Meehan encountered through her own Irish Catholic cultural background. Meehan radicalizes the traditional Marian role of intercessor by transposing it onto actual woman who are more oppositional than mediatory. In orthodox Catholic theology, Mary's function as mediatrix replicates the family dynamics of patriarchy in which the mother can at best mollify the stern judgments of the omnipotent father.[35] Meehan, on the other hand, extrapolates from "the strong matriarchal elements in Irish proletarian life in the city and amongst the rural dispossessed" a maternal role overtly resistant to patriarchal authority.[36] If in "Aubade," "the thunderbolts of a Catholic god" elicit "the useless tears of His mother" (*PT*, 36), just two poems later the ghost of the persona's actual mother accomplishes what Mary cannot by nullifying the threats of punishment directed towards her daughter for violating the sexual codes of a patriarchal church: "Fear not / the lightning bolts of a Catholic god" (*PT*, 39). But the exchange in "The Ghost of My Mother Comforts Me" seems strained and spurious, a point accentuated by the poem's interpolation of phrases from the Irish singer-songwriter Van Morrison. When these visionary encounters are grounded in actuality, the refractory power of these maternal figures is rendered more convincingly.

In "Hannah, Grandmother" from *Painting Rain*, Meehan recounts an episode in which as a young girl on the cusp of puberty she attends confession with her grandmother, who takes on the role of priestly counselor.

But in lieu of the submissive deference expected of the penitent, the grandmother advocates a more subversive posture, recommending that the girl *"tell them priests nothing,"* lest she provide them with a prurient *"thrill"* (*PR*, 45). Tellingly, the poem highlights the Marian context of this exchange, which occurs before a statue of the Blessed Mother and is followed by a prayer to her.

> As close as she came to the birds and the bees
> on her knees in front of the Madonna,
> Our Lady of the Facts of Life
>
> besides the confessional—
> oak door closing like a coffin lid
>
> neatly carpentered
> waxed and buffed
>
> In the well-made box of this poem
> her voice dies.
>
> She closes her eyes
>
> and lowers her brow to her joined hands.
> Prays hard:
>
> woman to woman. (*PR*, 45)

This encounter with "Our Lady of the Facts of Life," in the guise of the poet's grandmother, suggests the possibility of a different kind of Marianism, one that fosters, rather than represses, resistance to the prevailing authority structure. Such a possibility was realized by the practitioners of liberation theology whose radical revision of the Virgin Mary elucidates the position that Meehan ascribes to her grandmother here. The liberation theologian Leonardo Boff, for instance, divests the figure of the Virgin Mary of the trappings of regressive political and theological ideologies by relocating her more fully in her original scriptural and historical contexts and in the everyday struggles of Latin American peasants. From this process of transposition, he derives a counter-image of Mary as the catalyst for "a praxis of solidarity" with and among the marginalized and oppressed.[37] In the case of Meehan's poem, such a praxis takes the form of a transmission of female autonomy that thwarts the disciplinary apparatus of patriarchy.

Meehan's transmutation of Marian and mother goddess apparitions into "woman to woman" exchanges does not indicate a rejection of visionary experience so much as a desire to situate it more fully within ordinary communal life. This immersion of vision within the quotidian ensures that it does not coagulate into dogma but remains fluid. When poetic vision is incorporated, as Meehan insists it should be, in the everyday, when it is thrust into "a zone of contact with unresolved contemporaneity," it is detached from anterior forms of authority and kept from being consolidated into what Mikhail Bakhtin refers to as the "authoritative word."[38] Nowhere is this more apparent than in "St. John and My Grandmother—An Ode" from *Painting Rain.* As the title insinuates, the poem juxtaposes contrasting visionaries, one transcendental and sanctified, the other mundane and secular. Situated on the shoreline across from the holy island of Patmos, the putative site of the evangelist's apocalyptic revelations, the poet finds that the island's phantasmal presence—"it is hidden in a haze, / a rumour" (*PR*, 82)—induces her to daydream. She recalls her alternative to the Book of Revelations, her maternal grandmother Mary's daily recitation of her dreams to assembled family members. Drawn from Meehan's own childhood, this commonplace encounter with the uncanny has been identified by the poet herself as marking her initiation into the mysteries of visionary experience:

> There were no books in the house. But there was a great storytelling. My grandmother, the first thing she'd do in the morning was tell her dreams. When I was four, five, six. And that's where I found real poetry, as a living source. Not as something that exists in books, but something that exists out in the culture and the language.[39]

The poem establishes this connection even more forcefully:

> she'd tell her dreams to her gathered daughters,
> as apocalyptic in their cast as were St. John's.
>
> . . . .

The world was always signal portent,
every single thing stood for something else.
Her dreams, though I was not supposed to hear them,
could rivet, terrorise, warn or shrive you.
Her dreams were instruments of torture
for miscreant daughters who were out of line.
Her dream tongue my first access to poetry:
by her unwritten book I've lived, I'll die. (*PR*, 82–83)

In its delineation of the provenance of Meehan's own poetic vision, this poem recapitulates motifs associated with both Marian apparitions and her counter-vision of the mother goddess. The grandmother is presented as a surrogate of the latter: "Avatar of hearth mysteries, / true daughter of the moon, the shining one" (*PR*, 82). Yet like the Blessed Virgin, after whom she is named, her revelations have the apocalyptic cast that typically characterizes Marian apparitions. What distinguishes the grandmother's visions is that they evoke the numinous without granting it an external sanction. The risk of vision being rendered into doctrine is ever present, as the conversion of St. John's "hallucinatory / dreamscapes of the eternal now" into "the Word of God" (*PR*, 82) indicates and as Meehan herself recognized when she critiqued her own tendency to fetishize the mother goddess vision. This danger is overtly acknowledged and defused here. Having recounted in detail one of her grandmother's most sensational visions, the poet declares,

I sometimes tell this dream to my students
though it refuses a didactic read.
If they ask me where my poems come from
it's as good a place as any to begin:
Mary McCarthy's dream songs for her daughters,
as apocalyptic as the visions of St. John,
I heard them first before the age of reason.
They've stayed with me word for word
across half a century, I write one down now
in sight of Patmos, the island moving
like a trireme from me further into the haze

from which they both have come—
Mary McCarthy and the Evangelist John. (*PR*, 83)

These daily "dream songs" constitute the ultimate paradigm for the visionary experience that Meehan has aspired to cultivate in and through her poetry. Such visions, she suggests, possess a subliminal, subversive power. They linger in the psyche where they disrupt the hegemonic aspirations of "the age of reason." They are unsettling precisely because they do not aspire to the status of the authoritative word, but remain, like the haze-shrouded isle of Patmos glimpsed by the persona, merely "a rumour" (*PR*, 82)—a form of discourse that is anarchic, dispersive, groundless, altogether recalcitrant to modernity's effort to secure things by placing them on a rational foundation.

The formative influence of this childhood experience of the visionary quotidian is evident not just in the notion of poetic vision that Meehan advocates but in her emphasis on the performative and communal character of poetry, her insistence that "the real place where poetry happens . . . is with people in a room."[40] Meehan's effort "to take . . . poems out into the community" has led her from inner-city classrooms to detox programs to prisons.[41] Through sharing her poetic visions in such divergent settings, she seeks to establish a kind of ad-hoc "poetic community," based, as Gerald Bruns's paraphrase of Jean-Luc Nancy puts it, on "the sharing of ecstasy rather than of mind or spirit, language or myth."[42] The power of such communities lies in the fact that, in contrast to the crowds that gathered at Ballinspittle in the summer of 1985, they are never allowed to forfeit ecstatic vision to a totalizing meaning.

Epilogue

Religion and Poetry in Post-Catholic Ireland

The poets examined in the preceding chapters all grew to maturity in a culture where the influence of Catholicism was pervasive and, although increasingly challenged, still potent. Whether in the form of the psychic policing enacted through confession, a circumscription of the landscape's sacrality, sectarian appropriations of the Eucharist, a sacrificial imperative to atone for sinfulness, a sense of nuns and priests as exemplary figures, a Marian cult that enforced a code of sexual purity—Catholicism intruded upon their imaginations. Against the pressure it exerted, their poetry, to borrow Wallace Stevens's formulation, pressed back, transmuting this imposed material into new more pliable forms that bore a trace of the original's cultural heft. The extent and efficacy of this societal imprinting of Catholicism decreased dramatically in Ireland in the aftermath of the Second Vatican Council, leaving the poets born after that watershed moment less deeply marked by the stresses and inclinations fostered by their inherited faith. For these newer generations of Irish poets, Catholicism is less a matter of pressing immediate importance than one of passing historical interest. The secular milieu in which they dwell, although relatively recent for Ireland, has long been prevalent throughout the western world. Perhaps because Ireland remained saturated by religion long after it had dissipated elsewhere, the withdrawal of Catholicism to the margins of public and private life there still bears the shock of something new. It may be over a hundred years since Zarathustra came down from the mountain bearing the news of God's death, but in some places that message can still elicit a frisson of dread. Ireland, even in the twenty-first century, may be such a place, or so the Irish poet Dennis O'Driscoll's "Missing God," published in 2002, implies.

The poem's opening stanzas attribute the expulsion of the divine from modernity to familiar causes: a technological prowess that ensures the rise of "bread production . . . through / disease-resistant grains devised / scientifically to mitigate His faults" and that thereby nullifies the need to evoke "His grace . . . / before meals"; a growing belief in the autonomy of human rationality that renders obsolete the "oppressive father" worshipped and feared by more primitive cultures.[1] But the end of the poem's second stanza undercuts the secular self-assurance that usually accompanies our sense of having overcome the religious "infantilism" of the past. Its assertion that "we confess to missing Him at times" foregrounds an alternative meaning of the poem's title: not only has the *Deus* absconded, gone missing, but in his absence He is longed for, sadly missed.[2] The seventeen stanzas that follow, which each begin with the gentle imperative "Miss Him," solicit this act of repining by exposing the flattening of experience, both momentous and mundane, occasioned by the departure of the divine.

> Miss Him during the civil wedding
> when, at the blossomy altar
> of the registrar's desk, we wait in vain
> to be fed a line containing words
> like "everlasting" and "divine."
>
> . . . .
>
> Miss Him when we exclaim His name
> spontaneously in awe or anger
> as a woman in a birth ward
> calls to her long-dead mother.
>
> Miss Him when the linen-covered
> dining table holds warm bread rolls,
> shiny glasses of red wine.[3]

It is hard to read this accomplished poem and not hear the echoes of a famous precursor, Philip Larkin's "Church Going," which registers with a similar plaintiveness the loss of local habitation for the divine and its evaporation into airy nothingness. The resonances culminate in the last stanza of "Missing God." There, with poignant irony, our nostalgia for a moribund god is figured through the symbol of the Paraclete as we are left "standing in the brick / dome of a dovecote / after the birds have flown."[4] That is, of course, the position of Larkin's speaker, who, having stumbled into a vacant church, marks its superannuation when he declaims from its lectern "Here endeth" and then speculates on what the fate of the building will be as it "fall[s] completely out of use."[5] What is striking, though, is the temporal gap between these poems. Written in 1954, the year of Dennis O'Driscoll's birth, Larkin's poem precedes "Missing God" by almost fifty years. There is a strangely anachronistic aura about O'Driscoll's elegy for the divine. The fact that this poem seems like a museum piece to non-Irish readers testifies to Ireland's asynchronous relation to the thoroughgoing secularity characteristic of modernity, its belated entrance into a world where religion is no longer interwoven into the nation's social and cultural fabric.

As Catholicism recedes ever more rapidly from the mainstream to the periphery of Irish society, the disappearance of the divine will not occasion the plangent wistfulness that it does in O'Driscoll's poem but will simply be taken for granted. Even in this thoroughly secularized Ireland, however, there will be poets for whom registering the vicissitudes of a life lived solely on a natural plane will not suffice, for whom this realm will seem so vacuous, so desiccated, that their poetry will become a vehicle for soliciting forms of transcendence. To get a sense of what part Catholicism might play in such a quest, I want to turn briefly to the work of Seán Dunne (1956–1995), whose promising poetic career was cut short by his death from heart disease. Dunne was born a year after Paula Meehan, the last of the poets focused on in this study, but their poetry differs significantly in how it responds to their shared religious background. Like Meehan, Dunne grew up in a social context in which Catholicism was a central presence and, similarly, found himself repulsed by the oppressive moralism of the institutional church. But in contrast to Meehan, Dunne never commits his poetry to a critical revision of Catholic beliefs and practices. As he notes in his spiritual autobiography, *The Road to Silence* (1994), he jettisoned Catholicism in early adolescence. In his mid- to late twenties, as he struggled with a sense of existential meaninglessness, he began searching for alternative forms of spiritual sustenance.[6] That quest, recorded in his poetry as well as his prose, led him in the early 1980s to the Quakers when he found himself giving a poetry reading at Newtown, the famous Quaker school in Waterford, and then afterwards attending weekly Society of Friends meetings in his hometown of Cork. Over the next decade, he supplemented his dalliance with Quakerism with an interest in the nineteenth-century American Shakers, explorations of various forms of Buddhism, and most significantly, an extended foray into Catholic monasticism, specifically the Cistercians of Strict Observance or Trappists. Intrigued by the writings of the well-known American Trappist, Thomas Merton, Dunne, who worked as a freelance journalist, contracted to write an article about Mount Melleray, the Cistercian monastery in County Waterford. That visit in 1984 was followed by many more over the next decade as Dunne became a frequent guest at the monastery. What Dunne found in Mount Melleray and in Merton bore a close resemblance to what he discovered in the other religious traditions into which he delved—a profound commitment to silence as a means of acknowledging an ineffable Absolute and a posture of solicitude that allows "observed particulars [to] take on the mystery of revelation." The poem that employs that phrase as an epigraph, "Five Photographs by Thomas Merton," from Dunne's final book, *Time and the Island* (1996), could serve as a summa for all the other poems occasioned by his spiritual pilgrimage.[7]

The Hermitage

A house for quiet built in the woods,
one good place for a man alone;
Trees surround it and jets fly over
halfway through a psalm, words caught
in the slipstream and blown away.
It sits within the lens and seems
a shack for solitude in the wide world.

Still Life

A chair, a ladder, a bowl, wood
strewn with shavings on a plain floor.
Behind the chair, an old cup stained
with rainwater. Singled within
the frame he fixed, they are firm
and plain, mundane as the shadow
of chair on bowl, ladder-rung on chair.[8]

The spiritual aura conveyed in these first two sections of "Five Photographs by Thomas Merton" is indistinguishable from that evoked in earlier poems on a Quaker meeting or Shaker handiwork or a Zen tea ceremony. In this leap-frogging between various religious options, Seán Dunne epitomizes both the pluralism and privatization that characterizes the quest for transcendence in modern secularity.[9] With religious faith no longer yoked to public forms of identity, "the contemporary search for the spiritual" manifests itself, in Charles Taylor's apt phrase, as "a kind of individualized bricolage."[10]

What allowed the Catholic strand of Merton and Mount Melleray to be incorporated into Dunne's spiritual pastiche was precisely their marginality, a point that he implicitly makes in the title of his first poem on Merton, "Marginal Man." The peripheral position of the Trappists—the fact that they were "forever on the edge with the necessary trash / of poems or silence"—inoculated them from the taint of corruption associated with Catholicism in Ireland at the end of the twentieth century.[11] In future decades, as Irish Catholicism's social significance dwindles even further, as the stigma of its oppressive institutional past slowly fades, more of its material will become palatable for Irish poets who, like Sean Dunne, find themselves in need of spiritual nourishment. In the years to come, there will undoubtedly be Irish counterparts to contemporary American poets such as Mary Karr or Franz Wright who import Catholic images and doctrine into their poetry to ameliorate their existential angst.

But that poetry of "individualized bricolage" will relate to Catholicism in a markedly different manner from the poetry we have examined in this book. It is not that it will be less theologically sound than the poetry surveyed here, which, as we have seen, deviates frequently and profoundly from Catholic orthodoxy. But rather, the difference will be that for the poets of post-Catholic Ireland, the Catholic elements that enter their verse will have been chosen, selected precisely because they were amenable to the poet's imaginative and spiritual needs. That was not the case for the poets surveyed in the previous chapters. Having come of age when Catholicism was still a predominant force in Irish culture, each found aspects of Catholic practice and belief exerting a claim upon them and demanding a response, like the figure of the nun who entered Eiléan Ní Chuilleanáin's imagination unbidden.

The contrast is clearly evident if we juxtapose Dunne's work with that of his contemporary, Paula Meehan. If one judges on the basis of their poetry, Dunne appears to be more traditionally religious in temperament than Meehan, whose work gestures toward a transcendence that is distinctly nontheistic. Yet Meehan's poetic encounter with her inherited faith exhibits a greater depth and rigor than Dunne's, and would have done so even if her career had, like his, ended prematurely. Catholicism—in the form of a repressive Marianism that constrained female sexuality and that led to Anne Lovett's death in a grotto at Granard—imposed itself upon Meehan's poetic imagination in a way that it never did upon Dunne's. It came fully charged with a dangerous cultural potency, some of which was imparted to the poetry that set about defusing it. The act of critique that neutralizes and sublates this religious construct demands an intimate engagement with it. Instead of being simply evoked, it must be thoroughly worked through before the poet can appropriate it. This process of critical scrutiny, of separating the dross from the usable, the regressive from the revivifying, necessitates an attention to the particularities of the inherited Catholic material that is absent in the work of those who assimilate it in an already congenial form. Thus, Meehan's poetry carefully parses the conventional attributes associated with Marianism, exposes their roots in mother goddess cults, and refashions from that source a visionary experience that empowers rather than constricts women. The result of that dialectical exchange is a poetic derivative of Catholicism that, however far removed from its source, is more clearly delineated, more culturally resonant than Dunne's assimilation of a generalized monastic ethos.

Even when the outgrowth of this process remains unresolved—as with Heaney's notion of the marvelous hovering between secular gratuity and supernal grace—the Catholic rituals and doctrines from which it has been distilled leave their particular imprint upon the poetry. In Heaney's case, as we have seen, the contours of his poetic aperture to the marvelous are shaped by the dismantling of the Catholic sacrificial imperative in which he was so deeply inculcated. My premise throughout this book has been that twentieth-century Irish poetry attained distinctiveness through its struggle to transmute the debilitating elements Catholicism into something more enlivening, much as it did through its concomitant struggle with the traumatic aftereffects of British colonialism. As Ireland becomes as thoroughly post-Catholic as it is postcolonial, its poetry will have lost one of the few remaining cultural influences differentiating it from its Anglophone counterparts.

Notes

Bibliography

Index

Notes

Introduction

1. Russell Shorto, "The Irish Affliction," *New York Times* 13 February 2011, http://www.nytimes.com/2011/02/13/magazine/13Irish-t.html (accessed 11 February 2011).

2. Clifford Geertz has famously articulated this notion of religion as a "cultural system." See Clifford Geertz, *The Interpretation of Cultures* (New York: Basic Books, 1973), 87–125.

3. Dennis O'Driscoll, *Stepping Stones: Interviews with Seamus Heaney* (New York: Farrar, Straus, Giroux, 2008), 318.

4. Ibid., 318.

5. Ibid., 287.

6. Emmet Larkin, "The Devotional Revolution in Ireland, 1850–75," *American Historical Review* 77 (June 1972): 625–52. For a synopsis and updating of Larkin's foundational essay, see Louise Fuller, *Irish Catholicism since 1950: The Undoing of a Culture* (Dublin: Gill and Macmillan, 2002), xxiii–xxxviii.

7. Daniel Corkery, *Synge and Anglo-Irish Literature* (Dublin: Cork University Press, 1931), 12–13.

8. Ibid., 15.

9. Ibid., 20.

10. Ibid., 24.

11. Stopford A. Brooke and T. W. Rolleston, eds., *A Treasury of Irish Poetry in the English Tongue* (London: Macmillan, 1900), 150–51.

12. Ernest Boyd, *Ireland's Literary Renaissance* (New York: Knopf, 1916), 112, 107.

13. *A Treasury of Irish Poetry*, 422–25.

14. Boyd, 110–11.

15. Ibid., 109.

16. Ibid., 109.

17. In a later edition of *Irish Literary Renaissance,* while Boyd praises Joyce's artistry and asserts that "no Irish writer is more Irish than Joyce," he does not extend that claim to Joyce's relationship to his religious background, claiming that his purpose in *A Portrait of an Artist* and *Ulysses* seems to be "to empty Catholicism of all its spiritual content." Qtd. in

James Joyce: A Critical Heritage, vol. 1, *1902–1927*, ed. Robert Deming (New York: Barnes and Noble, 1970), 302–3.

18. Qtd. in Joseph Brooker, *Joyce's Critics: Transitions in Reading and Culture* (Madison: University of Wisconsin Press, 2004), 191.

19. Deming, ed., *James Joyce*, 1:165; Thomas MacGreevy, "The Catholic Element in *Work in Progress*," in *Our Exagmination Round His Factification for Incamination of Work in Progress* (Paris, 1929), 121, http://www.macgreevy.org (accessed 6 January 2011).

20. Deming, ed., *James Joyce*, 1:201.

21. Frederick Lang, *Ulysses and the Irish God* (Lewisburg, PA: Bucknell University Press, 1993), 16, 18, 169–74.

22. Mary Lowe-Evans, *Catholic Nostalgia in Joyce and Company* (Gainesville: University of Florida Press, 2008), 8, 162.

23. Charles Taylor, *A Secular Age* (Cambridge, MA: Harvard University Press, 2007), 360.

24. Ibid., 360, 299.

25. Ibid., 491, 515.

26. Richard Kearney, *Anatheism: Returning to God after God* (New York: Columbia University Press, 2010), xiv.

27. Ibid., 184.

28. Paul Ricoeur, *The Symbolism of Evil*, trans. Emerson Buchanan (Boston, MA: Beacon Press, 1967), 351–52.

29. James Joyce, *A Portrait of the Artist as a Young Man* (New York: Viking Press, 1964), 221.

30. Ricoeur, *Symbolism of Evil*, 352.

31. Kearney, *Anatheism*, 104.

32. See especially Joe Cleary, *Outrageous Fortune: Capital and Culture in Modern Ireland* (Dublin: Field Day, 2007), 111–80, and Emer Nolan, *Catholic Emancipations: Irish Fiction from Thomas Moore to James Joyce* (Syracuse, NY: Syracuse University Press, 2007), x–xvii.

33. Samuel Beckett, *Disjecta: Miscellaneous Writings and a Dramatic Fragment*, ed. Ruby Cohn (New York: Grove Press, 1984), 70.

34. Ibid., 74.

35. Ibid., 91, 68.

36. Denis Devlin, *Collected Poems*, ed. J.C.C. Mays (Winston-Salem, NC: Wake Forest University Press, 1989), 82.

37. Ibid., 82.

38. Ibid., 85–86.

39. O'Driscoll, *Stepping Stones*, 239, 238.

40. T. S. Eliot, "Religion and Literature," in *Selected Essays* (New York: Harcourt, Brace, 1950), 346.

41. Qtd. in Fuller, *Irish Catholicism since 1950*, 19.

42. Antoinette Quinn, *Patrick Kavanagh: A Biography* (Dublin: Gill and Macmillan, 2001), 187.

43. Donal Ó Drisceoil, "'The Best Banned in the Land': Censorship and Irish Writing since 1950," *Yearbook of English Studies* 35 (2005): 146–60.

44. Matthew Arnold, "The Study of Poetry," in *Essays, English and American*, ed. Charles Eliot (New York: Collier, 1910), 65.

45. T. S. Eliot, *The Use of Poetry and the Use of Criticism* (Cambridge, MA: Harvard University Press, 1933), 127.

46. Charles Taylor, *Sources of the Self: The Making of Modern Identity* (Cambridge, MA: Harvard University Press, 1989), 419.

47. Ibid., 428.

48. Charles Taylor, *A Secular Age*, 411.

1. Austin Clarke's (Anti-)Confessional Poetics

1. Austin Clarke, *Twice Round the Black Church*, 2nd ed. (Dublin: Moytura Press, 1990), 130.

2. Ibid., 136.

3. Ibid., 130.

4. Ibid., 87.

5. John Goodby, "'The Prouder Counsel of Her Throat': Towards a Feminist Reading of Austin Clarke," *Irish University Review* 29 (Autumn/Winter 1999): 328–29.

6. Robert Phillips, *The Confessional Poets* (Carbondale: Southern Illinois University Press, 1975), 5.

7. Michel Foucault, "About the Beginning of the Hermeneutics of the Self: Two Lectures at Dartmouth," *Political Theory* 21 (May 1993): 212–14.

8. Henry Charles Lea, *A History of Auricular Confession and Indulgences in the Latin Church* (London: Swan Sonnenschein, 1896), 1:27–30.

9. Hugh Connolly, *The Irish Penitentials and Their Significance for the Sacrament of Penance Today* (Dublin: Four Courts Press, 1995), 14.

10. Ibid., 32.

11. Ibid., 19, 131.

12. Foucault, "About the Beginning," 204.

13. Michel Foucault, *Abnormal: Lectures at the Collège de France, 1974–1975*, trans. Graham Burchell (New York: Picador, 2003), 175.

14. Ibid., 184.

15. Ibid., 185–86, 188.

16. Michel Foucault, *The History of Sexuality*, vol. 1, trans. Robert Hurley (New York: Pantheon, 1978), 19.

17. Foucault, *Abnormal*, 193.

18. Ibid., 202–3.

19. Foucault, *The History of Sexuality*, 1:61–62.

20. Richard Ellmann, *James Joyce*, 2nd ed. (Oxford: Oxford University Press, 1982), 49.

21. James M. O'Toole, "In the Court of Conscience: American Catholics and Confession, 1900–1975," in *Habits of Devotion: Catholic Religion Practice in Twentieth-Century America*, ed. James M. O'Toole (Ithaca, NY: Cornell University Press, 2004), 131–32.

22. Louise Fuller, *Irish Catholicism since 1950: The Undoing of a Culture* (Dublin: Gill and Macmillan, 2002), 21.

23. Tom Inglis, *Moral Monopoly: The Catholic Church in Modern Irish Society* (Dublin: Gill and Macmillan, 1987), 26.

24. S. J. Connolly, *Priests and People in Pre-Famine Ireland, 1780–1845* (Dublin: Gill and Macmillan, 1982), 122.

25. Qtd. in Inglis, *Moral Monopoly*, 149–50.

26. Patrick J. Corish, *The Irish Catholic Experience: A Historical Survey* (Wilmington, DE: Michael Glazier, 1985), 134.

27. William Carleton, *The Station; The Party Fight and Funeral; The Lough Derg Pilgrim. Traits and Stories of the Irish Peasantry, Part 2* (Bibliobazaar, 2007), 45.

28. Corish, *The Irish Catholic Experience*, 178–79, 211–12.

29. Austin Clarke, *Selected Poems*, ed. W. J. McCormack (London: Penguin Books, 1992), 214.

30. Gregory Schirmer, *The Poetry of Austin Clarke* (Notre Dame, IN: University of Notre Dame Press, 1983), 26.

31. Maurice Harmon, *Austin Clarke: A Critical Introduction* (Dublin: Wolfhound Press, 1989), 35.

32. Austin Clarke, *Collected Poems*, ed. R. Dardis Clarke (Manchester: Carcanet Press/The Bridge Press, 2008), 113. Hereafter, cited as *CPC* in text.

33. Harmon, *Austin Clarke*, 70.

34. See W. J. McCormark's note, Clarke, *Selected Poems*, 214–15.

35. Harmon, *Austin Clarke*, 70.

36. Michael Carroll, *Irish Pilgrimage: Holy Wells and Popular Catholic Devotion* (Baltimore, MD: Johns Hopkins University Press, 1999), 37–39.

37. Ibid., 39.

38. Vivian Mercier, "Mortal Anguish, Mortal Pride: Austin Clarke's Religious Lyrics," *Irish University Review* 4 (Spring 1974): 98.

39. G. Craig Tapping, *Austin Clarke: A Study of His Writings* (Dublin: Academy Press, 1981), 165.

40. Austin Clarke, *A Penny in the Clouds* (London: Routledge and Kegan Paul, 1968), 43.

41. See Clarke's note on this poem in *Collected Poems*, 545.

42. Gearóid Denvir, "Literature in Irish, 1800–1890: From the Act of Union to the Gaelic League," in *The Cambridge History of Irish Literature, Vol. 1 to 1890*, ed. Margaret Kelleher and Philip O'Leary (Cambridge: Cambridge University Press, 2006), 583.

43. Harmon, *Austin Clarke*, 83. In contrast to Harmon, Schirmer asserts that the poem "mocks" the speaker's attitude; see Schirmer, *The Poetry of Austin Clarke*, 49.

44. In an oft-quoted note to *Pilgrimage and Other Poems*, Clarke refers to how "assonance, more elaborate in Gaelic than in Spanish poetry, takes the clapper from the bell of rhyme. In simple patterns, the tonic word at the end of the line is supported by a vowel-rhyme in the middle of the next line." He goes on to suggest how such a technique may be approximated in English through the use of "cross-rhymes or vowel-rhyming, separately, one or more of the syllables of longer words, on or off accent . . ." (*Collected Poems*, 544).

45. Schirmer, *The Poetry of Austin Clarke*, 60.

46. Clarke, *Twice Round the Black Church*, 137.

47. See Clarke's note on this poem in *Collected Poems*, 546.

48. John Goodby offers a similar reading, asserting that the "eating of horses, thus becomes synonymous with the devouring of our creaturely selves, a denial of the body." John Goodby, "The Poetry of Austin Clarke," in *The Cambridge Companion to Contemporary Irish Poetry*, ed. Matthew Campbell (Cambridge: Cambridge University Press, 2003), 30.

49. Michel Foucault, *Psychiatric Power: Lectures at the Collège de France, 1973–1974*, ed. Jacques Lagrange, trans. Graham Burchell (London: Palgrave Macmillan, 2006), 77.

50. David Wheatley, "The Mercyseat and 'The Mansion of Forgetfulness': Samuel Beckett's *Murphy*, Austin Clarke's 'Mnemosyne Lay in Dust,' and Irish Poetic Modernism," *English Studies* 83 (December 2002): 535.

51. Maud Ellmann, *The Hunger Artists: Starving, Writing, and Imprisonment* (Cambridge, MA: Harvard University Press, 1993), 15. Using examples as varied as Richardson's Clarissa and the Irish hunger strikers at Long Kesh, Ellmann analyzes self-starvation as a form of resistance.

52. Wheatley, "The Mercyseat and 'The Mansion of Forgetfulness,'" 536.

53. Neil Corcoran, "The Blessings of Onan: Austin Clarke's *Mnemosyne Lay in Dust*," *Irish University Review* 13, no. 1 (Spring 1983): 46–47.

54. Thomas Duddy, *A History of Irish Thought* (London: Routledge, 2002), 38–39; Deirdre Carabine, *John Scottus Eriugena* (New York: Oxford University Press, 2000), 111.

55. Duddy, *A History of Irish Thought*, 39.

56. Ed Madden, writing from the perspective of contemporary queer theory, sees these late Clarke poems as still caught in the throes of heterosexism. Regardless of such lapses, the poems, when viewed in their cultural context, strike me as remarkably forward-looking in their acceptance of forms of sexuality that diverge from the heterosexual norm. See Madden's *Tiresian Poetics: Modernism, Sexuality, Voice, 1888–2001* (Cranbury, NJ: Fairleigh Dickinson University Press, 2008), 218–54.

2. Kavanagh's Parochialism: A Catholic Poetics of Place

1. Patrick Kavanagh, *Collected Poems*, ed. Antoinette Quinn (London: Penguin, 2005), 184. Hereafter, cited as *CPK* in text.

2. See S. T. Coleridge, "Lectures on Literature, #xiii," in *Imagination in Coleridge*, ed. John Spencer Hill (Totowa, NJ: Rowan and Littlefield, 1978), 171.

3. Patrick Kavanagh, *Collected Pruse* (London: MacGibbon and Kee, 1967), 282.

4. Declan Kiberd, *Irish Classics* (London: Granta Books, 2000), 599–600.

5. Kavanagh, *Collected Pruse*, 283.

6. Antoinette Quinn, *Patrick Kavanagh: A Critical Study* (Syracuse, NY: Syracuse University Press, 1991), 207. Whatever interpretive quibbles I might have with Quinn, like all who write on Kavanagh, I am deeply indebted to her assiduous work in producing the first comprehensive edition of his poetry based on accepted principles of textual scholarship.

7. Patrick Kavanagh, *A Poet's Country: Selected Prose*, ed. Antoinette Quinn (Dublin: Lilliput Press, 2003), 201.

8. Philip Sheldrake, *Spaces for the Sacred: Place, Memory, and Identity* (Baltimore, MD: Johns Hopkins University Press, 2001), 64.

9. Ibid., 62, 31.

10. Ibid., 64.

11. For a representative example, see Jonathan Allison, "Patrick Kavanagh and Anti-pastoral," in *The Cambridge Companion to Contemporary Irish Poetry*, ed. Matthew Campbell (Cambridge: Cambridge University Press, 2003), 42–58.

12. Quinn, *Patrick Kavanagh: A Critical Study*, 34. For a brief description of the sacramentality of Kavanagh's poetry, see Tom Stark, introduction to *No Earthly Estate: God and Patrick Kavanagh: An Anthology*, ed. Tom Stark (Dublin: Columba Press, 2002), 16–18.

13. Lene Klejs, "Seed Like Stars: Kavanagh's Nature," *Eire-Ireland* 18 (Spring 1983): 104.

14. Charles Taylor, *A Secular Age* (Cambridge, MA: Harvard University Press, 2007), 462–63. Such folk religious practices were in the past typically denigrated by scholars as mere superstition or as a corruption of the normative official religion. However, more recent studies of such phenomena have revealed the richness of the interplay of Christianity and "pagan" animism embodied in folk religion as well as the dynamism of its relationship to the prescribed doctrinal faith. See in particular, Ellen Badone, introduction, 3–21, and Jane Schneider, "Spirits and the Spirit of Capitalism," 24–54, in *Religious Orthodoxy and Popular Faith in European Society*, ed. Ellen Badone (Princeton, NJ: Princeton University Press, 1990) as well as William Christian Jr., *Local Religion in Sixteenth-Century Spain* (Princeton, NJ: Princeton University Press, 1981). Charles Taylor, drawing largely from scholarship focused on nineteenth-century France, condenses much of the current scholarly understanding of local religion. Despite falling prey to the reductionist view of folk religion as a debasement of its official counterpart, Kevin Whelan provides a succinct description of this phenomenon in an Irish context: "folk religion, based on the detritus of older religious modes and debased Christian motifs, . . . was strongest in the countryside, linked as it was to an animistic view of the universe and deriving much of its potency from calendar custom and awareness of a symbiotic relationship with nature. This rich vernacular sub-culture flourished most in self-contained traditional communities where

literacy and contact with the outside world was at a minimum" (2). See Kevin Whelan, "The Catholic Parish, the Catholic Chapel, and Village Development in Ireland," *Irish Geography* 16 (1983): 1–16.

15. Emmet Larkin, "The Devotional Revolution in Ireland, 1850–75," *American Historical Review* 77 (June 1972): 625–52.

16. Lawrence Taylor, *Occasions of Faith: An Anthropology of Irish Catholics.* (1995; reprint, Dublin: Lilliput Press, 1997), 58, 54.

17. Conchubhair Ó Fearghail, "The Evolution of Catholic Parishes in Dublin City from the Sixteenth to the Nineteenth Centuries," in *Dublin City and County: From Prehistory to Present,* ed. F.H.A. Aalen and Kevin Whalen (Dublin: Geography Press, 1992), 229; Patrick Kavanagh, *November Haggard: Uncollected Prose and Verse of Patrick Kavanagh,* ed. Peter Kavanagh (New York: Kavanagh Press, 1971), 69–70.

18. Charles Taylor, *A Secular Age,* 463, 443.

19. Ibid., 462–63.

20. Ó Fearghail, "The Evolution of Catholic Parishes," 229.

21. Lawrence Taylor, *Occasions of Faith,* 54.

22. Michael Carroll, *Irish Pilgrimage: Holy Wells and Popular Catholic Devotion* (Baltimore, MD: Johns Hopkins University Press, 1999), 20–21.

23. S. J. Connolly, *Priests and People in Pre-Famine Ireland, 1780–1845* (Dublin: Gill and Macmillan, 1982), 135–36; Lawrence Taylor, *Occasions of Faith,* 35–38.

24. S. J. Connolly, *Priests and People,* 138–48.

25. Kevin Whelan, "The Catholic Parish," 8–9. Whelan notes that the chapel-village was particularly prevalent in the "drumlin belt" of Monaghan, Cavan, and Leitrim (13). See also Lawrence Taylor, *Occasions of Faith,* 58.

26. Lawrence Taylor, *Occasions of Faith,* 67.

27. Ibid., 73.

28. Antoinette Quinn notes that it is unclear whether the description is derived from Kavanagh's own participation or from secondhand reports, *Patrick Kavanagh: A Critical Study,* 171–72.

29. Excerpted in Kavanagh, *Collected Pruse,* 69, 71–72.

30. Ibid., 72–73.

31. Ibid., 73–74.

32. Lawrence Taylor, *Occasions of Faith,* 46.

33. On the time frame for the composition and publication of this poem, see Quinn's note, Kavanagh, *Collected Poems,* 266.

34. Ibid., 267.

35. Lawrence Taylor, *Occasions of Faith,* 64–65.

36. Quinn, *Patrick Kavanagh: A Critical Study,* 214, 211.

37. William Christian Jr., *Local Religion in Sixteenth-Century Spain* (Princeton, NJ: Princeton University Press, 1981), 158.

38. Quinn interprets these lines differently, suggesting of Father Mat that "as a pagan poet he felt 'unhomed'" (*Patrick Kavanagh: A Critical Study*, 214). But the placement of the lines is problematic for such a reading since they immediately precede his renunciation of his "pagan" faith.

39. Sheldrake, *Spaces for the Sacred*, 114–15.

40. Lawrence Taylor, *Occasions of Faith*, 191.

41. Kavanagh, *A Poet's Country*, 272.

42. Michel de Certeau, *The Practice of Everyday Life*, trans. Steven Rendall (Berkeley: University of California Press, 1984), 109.

43. Patrick Kavanagh, *Collected Pruse*, 283.

44. Sheldrake, *Spaces for the Sacred*, 31.

45. This felicitous label comes from John McAuliffe, "Urban Hymns: The City, Desire, and Theology in Austin Clarke and Patrick Kavanagh," in *Critical Ireland: New Essays in Literature and Culture*, ed. Alan Gillis and Aaron Kelly (Dublin: Four Courts Press, 2001), 166–73.

46. Antoinette Quinn, *Patrick Kavanagh: A Biography* (Dublin: Gill and Macmillan, 2001), 200.

47. Antoinette Quinn, *Patrick Kavanagh: A Critical Study*, 171.

48. Victor Turner and Edith Turner, *Image and Pilgrimage in Christian Culture: Anthropological Perspectives* (New York: Columbia University Press, 1978), 136.

49. Quinn's claim that this poem is based upon "the myth of Ireland as a spiritual entity" overlooks the poem's extensive critique of the standardizing impetus inherent in this nationalist mythos. See Antoinette Quinn, *Patrick Kavanagh: A Critical Study*, 190.

50. Lawrence Taylor associates the Lough Derg pilgrimage with the Turner's concept of *communitas* but only elaborates briefly upon this connection. See *Occasions of Faith*, 193, 197.

51. Turner and Turner, *Image and Pilgrimage*, 250–51.

52. Ibid., 135.

53. Kavanagh, *A Poet's Country*, 106.

54. See Antoinette Quinn's note, Kavanagh, *Collected Poems*, 275–76.

55. Seamus Heaney, *The Government of the Tongue: Selected Prose, 1978–1987* (New York: Farrar, Straus, and Giroux, 1989), 5; hereafter cited as *GT* in the text.

56. Quinn, *Patrick Kavanagh: A Critical Study*, 400.

57. Michel Foucault, "Different Spaces," in *Aesthetics, Method, and Epistemology*, ed. James Faubion; trans. Robert Hurley et al. (New York: New Press, 1998), 175–86.

58. Joe Cleary, *Outrageous Fortune: Capital and Culture in Modern Ireland* (Dublin: Field Day Publications, 2007), 153, n. 72. Cleary's designation of this suburban space as a "domesticated neutralized landscape" does not, however, do justice to the dynamic hybridity that characterizes this zone in Kavanagh's Canal Bank poems.

59. Kavanagh, *November Haggard*, 45.

60. Kavanagh, *A Poet's Country*, 244.

61. De Certeau, *The Practice of Everyday Life*, 106.

62. Ibid., 106.

3. Partition and Communion in John Montague's Poetry

1. John Montague, *Collected Poems* (Winston-Salem, NC: Wake Forest University Press, 1995), 157. Hereafter cited as *CPM* in text.

2. The influence of Williams on Montague was noted early by Thomas Redshaw, the foremost scholarly advocate for Montague's poetry; Thomas D. Redshaw, "Location as Vocation: John Montague's 'The Northern Gate,'" *Canadian Journal of Irish Studies* 5, no. 2 (1979): 38. See also Paul Bowers, "John Montague and William Carlos Williams: Nationalism and Poetic Construction," *Canadian Journal of Irish Studies* 20, no. 2 (1994): 29–44.

3. John Montague, *The Figure in the Cave and Other Essays*, ed. Antoinette Quinn (Syracuse, NY: Syracuse University Press, 1989), 40; Seamus Deane, *Celtic Revivals* (Winston-Salem, NC: Wake Forest University Press, 1985), 154.

4. Ibid., 153.

5. Montague, *The Figure in the Cave*, 3, 170.

6. Daragh Smyth, *A Guide to Irish Mythology* (Dublin: Irish Academic Press, 1988), 108.

7. John Montague, *The Pear Is Ripe: A Memoir* (Dublin: Liberties Press, 2007), 181.

8. John Montague, "Revolution and the Shaping of Modern Ireland: A Reply to Conor Cruise O'Brien," in *The Celtic Consciousness*, ed. Robert O'Driscoll (New York: George Braziller, 1982), 438.

9. James Gleick, *Chaos: Making a New Science* (New York: Viking Press, 1987), 21–23.

10. Steven Matthews, *Irish Poetry: Politics, History, Negotiation: The Evolving Debate, 1969 to the Present* (New York, St. Martin's Press, 1997), 124.

11. Thomas Redshaw's "The Bounding Line: John Montague's *A New Siege* (1970)," *Canadian Journal of Irish Studies* 13, no. 1 (Spring 1987): 79–81. Redshaw's detailed analysis of the lineation of "A New Siege" highlights the dynamism of Montague's adaptation of the Anglo-Saxon hemistich.

12. Matthews, *Irish Poetry*, 131.

13. Nicholas Lash, *His Presence in the World: A Study of Eucharistic Worship and Theology* (Dayton, OH: Pflaum Press, 1968), 143.

14. John Montague, "Revolution and the Shaping of Modern Ireland," 437.

15. Steve Bruce, *Paisley: Religion and Politics in Northern Ireland* (Oxford: Oxford University Press, 2007), 46.

16. Ibid., 42–49.

17. This first appeared in the 1972 version of "The Bread God" that was incorporated in *The Rough Field*.

18. Bruce, *Paisley*, 48.

19. Jean-Luc Marion, *God Without Being*, trans. Thomas Carlson (Chicago: University of Chicago Press, 1991), 164.

20. Sarah Beckwith, *Christ's Body: Identity, Culture, and Society in Late Medieval Writings* (London: Routledge, 1993), 34. In rural Ireland even in the early twenty-first century, the Corpus Christi procession still functions as, to quote Beckwith, "a spectacle which stages community" (34).

21. David G. Holmes, "The Eucharistic Congress of 1932 and Irish Identity," *New Hibernia Review* 4, no. 1 (Spring 2000): 68.

22. Rev. P. Canon Boylan, ed., *Dublin—The Book of the Congress, 1932* (Wexford, Ireland: John English Press, 1934), 1:17–18.

23. Helena Concannon, *The Blessed Eucharist in Irish History* (Dublin: Browne and Nolan, 1932), 444.

24. Rev. P. Canon Boylan, ed., *Dublin—The Book of the Congress, 1932*, (Wexford, Ireland: John English Press, 1934), 2:434–35.

25. Holmes, "The Eucharistic Congress of 1932," 77.

26. Marion, *God Without Being*, 172.

27. Thomas Redshaw, "The Surviving Sign: John Montague's *The Bread God* (1968)," *Éire-Ireland* 17, no. 2 (Summer 1982): 78.

28. Marion, *God Without Being*, 175–76.

29. Liam Ó Dochartaigh, "*Ceol na mBréag*: Gaelic Themes in *The Rough Field*," *Well Dreams: Essays on John Montague*, ed. Thomas Redshaw (Omaha, NE: Creighton University Press, 2004), 201–3.

30. John Montague, *The Bread God: A Lecture . . .* (Dublin: Dolmen Press, 1968), ix.

31. Ó Dochartaigh, "*Ceol na mBréag*," 205.

32. Qtd. in John Caputo, *The Prayers and Tears of Jacques Derrida: Religion without Religion* (Bloomington: Indiana University Press, 1997), 129.

33. Daniel Tobin, "'Lines of Leaving/Lines of Returning': John Montague's Double Vision," *Well Dreams: Essays on John Montague*, ed. Thomas Redshaw (Omaha, NE: Creighton University Press, 2004), 156–57.

34. Marion, *God Without Being*, 178; Lash, *His Presence in the World*, 154–56. Ben Howard identifies the poet's physician brother as "the exemplar of *caritas*, of selfless brotherly love," but does connect this to eucharistic theology. See Ben Howard, "Unexpected Affirmations: 'Border Sick Call' (1995) and 'The Three Last Things' (1997)," in *Well Dreams: Essays on John Montague*, ed. Thomas Redshaw (Omaha, NE: Creighton University Press, 2004), 356.

35. Alessandro Gentili, "*Purgatorialità:* Reading Montague *Sub Species Dantis*," in *Well Dreams*, 296. Gentili notes that "the hilly upland landscape of snow and ice recalls the downward expanse of ice in the ninth circle of Dante's Hell."

36. John Freccero, *Dante: The Poetics of Conversion*, ed. Rachel Jakoff (Cambridge, MA: Harvard University Press, 1986), 161–66.

37. In asserting that "'Border Sick Call' crosses state borders, but not the more fundamental religious or tribal ones," Elmer Kennedy-Andrews seems to presume that the gnome-like old man is Catholic, but neither his name (MacGurren) nor any of his statements

definitively identify him as either Catholic or Protestant. See Elmer Kennedy-Andrews, "John Montague: Global Regionalist?" *Cambridge Quarterly* 35, no. 1 (2006): 47.

38. Maurice Merleau-Ponty qtd. in David Michael Levin, *The Body's Recollection of Being: Phenomenological Psychology and the Deconstruction of Nihilism* (London: Routledge and Kegan Paul, 1985), 249.

4. Transcending Sacrifice: How Heaney Makes Room for the Marvelous

1. Karl Miller, *Seamus Heaney in Conversation with Karl Miller* (London: Between the Lines, 2000), 36.

2. See "La Toilette" in Seamus Heaney, *Station Island* (New York: Farrar, Straus, Giroux, 1985), 14.

3. John Desmond, *Gravity and Grace: Seamus Heaney and the Force of Light* (Waco, TX: Baylor University Press, 2009), 5, 12.

4. Peggy O'Brien, *Writing Lough Derg: From William Carleton to Seamus Heaney* (Syracuse, NY: Syracuse University Press, 2006), 163–64.

5. Henry Hart, *Seamus Heaney: Poet of Contrary Progressions* (Syracuse, NY: Syracuse University Press, 1992), 36.

6. Dennis O'Driscoll, *Stepping Stones: Interviews with Seamus Heaney* (New York: Farrar, Straus, Giroux, 2008), 39–40.

7. Seamus Heaney, "Pilgrim's Journey," *Poetry Book Society Bulletin* 123 (Winter 1984); qtd. in Michael Parker's *Seamus Heaney: The Making of a Poet* (Iowa City: University of Iowa Press, 1993), 183. For this obscure reference as well as others, I am indebted to Parker's careful bibliographic research.

8. Benedict Kiely, "A Raid into Dark Corners: The Poems of Seamus Heaney," *Hollins Critic* 7, no. 4 (October 1970): 10; qtd. in Hart, *Seamus Heaney*, 34.

9. Rev. Charles Hart, *The Student's Catholic Doctrine* (London: Burns, Oates, and Washbourne, 1916), 52, 54. In his interviews with Dennis O'Driscoll, Heaney identifies this as the central textbook used in his theological education at St. Columb's, but mistakenly refers to its title as *Hart's Christian Doctrine*, 38.

10. Ibid., 301–2.

11. Rev. John C. McQuaid, *Wellsprings of Faith* (Dublin: Clonmore and Reynolds, 1956), 35.

12. Seamus Deane, *Celtic Revivals* (Winston-Salem, NC: Wake Forest University Press, 1985), 181.

13. Ibid., 174.

14. Friedrich Nietzsche, *On the Genealogy of Morals and Ecce Homo*, trans. Walter Kaufmann (New York: Vintage, 1989), 62.

15. Ibid., 140.

16. Ibid., 91.

17. Ibid., 92.

18. Ibid., 38.

19. Seamus Heaney, *Poems, 1965–1975* (New York: Farrar, Strauss, and Giroux, 1980), 215. Hereafter cited as *P.*

20. John Caputo, *Deconstruction in a Nutshell: A Conversation with Jacques Derrida* (New York: Fordham University Press, 1997), 144–45.

21. Seamus Heaney, *The Redress of Poetry* (New York: Farrar, Straus, Giroux, 1995), 15. Hereafter cited in the text as *RP.*

22. Seamus Heaney, *Opened Ground: Selected Poems 1966–1996* (New York: Farrar, Straus, Giroux, 1998), 423. Hereafter cited as *OG* in the text.

23. J. Hillis Miller, *The Disappearance of God: Five Nineteenth-Century Writers* (Cambridge, MA: Harvard University Press, 1963), 318.

24. Seamus Heaney, *Preoccupations: Selected Prose, 1968–1978* (New York: Farrar, Strauss, and Giroux, 1980), 94.

25. Christopher Devlin, S.J., ed., *The Sermons and Devotional Writings of Gerard Manley Hopkins* (London: Oxford University Press, 1959), 195. In this passage, Hopkins links "uncreated grace" to his notion of *instress,* the idea that all things manifest a divinely infused force—"are charged with God . . . and give off sparks and take fire." Hillis Miller echoes this in defining instress as "the pervasive energy of being" (289).

26. O'Driscoll, *Stepping Stones,* 444.

27. For an alternative description of Heaney's notion of grace, see John Desmond, *Gravity and Grace: Seamus Heaney and the Force of Light* (Waco, TX: Baylor University Press, 2009). Drawing upon parallels between Heaney and Simone Weil, Desmond identifies the grace manifested in Heaney's poetry as unequivocally supernatural and transcendent.

28. Seamus Heaney, *Preoccupations,* 56.

29. See Helen Vendler, *Seamus Heaney* (Cambridge, MA: Harvard University Press, 1998), 48, 126; Daniel Tobin, *Passage to the Center: Imagination and the Sacred in the Poetry of Seamus Heaney* (Lexington: University of Kentucky Press, 1999), 120–24.

30. Jean-Luc Nancy, "The Unsacrificeable," trans. Richard Stamp and Simon Sparks in *A Finite Thinking,* ed. Simon Sparks (Stanford, CA: Stanford University Press, 2003). Nancy charges artistic renditions of sacrifice with "dismissing the wearisome horror and pale glamor of split blood" and "replacing it with a rapturous horror," 67.

31. Wallace Stevens, *The Collected Poems of Wallace Stevens* (New York: Knopf, 1955), 240.

32. O'Driscoll, *Stepping Stones,* 195.

33. Seamus Heaney, *Field Work* (New York: Farrar, Strauss, and Giroux, 1979), 11. Hereafter cited as *FW* in the text.

34. Joan Stambaugh, *The Other Nietzsche* (Albany: SUNY Press, 1994), 55.

35. O'Driscoll, *Stepping Stones,* 211.

36. Michael Parker argues similarly that the poem critiques this act of veneration as "primitive, servile, immature" and associates it with "the political and moral defeatism and passiveness which impeded the Catholics' spiritual growth" (158).

37. Deane, *Celtic Revivals*, 183.

38. Max Horkheimer and Theodor Adorno, *Dialectic of Enlightenment: Philosophical Fragments*, ed. Gunzelin Noerr; trans. Edmund Jephcott (Stanford, CA: Stanford University Press, 2002), 43.

39. Lawrence Taylor, *Occasions of Faith*, 194.

40. O'Driscoll, *Stepping Stones*, 232.

41. Ibid., 259.

42. F. P. Carey, *Lough Derg and Its Pilgrimage*, 3rd ed. (Dublin: Irish Messenger Press, 1939), 16, 20.

43. Parker, *Seamus Heaney*, 182–83.

44. Richard Kearney, *Navigations: Collected Irish Essays 1976–2006* (Syracuse, NY: Syracuse University Press, 2006), 33.

45. Ibid., 36.

46. Ibid., 35.

47. Qtd. in Padraig O'Malley, *Biting at the Grave: The Irish Hunger Strikes and the Politics of Despair* (Boston, MA: Beacon Press, 1990), 52.

48. Ibid., 109.

49. Ibid., 118.

50. Kearney, *Navigations*, 50.

51. Allen Feldman, *Formations of Violence: The Narrative of the Body and Political Terror in Northern Ireland* (Chicago: University of Chicago Press, 1991), 220–21.

52. Ibid., 238, 236, 255.

53. O'Driscoll, *Stepping Stones*, 259.

54. Danny Morrison, introduction to *Hunger Strike: Reflections on the 1981 Hunger Strike*, ed. Danny Morrison (Dingle, Ireland: Brandon, 2006), 11.

55. Hannah Arendt, *The Human Condition* (Chicago: University of Chicago Press, 1958), 178.

56. Seamus Heaney, *The Cure at Troy: A Version of Sophocles' Philoctetes* (New York: Farrar, Strauss, and Giroux, 1991), 77.

57. Tom Collins, *The Irish Hunger Strike* (Dublin: White Island Book, 1986), 155. The fact that Collins's book offers extended sympathetic portraits of each of the hunger strikers invests these details with even more credibility.

58. Seamus Heaney, *Station Island* (London: Faber and Faber, 1984), 84. Hereafter cited as *SI* in text.

59. W. B. Yeats, *The Poems*, ed. Daniel Albright (London: J. M. Dent, 1990), 255.

60. Seamus Heaney, "Envies and Identifications: Dante and the Modern Poet," in *Finders Keepers: Selected Prose 1971–2001* (New York: Farrar, Strauss, and Giroux, 2002), 193.

61. Ibid., 195.

62. Seamus Heaney, *Sweeney Astray: A Version from the Irish* (New York: Farrar, Strauss, and Giroux, 1983), ii.

63. Michael Parker, *Seamus Heaney*, 196–98.

64. Daniel Tobin, *Passage to the Center*, 183.

65. Seamus Heaney, *Among School Children: A John Malone Memorial Lecture* (Belfast: John Malone Memorial Committee, 1983), 114–15; qtd. in Michael Parker, *Seamus Heaney*, 272 n189.

66. O'Driscoll, *Stepping Stones*, 249.

67. Jean-Luc Marion, "The Reason of the Gift," trans. Shane Mackinley and Nicolas de Warren, in *Givenness and God: Questions of Jean-Luc Marion*, ed. Ian Leask and Eoin Cassidy (New York: Fordham University Press, 2005), 121.

68. Daniel Tobin, *Passage to the Center*, 187–88.

69. Seamus Heaney, "Leaving the Island," in *James Joyce and Modern Literature*, ed. W. J. McCormack and Alistair Stead (London: Routledge and Kegan Paul, 1982), 74. This phrase is taken from Heaney's headnote to the poem. For this earlier version of canto 12 of "Station Island," I am once again indebted to Michael Parker. See Parker, *Seamus Heaney*, 265 n107.

70. On Joyce's exposure of ressentiment as key feature of the colonial condition anatomized in *Dubliners*, see Seamus Deane, "Dead Ends: Joyce's Finest Moments," in *Semicolonial Joyce* (Cambridge: Cambridge University Press, 2000), 33.

71. Seamus Heaney, "Leaving the Island," 75.

72. James Joyce, *A Portrait of the Artist as a Young Man* (New York: Viking Press, 1964), 221.

73. Vendler, *Seamus Heaney*, 113, 119.

74. Ibid., 151.

75. Henry Hart, "What Is Heaney Seeing in Seeing Things?" *Colby Quarterly* 30, no. 1 (March 1994): 36.

76. Jean-Luc Marion, *Being Given: Toward a Phenomenology of Givenness*, trans. Jeffrey Kosky (Stanford, CA: Stanford University Press, 2002), 124.

77. John Caputo, *The Weakness of God: A Theology of the Event* (Bloomington: Indiana University Press, 2006), 74.

78. Seamus Heaney, *The Haw Lantern* (New York: Farrar, Strauss, and Giroux, 1987), 33.

79. Ibid., 33.

80. Seamus Heaney, *Seeing Things* (New York: Farrar, Strauss, and Giroux, 1991), 52. Hereafter cited as *ST* in the text.

81. Henry Hart, "What Is Heaney Seeing," 38.

82. O'Driscoll, *Stepping Stones*, 317.

83. The paradox here is described in phenomenological terminology by Jean-Luc Marion, who indicates that "when givenness no longer gives an object or a being, but rather a pure given . . . the alternative between a shortage and a saturation of intuition becomes undecidable." In other words, with the ultimate experiences of givenness, it is impossible to determine whether they involve "saturated phenomena," those in which what is received through the senses (intuition) exceeds our conceptual framework (intention) and "poor phenomena," where what is received is so attenuated that it cannot even be conceptually

registered. In short, with such revelations, one is left unable to "decide between excess and shortage." See Marion, *Being Given*, 245–46.

84. Vendler, *Seamus Heaney*, 138.

85. O'Driscoll, *Stepping Stones*, 320.

86. Tobin, *Passage to the Center*, 273.

87. Vendler, *Seamus Heaney*, 147; Stevens, *The Collected Poems*, 9.

88. O'Driscoll, *Stepping Stones*, 475.

89. T. S. Eliot, *The Complete Poems and Plays* (New York: Harcourt, Brace and World, 1971), 136.

90. O'Driscoll, *Stepping Stones*, 425.

91. Seamus Heaney, *The Spirit Level* (New York: Farrar, Strauss, and Giroux, 1996), 30.

5. Relics and Nuns in Eiléan Ní Chuilleanáin's Poetry: Sifting the Remains of Irish Catholicism

1. Audrey Healy and Eugene McCaffrey, OCD, *St Thérèse in Ireland: Official Diary of the Irish Visit, April–June 2001* (Dublin: Columba Press, 2001), 12.

2. Don Mullan, *A Gift of Roses: Memories of the Visit to Ireland of the Relics of St. Thérèse* (Dublin: Wolfhound Press, 2001), 15.

3. Healy and McCaffrey, *St Thérèse in Ireland*, 10. It is worth noting that a 2005 government investigation known as the Ferns Report identified Bishop Comiskey as being culpable for having failed to report cases of child abuse by clergy in his diocese.

4. An exception to this would be a group of women who hosted a conference on women's ordination in Ireland at the same time as the visit of the relics and who enlisted St. Thérèse in their cause on the basis of the saint's expression in her personal writings of a desire to be a priest. See Mullen, *A Gift of Roses*, 191–96.

5. Eiléan Ní Chuilleanáin, "Nuns: A Subject for a Woman Writer," in *My Self, My Muse: Irish Women Poets Reflect on Life and Art*, ed. Patricia Boyle Haberstroh (Syracuse, NY: Syracuse University Press, 2001), 22.

6. Peter Sirr, "'How Things Begin to Happen': Notes on Eiléan Ní Chuilleanáin and Medbh McGuckian," *Southern Review* 31 (1995): 459.

7. Ní Chuilleanáin, "Nuns," 22.

8. Ibid., 23.

9. Michael Taussig, *The Devil and Commodity Fetishism in South America* (Chapel Hill, NC: University of North Carolina Press, 1980), 35.

10. Ní Chuilleanáin, "Nuns," 22.

11. J. J. Lee, "Women and the Church since the Famine," in *Women in Irish Society: The Historical Dimension*, ed. Margaret Mac Curtain and Donncha Ó Corrain (Westwood, CT: Greenwood Press, 1979), 42.

12. Ní Chuilleanáin, "Nuns," 23, 21.

13. Caroline Walker Bynum, *Fragmentation and Redemption: Essays on Gender and the Human Body in Medieval Religion* (New York: Zone Books, 1992), 186–88.

14. Mary Peckham Magray, *The Transforming Power of the Nuns: Women, Religion, and Cultural Change in Ireland, 1750–1900* (Oxford: Oxford University Press, 1998), 93.

15. Emmanuel Levinas, *Collected Philosophical Papers*, trans. by Alphonso Lingis (Pittsburg, PA: Duquesne University Press, 1998), 102, 106.

16. Eiléan Ní Chuilleanáin, *The Brazen Serpent* (Winston-Salem, NC: Wake Forest University Press, 1995), 16. Hereafter cited as *BS* in the text.

17. Guinn Batten's interpretation of this poem's conclusion touches upon this point by associating "the secret authority of the sister's relics" with the "missing narrative of woman and desire." See Guinn Batten's "Boland, McGuckian, Ní Chuilleanáin, and the Body of the Nation," in *The Cambridge Companion to Contemporary Irish Poetry*, ed. Matthew Campbell (Cambridge: Cambridge University Press, 2003), 174.

18. Rosemary Raughter, ed., *Religious Women and Their History: Breaking the Silence* (Dublin: Irish Academic Press, 2005), 116–18.

19. Eiléan Ní Chuilleanáin, *The Magdalene Sermon* (Loughcrew, Ireland: Gallery Press, 1989), 29. Hereafter cited as *MS* in the text.

20. Paul Stanfield, "How She Looks in That Company: Eiléan Ní Chuilleanáin as Feminist Poet," in *Contemporary Irish Women Poets: Some Male Perspectives*, ed. Alexander Gonzalez (Westport, CT: Greenwood Press, 1999), 109.

21. C. B. Macpherson, *The Political Theory of Possessive Individualism: Hobbes to Locke* (Oxford: Oxford University Press, 1962), 3.

22. Margaret Mac Curtain, *Ariadne's Thread: Writing Women into Irish History* (Galway: Arlen House, 2008), 319.

23. Mary Peckham Magray, *The Transforming Power of the Nuns: Women, Religion, and Cultural Change in Ireland, 1750–1900* (Oxford: Oxford University Press, 1998), 47.

24. Mac Curtain, *Ariadne's Thread*, 315, 318.

25. Yvonne McKenna, *Made Holy: Irish Women Religious at Home and Abroad* (Dublin: Irish Academic Press, 2006), 92.

26. For an extensive summary and analysis of this case, see Tom Inglis, *Truth, Power, and Lies: Irish Society and the Case of the Kerry Babies* (Dublin: University College of Dublin Press, 2003).

27. James MacKillop, *Oxford Dictionary of Celtic Mythology* (Oxford: Oxford University Press, 2004), 76, 192.

28. John J. Delaney, *Dictionary of Saints* (New York: Doubleday, 1980), 493.

29. Ní Chuilleanáin, "Nuns," 22, 28.

30. Ibid., 26.

31. For an astute analysis of this film's reversion to gothic conventions in its representation of nuns, see Elizabeth Cullingford, "'Our Nuns Are *Not* a Nation': Politicizing the Convent in Irish Literature and Film," *Éire-Ireland* 41, no. 1 and 2 (2006): 9–38.

32. Delaney, *Dictionary of Saints*, 381–82.

33. Frances Finnegan, *Do Penance or Perish: Magdalen Asylums in Ireland* (Oxford: Oxford University Press, 2004), 161–65.

34. Eamon Grennan, *Facing the Music: Irish Poetry in the Twentieth Century* (Omaha: Creighton University Press, 1999), 284.

35. Ibid., 285.

36. James M. Smith, *Ireland's Magdalen Laundries and the Nation's Architecture of Containment* (Notre Dame, IN: University of Notre Dame Press, 2007).

37. Ibid., 19.

38. Ibid., 42.

39. Ní Chuilleanáin, "Nuns," 29.

40. Eiléan Ní Chuilleanáin, *The Girl Who Married the Reindeer* (Winston-Salem, NC: Wake Forest University Press, 2002), 4. Hereafter cited as *GWMR* in the text.

41. Margaret Mac Curtain, "Late in the Field: Catholic Sisters in Twentieth-Century Ireland," in *Chattel, Servant, or Citizen: Women's Status in Church, State, and Society*, ed. Mary O'Dowd and Sabine Wichert (Belfast: Queen's University Press, 1995), 39–40.

42. For a more general analysis of jouissance in Ní Chuilleanáin focusing upon her comments on Bernini's statue of St. Theresa of Avila and her penchant for the baroque, see Dillon Johnston, "'Our Bodies' Eyes and Writing Hands': Secrecy and Sensuality in Ní Chuilleanáin's Baroque Art," in *Gender and Sexuality in Modern Ireland*, ed. Anthony Bradley and Maryann Gialanella Valiulis (Amherst: University of Massachusetts Press, 1997), 207–8.

43. For a description of Mannix Flynn's "extallation," see Geraldine Meaney, "The Gothic Republic: Dark Imaginings and White Anxieties," in *Single Motherhood in Twentieth-Century Ireland: Cultural, Historical and Social Essays*, ed. Maria Cinta Ramblado-Minero and Auxiliadora Pérez-Valdes (Lewiston, NY: Edwin Mellen Press, 2006), 26, as well as Mary Raftery, "Taking Mary Home," *Irish Times*, 15 April 2004, http://ireland.com/newspaper/opinion. More recently, James Smith has provided a detailed account of Mannix Flynn's memorial as well as an insightful analysis of the significance of its geographical location; see Smith, *Ireland's Magdalen Laundries*, 177–81.

44. Meaney, "The Gothic Republic," 26.

45. Maurice Blanchot, *The Writing of the Disaster*, trans. Ann Smock (Lincoln: University of Nebraska, 1995), 51.

46. Patricia Coughlan similarly asserts that this poem evokes the parallels between the Magdalen inmates and the sisters who ran the asylums. But when she argues, mistakenly I believe, that the persona who speaks the poem's last stanza is solely "the nun in charge," she underplays the extent of this congruence and lessens the potency of the poem's conclusion. See Patricia Coughlan, "'No Lasting Fruit at All': Containing, Recognition, and Relinquishing in *The Girl Who Married the Reindeer*," *Irish University Review* 37, no. 1 (Spring/Summer 2007): 165–66.

47. Smith, *Ireland's Magdalen Laundries*, 42, 70, 78.

48. Ibid., 37–40.

49. Ibid., 40.

6. Paul Durcan's Priests: Refashioning Irish Masculinity

1. John A. Murphy, "Priests and People in Modern Irish History," *Christus Rex* 23, no. 4 (1969): 258.

2. Maurice Elliott, "Paul Durcan—Duarchain," in *Poetry in Contemporary Irish Literature*, ed. Michael Kenneally (Gerrards Cross, UK: Colin Smythe, 1995), 304–5.

3. Fintan O'Toole, "In Light of Things as They Are: Paul Durcan's Ireland," in *The Kilfenora Teaboy: A Study of Paul Durcan*, ed. Colm Tóibín (Dublin: New Island Books, 1996), 30.

4. Ibid., 32.

5. Nicola Tallant, "Kidnapped by His Family and Put in a Mental Home," *Irish Independent*, 6 May 2007, http://www.independent.ie/unsorted/migration/kidnapped-by-his-family-and-put-in-a-mental-home (accessed 16 May 2011).

6. Ibid.

7. George Mosse, *The Image of Man: The Creation of Modern Masculinity* (Oxford: Oxford University Press, 1996), 49, 56.

8. Joseph Valente, "'Neither Flesh Nor Fish'; or How 'Cyclops' Stages the Double-Bind of Irish Manhood," in *Semicolonial Joyce*, ed. Derek Attridge and Marjorie Howes (Cambridge: Cambridge University Press, 2000), 97–98.

9. Ibid., 103–6.

10. See Joseph Valente, *The Myth of Manliness in Irish National Culture, 1880–1922* (Urbana: University of Illinois Press, 2011), 27–61, for an exhaustive analysis of Parnell's role as an exemplary of Irish masculinity.

11. Joseph Nugent, "The Sword and the Prayerbook: Ideals of Authentic Irish Manliness," *Victorian Studies* 50, no. 4 (Summer 2008): 602.

12. Ibid., 608.

13. Paul Dubois, *Contemporary Ireland* [*L'Irlande Contemporaine*] (Paris, 1907; Dublin: Manusel and Co. 1908), 495. Qtd. in Joseph Nugent, "Producing Priestliness," PhD diss. University of California, Berkeley, 2004, 159.

14. Bruce Biever, S.J., *Religion, Culture, and Values: A Cross-Cultural Analysis of Motivational Factors in Native Irish and Irish American Catholicism* (New York: Arno Press, 1976), 264, 568. Biever suggests that if the issue of social respect were deleted from the statement that the disparity in responses between Irish Catholics and Irish Americans would not be quite as great.

15. Ibid., 270, 594.

16. Harry Ferguson, "Men and Masculinities in Late-Modern Ireland," in *A Man's World? Changing Men's Practices in a Globalized World*, ed. Bob Pease and Keith Pringle (London: Zed Books, 2001), 120.

17. Paul Durcan, *Life Is a Dream: Forty Years Reading Poems, 1967–2007* (London: Harvill Secker, 2009), 32. Hereafter cited as *LD* in text.

18. Nugent, "Producing Priestliness," 137–39.

19. Paul Durcan, *The Berlin Wall Café* (1985; London: Harvill Press, 1995), 15. Hereafter cited as *BWC* in text.

20. Ferguson, "Men and Masculinities," 120.

21. Ruth Garde, "Against Mussolini: Art and the Fall of a Dictator at the Estorick Collection November 18, 2010," *Words, Pictures, Objects: Writings on Exhibitions and the Visual Arts*, http://ruthgarde.wordpress.com (accessed 6 April 2011).

22. Jean Blanchard, *The Church in Contemporary Ireland* (Dublin: Clonmore and Reynolds, 1963), 17, 19. Qtd. in Tom Inglis, *Moral Monopoly: The Catholic Church in Modern Irish Society* (Dublin: Gill and Macmillan, 1987), 39.

23. Ibid., 39–40.

24. Qtd. in Chrystel Hug, *The Politics of Sexual Morality in Ireland* (New York: St. Martin's, 1999), 92.

25. Qtd. in Louise Fuller, *Irish Catholicism since 1950: The Undoing of a Culture* (Dublin: Gill and Macmillan, 2002), 211.

26. Hug, *The Politics of Sexual Morality*, 118–21.

27. *Love Is for Life: Pastoral Letter of the Irish Bishops* (Dublin: Veritas, 1985), http://www.ewtn.com/library/BISHOPS/LOVELIFE.HTM (accessed 2 May 2011), sec. 187.

28. Qtd. in Hug, *The Politics of Sexual Morality*, 40–41.

29. Elizabeth Butler Cullingford, *Gender and History in Yeats' Love Poetry* (Syracuse, NY: Syracuse University Press, 1996), 233.

30. Mikhail Bakhtin, *Problems of Dostoevsky's Poetics*, ed. and trans. Caryl Emerson (Minneapolis: University of Minnesota Press, 1984), 123.

31. Hug, *The Politics of Sexual Morality*, 62.

32. Shawn Pogatchnik, "Irish Leaders Propose Amendment to Strict Divorce Law," *The Day* [New London, CT], 14 September 1995, 16, http://news.google.com/newspapers (accessed 20 July 2012).

33. Paul Durcan, *Greetings to Our Friends in Brazil* (London: Harvill Press, 1999), 193. Hereafter cited as *GB*.

34. The fact that subsequent revelations suggested that Michelle Smith's athletic success and muscular frame may have been the result of illegal doping doesn't negate the point behind Durcan's poetic evocation of her.

35. Mosse, *The Image of Man*, 77.

36. Ibid., 166.

37. Robert Duncan, *Selected Poems: Revised and Enlarged*, ed. Robert Bertholf (New York: New Directions Press, 1997), 64.

38. M. M. Bakhtin, *The Dialogic Imagination*, ed. Michael Holquist, trans. Caryl Emerson and Michael Holquist (Austin: University of Texas Press, 1981), 296–98.

39. James Penner, *Pinks, Pansies, and Punks: The Rhetoric of Masculinity in American Literary Culture* (Bloomington: Indiana University Press, 2010), 123–24.

40. Ibid., 124.

41. Paul Durcan, *Cries of an Irish Caveman: New Poems* (London: Harvill, 2001), 90.

42. Daniel Boyarin, "Paul and the Genealogy of Gender," *Representations* 41 (Winter 1993): 16, 11.

43. Qtd. in Nugent, "Producing Priestliness," 147.

44. Ibid., 147–48.

45. Mary Kenny, *Goodbye to Catholic Ireland* (Springfield, IL: Templegate Publishers, 2000), 213, 206.

46. Donald Cozzens, *The Changing Face of the Priesthood* (Collegeville, MN: Liturgical Press, 2000), 5.

47. Qtd. in Cozzens, *The Changing Face*, 81.

48. Robert Nash, S.J., *Don't Be a Priest* (Dublin: Irish Messenger Service, 1971), 6–7.

49. For a particularly virulent example of such discourse, see Michael Rose, *Goodbye, Good Men: How Liberals Brought Corruption into the Catholic Church* (Washington, DC: Regnery Press, 2002).

50. Ferguson, "Men and Masculinities," 123.

51. Martin McLoone, *Film, Media, and Popular Culture: Cityscapes, Landscapes, Soundscapes* (Dublin: Irish Academic Press, 2008), 117–26.

52. James Joyce, *Ulysses* (New York: Vintage Press, 1986), 171.

53. Ibid., 170.

7. Paula Meehan's Revised Marianism: The Apparitions of "Our Lady of the Facts of Life"

1. Karen Steele succinctly describes the poem's connection to this cultural crisis. See "Refusing the Poisoned Chalice: The Sexual Politics of Rita Ann Higgins and Paula Meehan," in *Homemaking: Women Writers and the Politics and Poetics of Home*, ed. Catherine Wiley and Fiona Barnes (New York: Garland, 1995), 323–26.

2. Tim Ryan and Jurek Kirakowski, *Ballinspittle: Moving Statues and Faith* (Cork: Mercier Press, 1985), 41.

3. Fintan O'Toole, "Seeing Is Believing," in *Seeing Is Believing: Moving Statues in Ireland*, ed. Colm Tóibín (Mountrath, Ireland: Pilgrim Press, 1985), 93; James S. Donnelly Jr., "Opposing the 'Modern World': The Cult of the Virgin Mary in Ireland, 1965–85," *Éire-Ireland* 40, no. 1/2 (Spring/Summer 2005): 230.

4. Ryan and Kirakowski, *Ballinspittle*, 9–10, 41. The authors estimate the crowds at Ballinspittle as half a million, 70 percent of whom claimed to have witnessed some form of apparition.

5. For a fuller account of these incidents and their sociopolitical significance, see Moira Maguire, "The Changing Face of Catholic Ireland: Conservatism and Liberalism in the Ann Lovett and Kerry Babies Scandal," *Feminist Studies* 27, no. 2 (Summer 2001): 335–58.

6. Eamonn McCann, "A Most Impressive Scene to Behold," in *Seeing Is Believing: Moving Statues in Ireland*, ed. Colm Tóibín (Mountrath, Ireland: Pilgrim Press, 1985), 36.

7. See Nicholas Perry and Loreto Echeverría, *Under the Heel of Mary* (London: Routledge, 1998).

8. James S. Donnelly Jr., "The Peak of Marianism in Ireland, 1930–1960," in *Piety and Power in Ireland, 1760–1960: Essays in Honour of Emmet Larkin*, ed. Stewart J. Brown and David W. Miller (Notre Dame, IN: Notre Dame University Press, 2000), 252–83.

9. James S. Donnelly Jr., "Opposing the 'Modern World,'" 188–96, 239–45.

10. Eavan Boland, "When the Spirit Moves," *New York Review of Books* 42, no. 1 (12 January 1995): 25.

11. Ibid., 27. My thanks to Jody Allen Randolph for directing me to this essay.

12. Wallace Stevens, *The Collected Poems of Wallace Stevens* (New York: Knopf, 1955), 240.

13. Paula Meehan, "An Interview with Paula Meehan," with John Hobbs, *Nua: Studies in Contemporary Irish Writing* 1, no. 1 (1997): 66.

14. Paula Meehan, *Painting Rain* (Winston-Salem, NC: Wake Forest University Press, 2009), 65. Hereafter cited as *PR* in the text.

15. Margaret Mac Curtain, *Ariadne's Thread: Writing Women into Irish History* (Galway: Arden House, 2008), 107–8.

16. Richard Kearney, *Postnationalist Ireland: Politics, Culture, Philosophy* (London: Routledge, 1997), 119.

17. Paula Meehan, *The Man Who Was Marked by Winter* (Loughcrew, Ireland: Gallery Press, 1991; rpt. Cheney: Eastern Washington University Press, 1994), 44. Hereafter cited as *MW* in text.

18. Elizabeth Butler Cullingford, "Virgins and Mothers: Sinéad O'Connor, Neil Jordan, and *The Butcher Boy*," *Yale Journal of Criticism* 15, no. 1 (2002): 189.

19. Ibid., 190.

20. Elizabeth Johnson, "Mary and the Female Face of God," *Theological Studies* 50, no. 3 (1989): 506.

21. Paula Meehan, *Return and No Blame* (Dublin, Ireland: Beaver Row Press, 1984), 7. Hereafter cited as *RNB* in text.

22. Paula Meehan, *Reading the Sky* (Dublin, Ireland: Beaver Row Press, 1985), 41–42. Hereafter cited as *RS* in text.

23. Paula Meehan, *Pillow Talk* (Loughcrew, Ireland: Gallery Press, 1994), 16. Hereafter cited as *PT* in text.

24. Joe Cleary, *Outrageous Fortune: Capital and Culture in Modern Ireland* (Dublin: Field Day, 2007), 183.

25. Ibid., 184–85.

26. Ibid., 199.

27. Ibid., 199.

28. Meehan, "An Interview with Paula Meehan," with John Hobbs, 64.

29. For a fuller account of Meehan's use of the shapeshifter motif, see Kathryn Kirkpatrick, "Between Country and City: Paula Meehan's Eco-Feminist Poetics," in *Out of the Earth: Eco-Critical Readings of Irish Texts*, ed. Christine Cusick (Cork: Cork University Press, 2010), 108–26.

30. Paula Meehan, "An Interview with Paula Meehan," with Eileen O'Halloran and Kelli Maloy, *Contemporary Literature* 43, no. 1 (2002): 13.

31. Walter Benjamin, *The Writer of Modern Life: Essays on Charles Baudelaire*, ed. Michael Jennings, trans. Howard Eiland et al. (Cambridge, MA: Harvard University Press, 2006), 107–8.

32. Paula Meehan, *Dharmakaya* (Winston-Salem, NC: Wake Forest University Press, 2002), 45. Hereafter cited as *D* in the text.

33. Robert Thurman, introduction to *The Tibetan Book of the Dead*, trans. Robert Thurman (New York: Bantam Books, 1994), 48.

34. Charles Molesworth, *Gary Snyder's Vision: Poetry and the Real Work* (Columbia: University of Missouri Press, 1983), 82.

35. Elizabeth Johnson, "The Marian Tradition and the Reality of Women," *Horizons* 12, no. 1 (1985): 128.

36. Meehan, "An Interview with Paula Meehan," with Eileen O'Halloran and Kelli Maloy, 6.

37. Leonardo Boff, *The Maternal Face of God: The Feminine and Its Religious Expressions*, trans. Robert Barr and John Diercksmeier (San Francisco: Harper and Row, 1987), 185.

38. M. M. Bakhtin, *The Dialogic Imagination*, ed. Michael Holquist, trans. Caryl Emerson and Michael Holquist (Austin: University of Texas Press, 1981), 346, 342.

39. Tracy Brain, "'Nobody's Muse': Pillow Talk with Paula Meehan," *Reviewing Ireland* (1995): 311.

40. Meehan, "An Interview with Paula Meehan," with Eileen O'Halloran and Kelli Maloy, 20.

41. Brain, "'Nobody's Muse,'" 312.

42. Gerald Bruns, *On the Anarchy of Poetry and Philosophy: A Guide for the Unruly* (New York: Fordham University Press, 2006), 81.

Epilogue: Religion and Poetry in Post-Catholic Ireland

1. *The Wake Forest Series of Irish Poetry*, vol. 1, ed. Jefferson Holdridge (Winston-Salem, NC: Wake Forest University Press, 2005), 121.

2. Ibid., 121.

3. Ibid., 121–22.

4. Ibid., 123.

5. Philip Larkin, *Collected Poems* (New York: Farrar, Strauss, and Giroux, 2003), 58.

6. Seán Dunne, *The Road to Silence: An Irish Spiritual Odyssey* (Dublin: New Island Books, 1994), 18–32.

7. Dunne seems to have borrowed that phrase from Esther de Waal's *A Seven Day Journey with Thomas Merton* (Ann Arbor, MI: Servant Publications, 1992), 35. De Waal, in turn, attributes it to a catalogue for an exhibition of David Jones's art and poetry.

8. Seán Dunne, *Collected*, ed. Peter Fallon (Loughcrew: Gallery Books, 2005), 178.

9. Charles Taylor, *A Secular Age* (Cambridge, MA: Harvard University Press, 2007), 299–300.

10. Charles Taylor, *Dilemmas and Connections: Selected Essays* (Cambridge, MA: Harvard University Press, 2011), 255.

11. Dunne, *Collected*, 91.

Bibliography

Allison, Jonathan. "Patrick Kavanagh and Anti-pastoral." In *The Cambridge Companion to Contemporary Irish Poetry*, ed. Matthew Campbell, 42–58. Cambridge: Cambridge University Press, 2003.

Arendt, Hannah. *The Human Condition*. Chicago: University of Chicago Press, 1958.

Arnold, Matthew. "The Study of Poetry." In *Essays, English and American*, ed. Charles Eliot. New York: Collier, 1910.

Badone, Ellen, ed. *Religious Orthodoxy and Popular Faith in European Society*. Princeton, NJ: Princeton University Press, 1990.

Bakhtin, M. M. *The Dialogic Imagination*, ed. Michael Holquist; trans. Caryl Emerson and Michael Holquist. Austin: University of Texas Press, 1981.

———. *Problems of Dostoevsky's Poetics*, ed. and trans. Caryl Emerson. Minneapolis: University of Minnesota Press, 1984.

Batten, Guinn. "Boland, McGuckian, Ní Chuilleanáin, and the Body of the Nation." In *The Cambridge Companion to Contemporary Irish Poetry*, ed. Matthew Campbell, 169–88. Cambridge: Cambridge University Press, 2003.

Beckett, Samuel. *Disjecta: Miscellaneous Writings and a Dramatic Fragment*, ed. Ruby Cohn. New York: Grove Press, 1984.

Beckwith, Sarah. *Christ's Body: Identity, Culture, and Society in Late Medieval Writings*. London: Routledge, 1993.

Benjamin, Walter. *The Writer of Modern Life: Essays on Charles Baudelaire*, ed. Michael Jennings; trans. Howard Eiland et al. Cambridge, MA: Harvard University Press, 2006.

Biever, S.J., Bruce. *Religion, Culture, and Values: A Cross-Cultural Analysis of Motivational Factors in Native Irish and Irish American Catholicism*. New York: Arno Press, 1976.

Blanchot, Maurice. *The Writing of the Disaster*, trans. Ann Smock. Lincoln: University of Nebraska, 1995.

Boff, Leonardo. *The Maternal Face of God: The Feminine and Its Religious Expressions*, trans. Robert Barr and John Diercksmeier. San Francisco: Harper and Row, 1987.

Boland, Eavan. "When the Spirit Moves." *New York Review of Books* 42, no. 1 (12 January 1995): 25–28.

Bowers, Paul. "John Montague and William Carlos Williams: Nationalism and Poetic Construction." *Canadian Journal of Irish Studies* 20, no. 2 (1994): 29–44.

Boyarin, Daniel. "Paul and the Genealogy of Gender." *Representations* 41 (Winter 1993): 1–33.

Boyd, Ernest. *Ireland's Literary Renaissance*. New York: Knopf, 1916.

Boylan, Rev. P. Canon, ed. *Dublin—The Book of the Congress, 1932*, 2 vols. Wexford, Ireland: John English Press, 1934.

Brain, Tracy. "'Nobody's Muse': Pillow Talk with Paula Meehan," *Reviewing Ireland* (1995): 305–13.

Brooke, Stopford A. and T. W. Rolleston, eds. *A Treasury of Irish Poetry in the English Tongue*. London: Macmillan, 1900.

Brooker, Joseph. *Joyce's Critics: Transitions in Reading and Culture*. Madison: University of Wisconsin Press, 2004.

Bruce, Steve. *Paisley: Religion and Politics in Northern Ireland* Oxford: Oxford University Press, 2007.

Bruns, Gerald. *On the Anarchy of Poetry and Philosophy: A Guide for the Unruly*. New York: Fordham University Press, 2006.

Bynum, Caroline Walker. *Fragmentation and Redemption: Essays on Gender and the Human Body in Medieval Religion*. New York: Zone Books, 1992.

Caputo, John. *Deconstruction in a Nutshell: A Conversation with Jacques Derrida*. New York: Fordham University Press, 1997.

———. *The Prayers and Tears of Jacques Derrida: Religion without Religion*. Bloomington: Indiana University Press, 1997.

———. *The Weakness of God: A Theology of the Event*. Bloomington: Indiana University Press, 2006.

Carabine, Deirdre. *John Scottus Eriugena*. New York: Oxford University Press, 2000.

Carey, F. P. *Lough Derg and Its Pilgrimage*, 3rd ed. Dublin: Irish Messenger Press, 1939.

Carleton, William. *The Station; The Party Fight and Funeral; The Lough Derg Pilgrim. Traits and Stories of the Irish Peasantry, Part 2*. Bibliobazaar, 2007.

Carroll, Michael. *Irish Pilgrimage: Holy Wells and Popular Catholic Devotion*. Baltimore, MD: Johns Hopkins University Press, 1999.

Christian, Jr., William. *Local Religion in Sixteenth-Century Spain* Princeton, NJ: Princeton University Press, 1981.

Clarke, Austin. *Collected Poems*, ed. R. Dardis Clarke. Manchester: Carcanet Press/ The Bridge Press, 2008.

———. *A Penny in the Clouds.* London: Routledge and Kegan Paul, 1968.

———. *Selected Poems*, ed. W. J. McCormack. London: Penguin Books, 1992.

———. *Twice Round the Black Church*, 2nd ed. Dublin: Moytura Press, 1990.

Cleary, Joe. *Outrageous Fortune: Capital and Culture in Modern Ireland.* Dublin: Field Day, 2007.

Coleridge, S. T. "Lectures on Literature, #xiii." In *Imagination in Coleridge*, ed. John Spencer Hill. Totowa, NJ: Rowan and Littlefield, 1978.

Collins, Tom. *The Irish Hunger Strike.* Dublin: White Island Book, 1986.

Concannon, Helena. *The Blessed Eucharist in Irish History.* Dublin: Browne and Nolan, 1932.

Connolly, Hugh. *The Irish Penitentials and Their Significance for the Sacrament of Penance Today.* Dublin: Four Courts Press, 1995.

Connolly, S. J. *Priests and People in Pre-Famine Ireland, 1780–1845.* Dublin: Gill and Macmillan, 1982.

Corcoran, Neil. "The Blessings of Onan: Austin Clarke's *Mnemosyne Lay in Dust.*" *Irish University Review* 13, no. 1 (Spring 1983): 43–53.

Corish, Patrick J. *The Irish Catholic Experience: A Historical Survey.* Wilmington, DE: Michael Glazier, 1985.

Corkery, Daniel. *Synge and Anglo-Irish Literature.* Dublin: Cork University Press, 1931.

Coughlan, Patricia. "'No Lasting Fruit at All': Containing, Recognition, and Relinquishing in *The Girl Who Married the Reindeer.*" *Irish University Review* 37, no. 1 (Spring/Summer 2007): 157–77.

Cozzens, Donald. *The Changing Face of the Priesthood.* Collegeville, MN: Liturgical Press, 2000.

Cullingford, Elizabeth Butler. *Gender and History in Yeats' Love Poetry.* Syracuse, NY: Syracuse University Press, 1996.

———. "'Our Nuns Are *Not* a Nation': Politicizing the Convent in Irish Literature and Film." *Éire-Ireland* 41, nos. 1 and 2 (2006): 9–38.

———. "Virgins and Mothers: Sinéad O'Connor, Neil Jordan, and *The Butcher Boy.*" *Yale Journal of Criticism* 15, no. 1 (2002): 185–210.

de Certeau, Michel. *The Practice of Everyday Life*, trans. Steven Rendall. Berkeley: University of California Press, 1984.

de Waal, Esther. *A Seven Day Journey with Thomas Merton*. Ann Arbor, MI: Servant Publications, 1992.

Deane, Seamus. *Celtic Revivals*. Winston-Salem, NC: Wake Forest University Press, 1985.

———. "Dead Ends: Joyce's Finest Moments." In *Semicolonial Joyce*, ed. Derek Attridge and Marjorie Howe, 21–36. Cambridge: Cambridge University Press, 2000.

Delaney, John J. *Dictionary of Saints*. New York: Doubleday, 1980.

Deming, Robert, ed. *James Joyce: A Critical Heritage*, vol. 1, *1902–1927*. New York: Barnes and Noble, 1970.

Denvir, Gearóid. "Literature in Irish, 1800–1890: From the Act of Union to the Gaelic League." In *The Cambridge History of Irish Literature, Vol. 1 to 1890*, ed. Margaret Kelleher and Philip O'Leary, 544–98. Cambridge: Cambridge University Press, 2006.

Desmond, John. *Gravity and Grace: Seamus Heaney and the Force of Light*. Waco, TX: Baylor University Press, 2009.

Devlin, S.J., Christopher, ed. *The Sermons and Devotional Writings of Gerard Manley Hopkins*. London: Oxford University Press, 1959.

Devlin, Denis. *Collected Poems*, ed. J.C.C. Mays. Winston-Salem, NC: Wake Forest University Press, 1989.

Donnelly, Jr., James S. "Opposing the 'Modern World': The Cult of the Virgin Mary in Ireland, 1965–85." *Éire-Ireland* 40, no. 1/2 (Spring/Summer 2005): 183–245.

———. "The Peak of Marianism in Ireland, 1930–1960." In *Piety and Power in Ireland, 1760–1960: Essays in Honour of Emmet Larkin*, ed. Stewart J. Brown and David W. Miller, 252–83. Notre Dame, IN: Notre Dame University Press, 2000.

Duddy, Thomas. *A History of Irish Thought*. London: Routledge, 2002.

Dunne, Seán. *Collected*, ed. Peter Fallon. Loughcrew: Gallery Books, 2005.

———. *The Road to Silence: An Irish Spiritual Odyssey*. Dublin: New Island Books, 1994.

Duncan, Robert. *Selected Poems: Revised and Enlarged*, ed. Robert Bertholf. New York: New Directions Press, 1997.

Durcan, Paul. *The Berlin Wall Café*. 1985. Reprint, London: Harvill Press, 1995.

———. *Cries of an Irish Caveman: New Poems*. London: Harvill Press, 2001.

———. *Greetings to Our Friends in Brazil*. London: Harvill Press, 1999.

———. *Life Is a Dream: Forty Years Reading Poems, 1967–2007*. London: Harvill Secker, 2009.

Eliot, T. S. "Religion and Literature." In *Selected Essays.* New York: Harcourt, Brace, and World, 1950.

———. *The Complete Poems and Plays.* New York: Harcourt, Brace and World, 1971.

———. *The Use of Poetry and the Use of Criticism.* Cambridge, MA: Harvard University Press, 1933.

Elliott, Maurice. "Paul Durcan—Duarchain." In *Poetry in Contemporary Irish Literature,* ed. Michael Kenneally, 304–28. Gerrards Cross, UK: Colin Smythe, 1995.

Ellmann, Maud. *The Hunger Artists: Starving, Writing, and Imprisonment* Cambridge, MA: Harvard University Press, 1993.

Ellmann, Richard. *James Joyce,* 2nd ed. Oxford: Oxford University Press, 1982.

Feldman, Allen. *Formations of Violence: The Narrative of the Body and Political Terror in Northern Ireland.* Chicago: University of Chicago Press, 1991.

Ferguson, Harry. "Men and Masculinities in Late-Modern Ireland." In *A Man's World? Changing Men's Practices in a Globalized World,* ed. Bob Pease and Keith Pringle, 118–34. London: Zed Books, 2001.

Finnegan, Frances. *Do Penance or Perish: Magdalen Asylums in Ireland.* Oxford: Oxford University Press, 2004.

Foucault, Michel. *Abnormal: Lectures at the Collège de France, 1974–1975,* trans. Graham Burchell. New York: Picador, 2003.

———. "About the Beginning of the Hermeneutics of the Self: Two Lectures at Dartmouth," *Political Theory* 21 (May 1993): 198–227.

———. "Different Spaces" in *Aesthetics, Method, and Epistemology,* ed. James Faubion; trans. Robert Hurley et al. New York: New Press, 1998.

———. *The History of Sexuality,* vol. 1, trans. Robert Hurley. New York: Pantheon, 1978.

———. *Psychiatric Power: Lectures at the Collège de France, 1973–1974,* ed. Jacques Lagrange; trans. Graham Burchell. London: Palgrave Macmillan, 2006.

Freccero, John. *Dante: The Poetics of Conversion,* ed. Rachel Jakoff. Cambridge, MA: Harvard University Press, 1986.

Fuller, Louise. *Irish Catholicism since 1950: The Undoing of a Culture.* Dublin: Gill and Macmillan, 2002.

Garde, Ruth. "Against Mussolini: Art and the Fall of a Dictator at the Estorick Collection November 18, 2010." *Words, Pictures, Objects: Writings on Exhibitions and the Visual Arts.* http://ruthgarde.wordpress.com (accessed 6 April 2011).

Geertz, Clifford. *The Interpretation of Cultures.* New York: Basic Books, 1973.

Gentili, Alessandro. "*Purgatorialità:* Reading Montague *Sub Species Dantis.*" In *Well Dreams: Essays on John Montague*, ed. Thomas Redshaw, 289–99. Omaha, NE: Creighton University Press, 2004.

Gleick, James. *Chaos: Making a New Science.* New York: Viking Press, 1987.

Goodby, John. "The Poetry of Austin Clarke." In *The Cambridge Companion to Contemporary Irish Poetry*, ed. Matthew Campbell, 21–41. Cambridge: Cambridge University Press, 2003.

———. "'The Prouder Counsel of Her Throat': Towards a Feminist Reading of Austin Clarke." *Irish University Review* 29 (Autumn/Winter 1999): 321–40.

Grennan, Eamon. *Facing the Music: Irish Poetry in the Twentieth Century.* Omaha, NE: Creighton University Press, 1999.

Harmon, Maurice. *Austin Clarke: A Critical Introduction.* Dublin: Wolfhound Press, 1989.

Hart, Rev. Charles. *The Student's Catholic Doctrine.* London: Burns, Oates, and Washbourne, 1916.

Hart, Henry. *Seamus Heaney: Poet of Contrary Progressions.* Syracuse, NY: Syracuse University Press, 1992.

———. "What Is Heaney Seeing in Seeing Things?" *Colby Quarterly* 30, no. 1 (March 1994): 33–42.

Healy, Audrey, and Eugene McCaffrey, OCD. *St Thérèse in Ireland: Official Diary of the Irish Visit, April–June 2001.* Dublin: Columba Press, 2001.

Heaney, Seamus. *The Cure at Troy: A Version of Sophocles' Philoctetes.* New York: Farrar, Strauss, and Giroux, 1991.

———. *Field Work.* New York: Farrar, Strauss, and Giroux, 1979.

———. "Envies and Identifications: Dante and the Modern Poet." In *Finders Keepers: Selected Prose 1971–2001*, 184–97. New York: Farrar, Strauss, and Giroux, 2002.

———. *The Government of the Tongue: Selected Prose, 1978–1987.* New York: Farrar, Straus, and Giroux, 1989.

———. *The Haw Lantern.* New York: Farrar, Strauss, and Giroux, 1987.

———. "Leaving the Island." In *James Joyce and Modern Literature*, ed. W. J. McCormack and Alistair Stead, 74–75. London: Routledge and Kegan Paul, 1982.

———. *Opened Ground: Selected Poems, 1966–1996.* New York: Farrar, Straus, Giroux, 1998.

———. *Poems, 1965–1975.* New York: Farrar, Strauss, and Giroux, 1980.

———. *Preoccupations: Selected Prose, 1968–1978.* New York: Farrar, Strauss, and Giroux, 1980.

———. *The Redress of Poetry*. New York: Farrar, Straus, Giroux, 1995.

———. *Seeing Things*. New York: Farrar, Strauss, and Giroux, 1991.

———. *The Spirit Level*. New York: Farrar, Strauss, and Giroux, 1996.

———. *Station Island*. New York: Farrar, Straus, Giroux, 1985.

———. *Sweeney Astray: A Version from the Irish*. New York: Farrar, Strauss, and Giroux, 1983.

Holdridge, Jefferson, ed. *The Wake Forest Series of Irish Poetry*, vol. 1. Winston-Salem, NC: Wake Forest University Press, 2005.

Holmes, David G. "The Eucharistic Congress of 1932 and Irish Identity." *New Hibernia Review* 4, no. 1 (Spring 2000): 55–78.

Horkheimer, Max, and Theodor Adorno. *Dialectic of Enlightenment: Philosophical Fragments*, ed. Gunzelin Noerr; trans. Edmund Jephcott. Stanford, CA: Stanford University Press, 2002.

Howard, Ben. "Unexpected Affirmations: 'Border Sick Call' (1995) and 'The Three Last Things' (1997)." In *Well Dreams: Essays on John Montague*, ed. Thomas Redshaw, 348–62. Omaha, NE: Creighton University Press, 2004.

Hug, Chrystel. *The Politics of Sexual Morality in Ireland*. New York: St. Martin's, 1999.

Inglis, Tom. *Moral Monopoly: The Catholic Church in Modern Irish Society*. Dublin: Gill and Macmillan, 1987.

———. *Truth, Power, and Lies: Irish Society and the Case of the Kerry Babies*. Dublin: University College of Dublin Press, 2003.

Johnson, Elizabeth. "The Marian Tradition and the Reality of Women." *Horizons* 12, no. 1 (1985): 116–35.

———. "Mary and the Female Face of God." *Theological Studies* 50, no. 3 (1989): 500–526.

Johnston, Dillon. "'Our Bodies' Eyes and Writing Hands': Secrecy and Sensuality in Ní Chuilleanáin's Baroque Art." In *Gender and Sexuality in Modern Ireland*, ed. Anthony Bradley and Maryann Gialanella Valiulis, 187–211. Amherst: University of Massachusetts Press, 1997.

Joyce, James. *A Portrait of the Artist as a Young Man*. New York: Viking Press, 1964.

———. *Ulysses*. New York: Vintage Press, 1986.

Kavanagh, Patrick. *Collected Poems*, ed. Antoinette Quinn. London: Penguin, 2005.

———. *Collected Pruse*. London: MacGibbon and Kee, 1967.

———. *November Haggard: Uncollected Prose and Verse of Patrick Kavanagh*, ed. Peter Kavanagh. New York: Kavanagh Press, 1971.

———. *A Poet's Country: Selected Prose*, ed. Antoinette Quinn. Dublin: Lilliput Press, 2003.

Kearney, Richard. *Anatheism: Returning to God after God*. New York: Columbia University Press, 2010.

———. *Navigations: Collected Irish Essays 1976–2006*. Syracuse, NY: Syracuse University Press, 2006.

———. *Postnationalist Ireland: Politics, Culture, Philosophy*. London: Routledge, 1997.

Kennedy-Andrews, Elmer. "John Montague: Global Regionalist?" *Cambridge Quarterly* 35, no. 1 (2006): 31–48.

Kenny, Mary. *Goodbye to Catholic Ireland*. Springfield, IL: Templegate Publishers, 2000.

Kiberd, Declan. *Irish Classics*. London: Granta Books, 2000.

Kirkpatrick, Kathryn. "Between Country and City: Paula Meehan's Eco- Feminist Poetics." In *Out of the Earth: Eco-Critical Readings of Irish Texts*, ed. Christine Cusick, 108–26. Cork: Cork University Press, 2010.

Klejs, Lene. "Seed Like Stars: Kavanagh's Nature." *Eire-Ireland* 18 (Spring 1983): 98–108.

Lang, Frederick. *Ulysses and the Irish God*. Lewisburg, PA: Bucknell University Press, 1993.

Lash, Nicholas. *His Presence in the World: A Study of Eucharistic Worship and Theology*. Dayton, OH: Pflaum Press, 1968.

Larkin, Emmet. "The Devotional Revolution in Ireland, 1850–75." *American Historical Review* 77 (June 1972): 625–52.

Larkin, Philip. *Collected Poems*. New York: Farrar, Strauss, and Giroux, 2003.

Lea, Henry Charles. *A History of Auricular Confession and Indulgences in the Latin Church*, vol. 1. London: Swan Sonnenschein, 1896.

Lee, J. J. "Women and the Church since the Famine." In *Women in Irish Society: The Historical Dimension*, ed. Margaret Mac Curtain and Donncha Ó Corrain, 7–45. Westwood, CT: Greenwood Press, 1979.

Levin, David Michael. *The Body's Recollection of Being: Phenomenological Psychology and the Deconstruction of Nihilism*. London: Routledge and Kegan Paul, 1985.

Levinas, Emmanuel. *Collected Philosophical Papers*, trans. Alphonso Lingis. Pittsburg, PA: Duquesne University Press, 1998.

Love Is for Life: Pastoral Letter of the Irish Bishops. Dublin: Veritas, 1985. http://www.ewtn.com/library/BISHOPS/LOVELIFE.HTM (accessed 2 May 2011).

Lowe-Evans, Mary. *Catholic Nostalgia in Joyce and Company*. Gainesville: University of Florida Press, 2008.

Mac Curtain, Margaret. *Ariadne's Thread: Writing Women into Irish History*. Galway: Arlen House, 2008.

———. "Late in the Field: Catholic Sisters in Twentieth-Century Ireland." In *Chattel, Servant, or Citizen: Women's Status in Church, State, and Society*, ed. Mary O'Dowd and Sabine Wichert. Belfast: Queen's University Press, 1995.

MacGreevy, Thomas. "The Catholic Element in *Work in Progress*." In *Our Exagmination Round His Factification for Incamination of Work in Progress*. Paris, 1929, 121–27. http://www.macgreevy.org (accessed 3 February 2011).

MacKillop, James. *Dictionary of Celtic Mythology*. Oxford: Oxford University Press, 1998.

Macpherson, C. B. *The Political Theory of Possessive Individualism: Hobbes to Locke*. Oxford: Oxford University Press, 1962.

Madden, Ed. *Tiresian Poetics: Modernism, Sexuality, Voice, 1888–2001*. Cranbury, NJ: Fairleigh Dickinson University Press, 2008.

Magray, Mary Peckham. *The Transforming Power of the Nuns: Women, Religion, and Cultural Change in Ireland, 1750–1900*. Oxford: Oxford University Press, 1998.

Maguire, Moira. "The Changing Face of Catholic Ireland: Conservatism and Liberalism in the Ann Lovett and Kerry Babies Scandal," *Feminist Studies* 27, no. 2 (Summer 2001): 335–58.

Marion, Jean-Luc. *Being Given: Toward a Phenomenology of Givenness*, trans. Jeffrey Kosky. Stanford, CA: Stanford University Press, 2002.

———. *God Without Being*, trans. Thomas Carlson. Chicago: University of Chicago Press, 1991.

———. "The Reason of the Gift," trans. Shane Mackinley and Nicolas de Warren. In *Givenness and God: Questions of Jean-Luc Marion*, ed. Ian Leask and Eoin Cassidy, 101–34. New York: Fordham University Press, 2005.

Matthews, Steven. *Irish Poetry: Politics, History, Negotiation: The Evolving Debate, 1969 to the Present*. New York: St. Martin's Press, 1997.

McAuliffe, John. "Urban Hymns: The City, Desire, and Theology in Austin Clarke and Patrick Kavanagh." In *Critical Ireland: New Essays in Literature and Culture*, ed. Alan Gillis and Aaron Kelly, 166–73. Dublin: Four Courts Press, 2001.

McCann, Eamonn. "A Most Impressive Scene to Behold." In *Seeing Is Believing: Moving Statues in Ireland*, ed. Colm Tóibín, 33–38. Mountrath, Ireland: Pilgrim Press, 1985.

McKenna, Yvonne. *Made Holy: Irish Women Religious at Home and Abroad*. Dublin: Irish Academic Press, 2006.

McLoone, Martin. *Film, Media, and Popular Culture: Cityscapes, Landscapes, Soundscapes*. Dublin: Irish Academic Press, 2008.

McQuaid, Rev. John C. *Wellsprings of Faith*. Dublin: Clonmore and Reynolds, 1956.

Meaney, Geraldine. "The Gothic Republic: Dark Imaginings and White Anxieties." In *Single Motherhood in Twentieth-Century Ireland: Cultural, Historical, and Social Essays*, ed. Maria Cinta Ramblado-Minero and Auxiliadora Pérez-Valdes, 13–28. Lewiston, NY: Edwin Mellen Press, 2006.

Meehan, Paula. *Dharmakaya*. Winston-Salem, NC: Wake Forest University Press, 2002.

———. "An Interview with Paula Meehan," with John Hobbs. *Nua: Studies in Contemporary Irish Writing* 1, no. 1 (1997): 53–68.

———. "An Interview with Paula Meehan," with Eileen O'Halloran and Kelli Maloy. *Contemporary Literature* 43, no. 1 (2002): 1–27.

———. *The Man Who Was Marked by Winter*. 1991. Reprint, Cheney, WA: Eastern Washington University Press, 1994.

———. *Painting Rain*. Winston-Salem, NC: Wake Forest University Press, 2009.

———. *Pillow Talk*. Loughcrew, Ireland: Gallery Press, 1994.

———. *Reading the Sky*. Dublin, Ireland: Beaver Row Press, 1985.

———. *Return and No Blame*. Dublin, Ireland: Beaver Row Press, 1984.

Mercier, Vivian. "Mortal Anguish, Mortal Pride: Austin Clarke's Religious Lyrics." *Irish University Review* 4 (Spring 1974): 91–99.

Miller, J. Hillis. *The Disappearance of God: Five Nineteenth-Century Writers*. Cambridge, MA: Harvard University Press, 1963.

Miller, Karl. *Seamus Heaney in Conversation with Karl Miller*. London: Between the Lines, 2000.

Molesworth, Charles. *Gary Snyder's Vision: Poetry and the Real Work*. Columbia: University of Missouri Press, 1983.

Montague, John. *The Bread God: A Lecture, with Illustrations in Verse on the Recent History of the Church in the Ancient Parish of Errigal Kieran*. Dublin: Dolmen Press, 1968.

———. *Collected Poems*. Winston-Salem, NC: Wake Forest University Press, 1995.

———. *The Figure in the Cave and Other Essays*, ed. Antoinette Quinn. Syracuse, NY: Syracuse University Press, 1989.

———. *The Pear Is Ripe: A Memoir*. Dublin: Liberties Press, 2007.

———. "Revolution and the Shaping of Modern Ireland: A Reply to Conor Cruise O'Brien." In *The Celtic Consciousness*, ed. Robert O'Driscoll, 427–39. New York: George Braziller, 1982.

Morrison, Danny. Introduction to *Hunger Strike: Reflections on the 1981 Hunger Strike*, ed. Danny Morrison, 7–20. Dingle, Ireland: Brandon, 2006.

Mosse, George. *The Image of Man: The Creation of Modern Masculinity.* Oxford: Oxford University Press, 1996.

Mullan, Don. *A Gift of Roses: Memories of the Visit to Ireland of the Relics of St Thérèse.* Dublin: Wolfhound Press, 2001.

Murphy, John A. "Priests and People in Modern Irish History." *Christus Rex* 23, no. 4 (1969): 235–59.

Nancy, Jean-Luc. *A Finite Thinking*, ed. Simon Sparks; trans. Richard Stamp and Simon Sparks. Stanford, CA: Stanford University Press, 2003.

Nash, S.J., Robert. *Don't Be a Priest.* Dublin: Irish Messenger Service, 1971.

Ní Chuilleanáin, Eiléan. *The Brazen Serpent.* Winston-Salem, NC: Wake Forest University Press, 1995.

———. *The Girl Who Married the Reindeer.* Winston-Salem, NC: Wake Forest University Press, 2002.

———. *The Magdalene Sermon.* Loughcrew, Ireland: Gallery Press, 1989.

———. "Nuns: A Subject for a Woman Writer." In *My Self, My Muse: Irish Women Poets Reflect on Life and Art*, ed. Patricia Boyle Haberstroh, 16–31. Syracuse, NY: Syracuse University Press, 2001.

Nietzsche, Friedrich. *On the Genealogy of Morals and Ecce Homo*, trans. Walter Kaufmann. New York: Vintage, 1989.

Nolan, Emer. *Catholic Emancipations: Irish Fiction from Thomas Moore to James Joyce.* Syracuse, NY: Syracuse University Press, 2007.

Nugent, Joseph. "Producing Priestliness." Ph.D. diss., University of California, Berkeley, 2004.

———. "The Sword and the Prayerbook: Ideals of Authentic Irish Manliness." *Victorian Studies* 50, no. 4 (Summer 2008): 587–613.

O'Brien, Peggy. *Writing Lough Derg: From William Carleton to Seamus Heaney.* Syracuse, NY: Syracuse University Press, 2006.

Ó Dochartaigh, Liam. "*Ceol na mBréag*: Gaelic Themes in *The Rough Field*." In *Well Dreams: Essays on John Montague*, ed. Thomas Redshaw, 194–210. Omaha, NE: Creighton University Press, 2004.

Ó Drisceoil, Donal. "'The Best Banned in the Land': Censorship and Irish Writing since 1950." *Yearbook of English Studies* 35 (2005): 146–60.

O'Driscoll, Dennis. *Stepping Stones: Interviews with Seamus Heaney.* New York: Farrar, Straus, Giroux, 2008.

Ó Fearghail, Conchubhair. "The Evolution of Catholic Parishes in Dublin City from the Sixteenth to the Nineteenth Centuries." In *Dublin City and County:*

From Prehistory to Present, ed. F.H.A. Aalen and Kevin Whalen, 229–50. Dublin: Geography Press, 1992.

O'Malley, Padraig. *Biting at the Grave: The Irish Hunger Strikes and the Politics of Despair.* Boston, MA: Beacon Press, 1990.

O'Toole, Fintan. "In Light of Things as They Are: Paul Durcan's Ireland." In *The Kilfenora Teaboy: A Study of Paul Durcan*, ed. Colm Tóibín, 26–41. Dublin: New Island Books, 1996.

———. "Seeing Is Believing." In *Seeing Is Believing: Moving Statues in Ireland*, ed. Colm Tóibín, 89–95. Mountrath, Ireland: Pilgrim Press, 1985.

O'Toole, James M. "In the Court of Conscience: American Catholics and Confession, 1900–1975." In *Habits of Devotion: Catholic Religion Practice in Twentieth-Century America*, ed. James M. O'Toole, 131–86. Ithaca, NY: Cornell University Press, 2004.

Parker, Michael. *Seamus Heaney: The Making of a Poet.* Iowa City: University of Iowa Press, 1993.

Penner, James. *Pinks, Pansies, and Punks: The Rhetoric of Masculinity in American Literary Culture.* Bloomington: Indiana University Press, 2010.

Perry, Nicholas, and Loreto Echeverría. *Under the Heel of Mary.* London: Routledge, 1998.

Phillips, Robert. *The Confessional Poets.* Carbondale: Southern Illinois University Press, 1975.

Pogatchnik, Shawn. "Irish Leaders Propose Amendment to Strict Divorce Law," *The Day* [New London, CT] 14 September 1995, 16. http://news.google.com/newspapers (accessed 20 July 2012).

Quinn, Antoinette. *Patrick Kavanagh: A Biography.* Dublin: Gill and Macmillan, 2001.

———. *Patrick Kavanagh: A Critical Study.* Syracuse, NY: Syracuse University Press, 1991.

Raftery, Mary. "Taking Mary Home." *Irish Times.* 15 April 2004. http://ireland.com/newspaper/opinion (accessed 12 December 2007).

Raughter, Rosemary, ed. *Religious Women and Their History: Breaking the Silence.* Dublin: Irish Academic Press, 2005.

Redshaw, Thomas. "The Bounding Line: John Montague's *A New Siege* (1970)." *Canadian Journal of Irish Studies* 13, no. 1 (Spring 1987): 75–105.

———. "Location as Vocation: John Montague's 'The Northern Gate.'" *Canadian Journal of Irish Studies* 5, no. 2 (1979): 38–52.

———. "The Surviving Sign: John Montague's *The Bread God* (1968)." *Éire-Ireland* 17, no. 2 (Summer 1982): 56–91.

Ricoeur, Paul. *The Symbolism of Evil*, trans. Emerson Buchanan. Boston, MA: Beacon Press, 1967.

Rose, Michael. *Goodbye, Good Men: How Liberals Brought Corruption into the Catholic Church*. Washington, DC: Regnery Press, 2002.

Ryan, Tim, and Jurek Kirakowski. *Ballinspittle: Moving Statues and Faith*. Cork: Mercier Press, 1985.

Schirmer, Gregory. *The Poetry of Austin Clarke*. Notre Dame, IN: University of Notre Dame Press, 1983.

Sheldrake, Philip. *Spaces for the Sacred: Place, Memory, and Identity*. Baltimore, MD: Johns Hopkins University Press, 2001.

Shorto, Russell. "The Irish Affliction." *New York Times* 9 February 2011. http://www.nytimes.com/2011/02/13/magazine/13Irish-t.html (accessed 11 February 2011).

Sirr, Peter. "'How Things Begin to Happen': Notes on Eiléan Ní Chuilleanáin and Medbh McGuckian." *Southern Review* 31 (1995): 450–67.

Smith, James M. *Ireland's Magdalen Laundries and the Nation's Architecture of Containment*. Notre Dame, IN: University of Notre Dame Press, 2007.

Smyth, Daragh. *A Guide to Irish Mythology*. Dublin: Irish Academic Press, 1988.

Stambaugh, Joan. *The Other Nietzsche*. Albany: State University of New York Press, 1994.

Stanfield, Paul. "How She Looks in That Company: Eiléan Ní Chuilleanáin as Feminist Poet." In *Contemporary Irish Women Poets: Some Male Perspectives*, ed. Alexander Gonzalez, 103–21. Westport, CT: Greenwood Press, 1999.

Stark, Tom. Introduction to *No Earthly Estate: God and Patrick Kavanagh: An Anthology*, ed. Tom Stark, 9–42. Dublin: Columba Press, 2002.

Steele, Karen. "Refusing the Poisoned Chalice: The Sexual Politics of Rita Ann Higgins and Paula Meehan." In *Homemaking: Women Writers and the Politics and Poetics of Home*, ed. Catherine Wiley and Fiona Barnes, 313–33. New York: Garland, 1995.

Stevens, Wallace. *The Collected Poems of Wallace Stevens*. New York: Knopf, 1955.

Tallant, Nicola. "Kidnapped by His Family and Put in a Mental Home." *Irish Independent*. 6 May 2007. http://www.independent.ie/unsorted/migration/kidnapped-by-his-family-and-put-in-a-mental-home (accessed 16 May 2011).

Tapping, G. Craig. *Austin Clarke: A Study of His Writings*. Dublin: Academy Press, 1981.

Taussig, Michael. *The Devil and Commodity Fetishism in South America*. Chapel Hill, NC: University of North Carolina Press, 1980.

Taylor, Charles. *Dilemmas and Connections: Selected Essays*. Cambridge, MA: Harvard University Press, 2011.

———. *A Secular Age*. Cambridge, MA: Harvard University Press, 2007.

———. *Sources of the Self: The Making of Modern Identity*. Cambridge, MA: Harvard University Press, 1989.

Taylor, Lawrence. *Occasions of Faith: An Anthropology of Irish Catholics*. 1995. Reprint, Dublin: Lilliput Press, 1997.

Thurman, Robert, ed. *The Tibetan Book of the Dead*. New York: Bantam Books, 1994.

Tobin, Daniel. "'Lines of Leaving/Lines of Returning': John Montague's Double Vision." In *Well Dreams: Essays on John Montague*, ed. Thomas Redshaw, 147–66. Omaha, NE: Creighton University Press, 2004.

———. *Passage to the Center: Imagination and the Sacred in the Poetry of Seamus Heaney*. Lexington: University of Kentucky Press, 1999.

Turner, Victor, and Edith Turner. *Image and Pilgrimage in Christian Culture: Anthropological Perspectives*. New York: Columbia University Press, 1978.

Valente, Joseph. *The Myth of Manliness in Irish National Culture, 1880–1922*. Urbana: University of Illinois Press, 2011.

———. "'Neither Flesh Nor Fish'; or How 'Cyclops' Stages the Double-Bind of Irish Manhood." In *Semicolonial Joyce*, ed. Derek Attridge and Marjorie Howe, 96–127. Cambridge: Cambridge University Press, 2000.

Vendler, Helen. *Seamus Heaney*. Cambridge, MA: Harvard University Press, 1998.

Wheatley, David. "The Mercyseat and 'The Mansion of Forgetfulness': Samuel Beckett's *Murphy*, Austin Clarke's 'Mnemosyne Lay in Dust,' and Irish Poetic Modernism." *English Studies* 83 (December 2002): 527–40.

Whelan, Kevin. "The Catholic Parish, the Catholic Chapel, and Village Development in Ireland." *Irish Geography* 16 (1983): 1–16.

Yeats, W. B. *The Poems*, ed. Daniel Albright. London: J. M. Dent, 1990.

Index